CHALLENGES OF EQUALITY

Judaism, State, and Education in Nineteenth-Century France

CHALLENGES of EQUALITY

JEFFREY HAUS

WAYNE STATE UNIVERSITY PRESS   DETROIT

© 2009 by Wayne State University Press, Detroit, Michigan 48201. All rights reserved. No part of this book may be reproduced without formal permission. Manufactured in the United States of America.
13 12 11 10 09   5 4 3 2 1

Library of Congress Cataloging-in-Publication Data

Haus, Jeffrey.
Challenges of equality : Judaism, state, and education in nineteenth-century France / Jeffrey Haus.
    p. cm.
Includes bibliographical references and index.
ISBN 978-0-8143-3380-8 (cloth : alk. paper)
1. Jewish religious education of adults—France—History—19th century. 2. Rabbis—Education—France—19th century. 3. Rabbinical seminaries—France—History—19th century. 4. Jews—France—Politics and government—19th century. 5. Jews—France—History—19th century. 6. Judaism and state—France—History—19th century. 7. Judaism—France—History—19th century. I. Title.

BM85.F8H38 2009
296.071'144—dc22

2008037316

Designed by Maya Rhodes
Typeset by E. T. Lowe Publishing Company
Composed in Adobe Garamond and Serlio LH

Contents

Preface and Acknowledgments vii
Introduction 1

PART I: JEWISH PRIMARY EDUCATION AND THE STATE, 1808–1870

1. Foundations 9
2. Roadblocks to Regeneration 28
3. Redefinition and Consolidation 43

PART II: RABBINICAL EDUCATION AND THE STATE, 1808–1906

4. How Much Latin Should a Rabbi Know? 65
5. A Tale of Two Cities: From Metz to Paris 91

PART III: TOWARD SEPARATION, 1875–1906

6. Challenges of Equality: Financial Anticlericalism 115
7. Jewish Education and Jewish Space 134
8. "Just Proportions": Financial Anticlericalism and Rabbinical Space 151

Conclusion 160

Notes 167
Bibliography 205
Index 221

Preface and Acknowledgments

This book began with a basic question: How did French anticlerical legislation affect French Jews during the first half of the Third Republic (roughly 1875–1906)? Searching for the answer led me to focus on education, which was one of the main targets of anticlerical activity. My research into schools took me to France, where I combed the holdings of the Archives Nationales, the Consistoire de Paris, and the Consistoire Central. The sources quickly convinced me that what happened during the Third Republic had roots in the early nineteenth century, and I expanded my study accordingly. I had originally intended to focus on the legislative and intellectual aspects of the question, but early on discovered a new, unexplored thread: the financial relationship between French Judaism and the French state. I followed that thread back to legal thinking, which took me to the Archives du Conseil d'État in Paris. This rich resource provided valuable insight into government views of Judaism in particular, and church-state relations generally. The analytical narrative that follows contains the results of this complex investigation.

While I was working on this project, the French government banned from the public schools all religious symbolism and clothing (e.g., headscarves for Muslims, *kippot* for Jews, and crucifixes for Christians). The so-called "Veil Law" of 2004 generated a good deal of controversy, both in France and internationally.[1] I did not set out to write about Jews and French schools as an analogy for Muslims and French schools; nor did I seek to comment on contemporary French attitudes toward religion. Nevertheless, as I tell my students, sometimes we find relevance and sometimes relevance finds us. Such is the case with this book, which explores the intertwining of politics and religion in an age seemingly removed from contemporary identity politics.

Upon closer examination, the case of Jews and education in the nineteenth century has much to teach us about the way in which broad conceptions respond to specific realities. Nineteenth-century French Jews had to manage government expectations of them and their religion while forging conceptions of themselves as both Jews and citizens of France. A predisposition toward achieving acceptance necessarily limited the points of view available to acculturating French Jews at that time; simply put, with full cultural separatism off the table, they had to explore other options. The reader, therefore, will not find in this book the intellectual or political militancy that characterizes contemporary debate. Yet this absence should not suggest any lack of commitment or passion on the part of the Jewish leaders discussed in the following pages. Even after going over this material many times, I am still struck by their extraordinary dedication to learning, to their fellow Jews, and to the country they loved.

This study would not have appeared without the help of a number of individuals and institutions. I could not have undertaken the initial primary research without the generous support of the Tauber Institute for the Study of European Jewry and the Frances and Jeffrey Sachar Fund at Brandeis University, and the Memorial Foundation for Jewish Culture. I was also privileged to work with the collection of French Judaica at Brandeis University, and to view key holdings at the library of the Jewish Theological Seminary of America. In France, the benefits of being an exchange fellow at the École Normale Supérieure in Paris—from the use of their extensive library to the hospitality of their dormitory—are too numerous to mention. The access I was afforded to the Archives of the Central Consistory (where I was helped by the wise counsel of the director, M. Philippe Landau), the Archives Nationales, and the Archives of the Conseil d'État were vital to my research. Likewise, the assistance I received from the staff of the Bibliothéque de l'Alliance Israélite Universelle and its director, M. Jean-Claude Kuperminc, proved invaluable.

I am indebted to those who served as sounding boards at various stages of the project. I especially appreciate the friendship and support of Richard Latner, Henry Samuel Levinson, Gregory Grieve, Sarah Krive, and Maud Mandel, all of whom read early parts of the manuscript and contributed valuable comments. At Kalamazoo College, I have benefited from the insights of Joseph Bangura and Espelencia Baptiste, both of whom helped me tighten my argument as the project neared completion. Throughout my career Frances Malino, who helped me enter this field in the first place, has always provided me with constructive comments, a sympathetic ear, and more than one pat on the back. I am honored to call her a mentor, colleague, and friend.

I am also deeply grateful for the encouragement of my colleagues at Tulane University, the University of North Carolina at Greensboro, and

Kalamazoo College, all of whom gave me the space, time, and support necessary to finish this book. Thanks also to the many scholars who listened to my conference presentations of this material over the years, challenged my assumptions, and asked questions that helped strengthen the final product.

The staff at Wayne State University Press has done a wonderful job of shepherding this project to a fruitful end. Kathryn Wildfong believed in this project from the moment I presented it to her, and has been a most gracious, supportive, and effective editor. Kristin Harpster Lawrence and the production department at WSUP have been patient and efficient, and have taken great care to present my work in the best possible light. Eric Schramm copyedited the manuscript, saving me from myself stylistically on a number of occasions. Many thanks also to the manuscript's anonymous readers and to the members of the WSUP editorial board, who pushed me to improve the manuscript. Any shortcomings in this book are my responsibility alone.

Finally, I could not have completed the book without an understanding and loving family. My daughters Shira, Nava, and Mazal have provided a welcome distraction and a reason to return to the twenty-first century after spending so much of my time in the nineteenth. My wife, Rachel, has listened to me talk about this project from its nascent stage. Her support for it, and for me, has never wavered despite the many sacrifices my work has demanded. I dedicate this book to her with gratitude and love, for it could not have been completed without her.

Introduction

On January 4, 1812, Félix-Julien-Jean Bigot de Préameneu wrote a letter. In his capacity as Napoleon Bonaparte's Minister of Religions, he wrote many letters, but this one must have seemed a particular chore. For more than three years, the leaders of the Jewish Consistory—the officially recognized administrative structure charged with integrating French Jews and operating French Jewish institutions—had petitioned his office for permission to establish a national system of Jewish schools. Despite Préameneu's efforts to ignore or dissuade them, their pleas had grown louder and more frequent. In September of 1811, the consistorial leadership had written in an impatient tone, asking once again for authorization to open both a central rabbinical school and Jewish primary schools. The leaders argued that stonewalling the issue of Jewish schooling directly contradicted Napoleon's own instructions for the regeneration of French Jewry. They also reminded Préameneu that the school issue held "the highest importance for the Jews of the Empire" and that he long ago had promised to settle the matter. Meanwhile, the continuing absence of Jewish schools exercised a deleterious moral effect on young French Jews.[1] Jewish education offered the best defense against the growing religious indifference within French Jewry that threatened the survival of French Judaism. French Jews, the leaders warned, could not remain "in this state of abandon contrary to the principles of their religion."[2] Still skeptical of these arguments, Préameneu had decided to answer them once and for all.

Préameneu's reply outlined many of the issues that framed the educational debates between French Judaism and the French state in the nineteenth century: providing for fair and equal treatment under the law; ensuring the "proper" moral development of French Jewish schoolchildren; struggling to define utility and efficiency in Jewish schooling; and above all, determining the responsibilities of Judaism and state in the general process of national integration. Subsequent negotiations over Jewish education also highlighted broader tensions regarding the relationship between French Judaism and the French state, and the conceptual connection between French Judaism and French citizenship.

One area that Préameneu did not address proved equally important: the influence of government funding—and consistorial attempts to obtain it—on Jewish education. His omission of financial issues, however, did not remove them from the conversation. Rather, like many other French administrators, he subsumed such matters in ideological and administrative questions. Consequently, debate over French Jewish schooling became intricately interwoven with attitudes toward Jewish status in France and the ways in which French Jews navigated the process of integration.

Historians of post-Revolutionary French Jewry have followed this orientation. Their work tends to view the relationship between Judaism and state as ideologically oriented, fully bent on integrating Jews into French society. According to this traditional line of interpretation, both assimilating Jews and government officials viewed Jewish particularism as an impediment on the path toward full integration. The melding of "Jewish" and "French" subsequently played out as an ideological process, with intellectual and political leaders developing integration formulas that then trickled down to the masses.[3]

This research yielded a vast and important body of literature that has framed the study of French Jewry for decades. Still, its largely intellectual focus provided a limited view of Jewish integration. Paula Hyman added an important dimension to this interpretation by emphasizing the influence of economic and social factors on Jewish integration, and how those factors engendered Jewish responses to political developments.[4] Both approaches, however, convey a sense of French Jewish integration as somehow separate from the general experience of nineteenth-century France. Hyman sees forces influencing Jewish integration as emanating either from within French Jewry or from outside it. Certainly, French Jews faced different challenges and problems along the road to becoming integrated French citizens; but they were neither physically nor intellectually walled off from the rest of the country. Although, as Hyman notes, the Jews of Alsace tended to be more culturally and socially insulated than their counterparts in the south,[5] their cultural and religious traditions met French traditions at some point. This intermingling produced Franco-Judaism, however one wishes to characterize that phenomenon.

Historians of French Jewry have thus concentrated on either the general social and legislative forces stimulating these changes, or on developments in the economic lives of individuals that spurred them to change their views of Judaism. Few, however, have investigated the interaction of practical, material issues with the political and social forces that redrew the boundaries of French Jewish communal life. Derek Penslar's work on European Jewish political economy and philanthropy has certainly broken new ground in this regard. Penslar argues that the central European leaders of the Jewish Enlightenment (known by the Hebrew term *haskalah*, whose leaders were dubbed *maskilim*) sought to change the economic activities of their less acculturated co-religionists as much as they sought to enlighten them intellectually. Practical material changes, they believed, would encourage simultaneous cultural and social integration. Penslar's *maskilim* thus saw economic and social forces as interactive, mutually reinforcing factors producing the inferior condition from which they sought to extricate their fellow Jews.[6]

Penslar's study, though, deals mostly with German-speaking central Europe, where Jews lived under political and social conditions that did not necessarily exist in France. Central European *maskilim* operated in a region where Jews had not yet received full political emancipation; nor had a central government structure devised any sort of working plan for integrating them. In France, Jewish legal emancipation came in 1791, meaning that the French Jews who lobbied for schools in the nineteenth century did so as *citizens*. Their concept of *utility* worked in tandem with a conception of legal *equality*, which they interpreted as endowing them with civil liberties equal to Christian citizens. Although French *maskilim* were deeply influenced by the Prussian *haskalah*, they harbored different expectations of the state's partnership in the integration process. For them, France represented more than simply the agent of emancipation: integrated French Jews saw the French state as a place in which they could carve out a niche for an integrated Judaism whose political equality was already a *fait accompli*.

Consequently, while Jewish philanthropy concentrated on the utilitarian ends that Penslar identifies, French Jewish leaders defined utility differently than their central European counterparts. Utility connoted the moral, intellectual, economic, and ultimately political compatibility between Jewishness and Frenchness. Assertions of equality meanwhile affirmed the right of Jews to preserve a degree of religious and cultural difference. Combining the two terms enabled French Jewish leaders to demonstrate their unity with France while validating their continuing distinctiveness.

This book seeks to move further in the direction initiated by Penslar, exploring one of the primary areas where utility and equality—and thus, "Frenchness" and "Jewishness"—intersected in the nineteenth century. Specifically, it examines debates over the most appropriate way to educate

French Jews and the financial responsibility for providing that education. In so doing, this study will address several significant lacunae in the historiography of French Jewry. First, the field lacks a detailed study of Jewish education in France. While broader histories of French Jewry mention education, few have dealt with it as their primary subject.[7] Schools, though, often embody the ideals of their founders (in theory if not always in practice); studying the development of French Jewish education therefore reveals Jewish attitudes toward Judaism, France, and the relationship between the two. While parochial schools hardly constituted the focal point of French Jewish activity, they did represent staging areas where consistorial leaders and French bureaucrats molded broader dialogues about the relationship between Judaism and state.

Disagreements over Jewish education also highlight the diversity of nineteenth-century French Jewry. These factional divisions shaped communal dynamics and educational strategies alike. Government legislation understandably painted Jews with a broad brush, treating them as one unified entity (which they were, according to French law). Yet the development of Jewish education policy within the Jewish communities themselves points to a persistent diversity that did not dissipate over time. Nor did it adhere to the regional divisions so common to the historiography of French Jewry: that the Jews of the northeast were conservative and resistant to change, for example, or that the Jews of Bordeaux were completely assimilated or, at least, acculturated. With state officials generally assuming Jewish unity, however, Jewish leaders had no choice but to respond as though they were, in fact, unified. The century-long wrangling over financing French Jewish schooling—how to pay for it, who should pay for it, and whether it even merited any support at all—therefore influenced not only attitudes toward Jewish learning in France, but the ways in which French Jews portrayed themselves to their fellow citizens.

Because financial considerations shaped the expectations of government officials and the responses of Jewish leaders, they also molded the interaction between them. In addition to reinterpreting the intellectual context of this interaction, this study will extract the often subtle influence of finances based on the point of contact that the schools provided. Previously unpublished materials construct an evolving relationship between Judaism and state that defies blanket generalization. At times, money drew the civil and Jewish realms closer together; at other times, it pushed them further apart. While Jewish leaders sought to frame their communal activities in broad ideological terms, the evidence suggests that they frequently did so with at least one eye upon their balance sheets. Government money thus represented a powerful vehicle for state influence in Jewish affairs. True, financial issues did not single-handedly determine the outcome of the integration process; but the financial lever helped to move French Jewish leaders in certain directions. Money might not constitute the only determinant of this story, but it often played an influential role in it.

In addition, financial influence cut both ways. As we shall see in the case of the rabbinical school, official state views of Jewish educational priorities could change according to specific practical considerations. Financial issues functioned as barometers of state attitudes toward Judaism and Jewish attitudes toward the state. The process of gaining government authorization put a civic stamp on Jewish educational institutions, demanding that they conform to government models in order to open and operate. For Jewish schools, government approval often proved as important as the money itself (which was often inadequate). The appropriation of state funding cemented the legitimacy of Jewish education, providing a tangible sign that Judaism marched on the integrationist path demanded by emancipation. Acquiring and maintaining vital state financial support thus earmarked French Judaism as an agent for integrating and forming Jewish citizens. This function in turn became a central pillar of French Jewish institutional culture, shaping the scope and content of official Jewish communal activity.

Money also helped to delineate boundaries between Jewish and civic space. By selectively supporting only certain types of activities, French officials determined what served the public interest and what did not. In so doing, they passed judgment on which activities were "French" and which were parochially "Jewish." Where these borders remained ambiguous, money helped identify the common ground of both "French" and "Jewish" by bringing the state's authority to bear. This dynamic adds an intriguing dimension to the notion of "marking money," the idea that some money is different than other money, based upon its source, function, and purpose.[8] The appropriation of government money denoted the legitimacy of the Consistory by literally conveying civic approval of consistorial institutions, validating the consistorial conception of French Jews and French Judaism. As a result, consistorial leaders worked hard to obtain government money for their rabbinical academy and primary schools, even though those funds could not support the entire Jewish educational structure. The educational dialogue between Jewish and civil officials thus points toward both Jewish and non-Jewish perceptions of Judaism's proper role in nineteenth-century France.

For French Jews, these perceptions went beyond usual definitions of what many scholars term "identity," which focuses on standards of group membership and group consciousness.⁹ Rather, they reflected ideas about Judaism's practical role in the lives of French Jews. For both Jewish and non-Jewish officials, French Judaism represented a useful tool for imbuing morality and promoting integration. While many French Jews may have considered Judaism merely a sentimental attachment, persistent conflicts over the conduct and content of Jewish education suggest a lingering ambiguity about the definition of post-emancipation French Judaism. The inability of the Jewish Consistory to rally support for establishing a national Jewish primary school system spoke to this fragmented range of opinion, as did the generally weak financial support for the central rabbinical school and continual disagreement over its curriculum.

If the appropriation of funds reflected the spectrum of views regarding the relationship between Judaism and state, conflicting attitudes toward money shaped the interaction between the two. Scholars of French material culture have pointed out that money in nineteenth-century France could at once represent power, liberty, success, nobility, and the root of all evil.¹⁰ Such contrasting interpretations in turn produced paradoxical social views of money. As Victoria Thompson aptly notes, while nineteenth-century French working-class activists saw low wages as the crucial factor producing poverty, asking for higher pay risked drawing criticism for greed and selfishness. French labor organizers therefore had to align their arguments with prevalent moral interpretations of poverty.¹¹ Similarly, Jewish educational plans had to conform to government academic and cultural standards in order to attract support. Repeated shifts in government regimes during the nineteenth century produced ripples in Jewish educational thinking as notions of those standards changed.

Within this environment, few issues proved as enduringly controversial as Jewish education. Throughout the nineteenth century, the question of how best to educate Jews vexed both French bureaucrats trying to establish a national school system and Jewish officials trying to stake out a preserve for Judaism in the post-emancipation era. The main sticking point concerned where Jewish schooling fit into the developing framework of French education. Financial issues formed the main nexus for larger educational debates. When Jews funded their own schools, civil officials tended to leave them alone; the involvement of state money, however, raised questions of sovereignty, educational efficacy, and the obligations of Jewish citizenship. Addressing these concerns from a standpoint of equality and utility challenged French Jewish leaders to define the relationship between Judaism and state in a language that both Jews and non-Jews could understand.

I
Jewish Primary Education and the State, 1808–1870

1

Foundations

The Historical Setting

Like France itself, French Jewry hardly constituted a cohesive, unified entity by the 1790s, or even by the beginning of the nineteenth century. Conceptions of the relationship between being Jewish and being French in the aftermath of the Revolution were equally diverse. As some scholars have suggested, French Jews repeatedly adapted their sense of themselves in response to changing political, intellectual, social, and economic forces.[1] Debates over Jewish education in France took similar twists and turns in the course of the nineteenth century. While these negotiations were products of specific points in time, they unfolded against a backdrop of ideas and expectations emanating from the historical context in which French Jews found themselves.

At the time of the French Revolution in 1789, Jews constituted a tiny minority within France. Numbering between 40,000 and 50,000 souls, French Jewry made up less than 1 percent of France's approximately five million inhabitants. Geographically, French Jews lived in three main areas. While Paris and its environs would become the largest population center by the end of the nineteenth century, in 1800 the bulk of the Jewish population—around 30,000—resided in the northeastern departments of Alsace and Lorraine. Alsatian Jews spoke mostly Yiddish and German and followed the Ashkenazic religious ritual, which placed a great weight on rabbinic authority. Some resided in larger urban centers, such as Strasbourg, Metz, and Mulhouse, while others dwelled in smaller towns and communes. Paula Hyman counts Jews living in about 16 percent of Alsace's 1,150 communes on the eve of the Revolution; after their emancipation in 1791, Jews migrated within the region to larger urban areas. As the Alsatian Jewish population expanded in the nineteenth century, its demographic concentration also increased.[2]

Many Alsatian Jews lived in poverty; others lived comfortably; a few were more than comfortable. Most engaged in trade of some sort, while some prospered in the textile industry.[3] Alsatian Jews, like their counterparts elsewhere in Europe, maintained a corporate communal structure that oversaw all aspects of Jewish civic and religious life. As an autonomous structure, the Jewish community (in Hebrew, *kahal*) administered justice to its members according to Jewish religious law (*halakhah*), and saw to the operation and maintenance of Jewish religious edifices and institutions. Its leaders, or syndics, tended to come from the wealthiest men in the community. The syndics managed the payment of communal taxes to the secular authorities and served as the main liaison between them and the Jewish community they served. The *kahal* financed its operation through the levying of taxes among its members, usually on some sort of sliding scale in which the richest members paid the most.[4]

The second largest Jewish population in France at the end of the eighteenth century was the 5,000 or so Sephardic Jews of Bordeaux. This community had largely descended from Iberian Jewish converts to Catholicism (*conversos*), some of whom secretly retained Jewish religious practices. Many of these *conversos* had left Spain and Portugal in the fifteenth century seeking commercial opportunity, which some found in southwestern France. A number of *bordelais* Sephardim, particularly international merchants such as the Gradis family, had achieved considerable economic success and with it a certain social integration.[5] By the beginning of the eighteenth century, the Sephardim of Bordeaux emerged as an openly Jewish community whose status as a corporate community provided relative protection from wide-scale persecution. Their religious tradition emphasized traditional observance, to be sure, but with a greater acceptance of rationalist thinking and a rabbinate more deferential to lay authorities.[6] The Sephardim of Bordeaux also adopted a more insular attitude toward their fellow Jews, resisting Jewish immigration from the Papal States and the Yiddish-speaking regions to the northeast. After the Revolution, their leaders sought to prevent legal unification with the Ashkenazic population of the northeast, fearing both financial liability for Alsatian communal debts (a real concern) and the loss of their social distinctions.

The third major Jewish population center on the eve of the Revolution was in the papal states of Avignon, Carpentras, Cavaillon, and l'Isle-sur-Sogue. These Jews eventually entered Sephardic society and expanded Jewish settlement to cities such as Lyon and Paris. Although papal Jews melded well with their Sephardic brothers and sisters, they retained certain linguistic distinctions and engaged in broader commercial activity. Like the Sephardim of Bordeaux, these communities constructed hierarchical communal structures, which saw to internal activities such as the administration of poor relief and maintenance of religious structures.[7]

Prior to 1789, this communal organization had provided a loose educational structure for French Jews. While formal academies for rabbinical study and scholarship existed in Alsace and Lorraine through the Middle Ages, Jewish elementary education during this period remained dependent on local attitudes and customs. Some communities might have provided organized schools, but their capacity was limited. The schools that did exist provided traditional religious instruction: at worst literacy in Hebrew and the prayer liturgy, at best study of the traditional biblical texts necessary for advanced talmudic learning. Organized elementary schools, however, tended to be rare; a more common arrangement was for a family or group of families to hire a private tutor, or *melammed,* to teach small groups (usually boys, although girls could also be educated in this manner).[8]

In any case, this traditional arrangement did not provide broad, systematic elementary education and mostly excluded secular learning. Jay Berkovitz observes that, in an effort to formalize Jewish elementary schooling in the eighteenth century, leaders of the Metz and Bordeaux communities organized elementary schools for boys and attempted to compel parents to send their sons for lessons. These institutions, however, remained largely traditional in content, and were as concerned with keeping idle youths off the streets as with systematizing religious instruction. Like earlier models, these schools aimed their instruction at boys rather than girls.[9]

Attempts to regularize Jewish schools, though limited in scope, reflected the growing significance of educational issues within French Jewish life. This emphasis, in turn, mirrored the increasing attention paid to education by French Enlightenment thinkers. To them, learning constituted either a vehicle for political, economic, and social progress or at least a method for social control.[10] These concerns dovetailed with growing debate over the legal status of Jews in France. Both supporters and foes of equality offered similar diagnoses for the persecution and poverty afflicting European Jews: Jews existed in a state of social, political, and economic isolation, either willfully (as opponents of emancipation would argue) or through the neglect and shortsightedness of an oppressive, unenlightened society.

Not everyone agreed, however, on the proper remedy for this condition. Some, like the Prussian scholar Johann David Michaelis, held that because of what he considered their inherent nature, Jews could never be reformed and should remain segregated. Others, such as the British thinker John Toland, maintained that Jews should receive equal status as a matter of course with no preconditions. A third group, typified by the Prussian writer Christian Wilhelm von Dohm and the French cleric Abbé Henri Grégoire, argued that extending equal rights to the Jews would encourage them to change their traditional social and economic ways, thereby effecting their rehabilitation. In order for this approach to succeed, however, certain conditions ought to be attached to any amelioration of Jewish status as incentives for Jews to reform.[11] These different schools of thought set the terms for the debate over Jewish legal status in France, assuming a set of pervasive characteristics common to all French Jews and in need of immediate modification.

While some Jews—most notably the Polish immigrant Zalkind Hourwitz[12]—tried to combat notions of Jewish inferiority, they still found themselves in a reactive position, needing to portray themselves in the light of general preconceived notions. Ronald Schechter has argued that French Jews actually used this dynamic to their advantage during the eighteenth century, "appropriating" unflattering gentile characterizations of them and reinterpreting them in a positive light.[13] This strategy apparently carried through the Revolutionary era, as French Jews sought to recast their image according to French cultural standards.

The extension of full legal emancipation to French Jewry institutionalized expectations of Jewish integration, eventually giving rise to competing visions for educating Jews. In 1791, after two years of debate, the French National Assembly declared the emancipation of the Jews of France. The proclamation extended to French Jewry equal rights of citizenship under the French Constitution, the first time that a European nation had granted full legal rights to its Jewish inhabitants. Equality did not, however, come free of obligations. In exchange for citizenship, the National Assembly expected French Jews to abandon all aspects of corporate collective existence and to assume individual relationships with the French state and their fellow citizens.

Emancipation created a set of political and cultural assumptions that influenced the decision making of both government and Jewish leaders. Despite lofty expectations, the details of the integration process remained undefined until the beginning of the nineteenth century. Following a *coup d'état* in 1799, Napoleon Bonaparte became First Consul of France. Under his rule, the French government began to assume a more centralized bureaucratic organization based upon centrally decreed administrative standards.[14] Religion, which Napoleon viewed as an agent for fostering public morality and loyalty to his regime, soon fell under government auspices. In 1801, the First Consul negotiated a *concordat* with Pope Pius VII that altered the course of church-state relations in France. The terms of the agreement provided the Bonapartist regime with control over the institutions and personnel of French Catholicism. With this settlement, French Catholicism began to serve the regime as what Adrien Dansette has called a *religion-gendarme,* enlisting the Catholic clergy as an administrative and moral extension of state authority in order to legitimize and consolidate Napoleon's authority.[15] The new system of religious administration also instituted civil salaries for the Catholic clergy, tying the Church's material interests to the state's political survival. The government soon expanded the system to include French Protestantism. The union between the religious and civil apparatus established by the *concordat,* though challenged at times during a turbulent century, would outlast the Empire and remain on the books until the separation of church and state in 1905.

Meanwhile, by the first decade of the nineteenth century, the traditional Jewish communal structure had weakened considerably. While this trend had a minimal impact upon the more acculturated Jews of Bordeaux, it produced anxiety among the Jewish leadership of the northeastern provinces whose authority emancipation had significantly undermined. In the regions of Alsace and Lorraine, local Jewish leaders found their ability to generate support for Jewish institutions greatly diminished. Before emancipation, Jewish communities could tax their members in order to maintain institutions such as synagogues, schools, and cemeteries. Emancipation undid this system, rendering membership and submission to Jewish communal authorities voluntary. In addition, the strife that followed the Revolution threatened the economic, political, and physical security of French Jewry, especially in Alsace.[16] Emancipation and its aftermath thus stripped the remnants of the French Jewish communities of their traditional resources and left them no clear mandate for the future. Under these conditions, prominent French Jews such as Berr Isaac Berr petitioned the Minister of Religions, Jean Portalis, for government intervention and for the inclusion of French Judaism in the civil religious administration.[17]

In 1806, the now self-proclaimed Emperor Napoleon convened an Assembly of Jewish Notables charged with clarifying the terms of Jewish emancipation. The following year, he assembled a group of French rabbinical leaders—which he audaciously dubbed the Great Sanhedrin, after the rabbinical high court of antiquity—as a means of stamping the decisions of the Notables with religious legitimacy. Both bodies affirmed Jewish loyalty to the state and the compatibility of Jewish integration with French national goals. In addition, they outlined an ideology committed to the mission of integrating less enlightened Jews into the French nation. This process, to which the Abbé Grégoire had attached the term *régénération* in an essay published in 1789, implied economic as well as cultural integration. French Jews were expected to abandon those economic activities traditionally associated with Jews—money lending, for example—and turn toward more "productive" sectors of the economy such as the artisan trades.[18]

The commitments made by the Notables and the Sanhedrin gained institutional expression in 1808 when Judaism became the third state religion in France. After extensive negotiations, the Imperial government created an administrative structure to oversee the religious activities of French Judaism and to promote the process of Jewish regeneration. This administration, dubbed the Consistory after its Protestant counterpart, would also serve as the official political intermediary between the state and French Judaism. Like the rest of the French bureaucracy, the Jewish Consistory was organized hierarchically. A Central Consistory in Paris oversaw seven subordinate consistories spread geographically throughout the departments of France. Within the consistorial structure, French Jewish leaders rebuilt an infrastructure of official Jewish institutions. Although its authority was never as absolute in practice as the law seemed to envision, the consistorial leadership controlled the construction of synagogues as well as the education and ordination of French rabbis, and played a significant role in the distribution of charity. In addition, the consistories oversaw the establishment of Jewish educational institutions.[19]

The expectation that the Consistory would advance the process of Jewish regeneration created tension between consistorial and state officials. Throughout the nineteenth century, Jewish leaders had to balance their mission to regenerate and integrate French Jews with their commitment to preserve Jewish continuity. Both goals led directly to the question of education. If Jews were to integrate, they needed to study secular subjects such as French history and language; yet how much of this knowledge did Jews need to become integrated, and in what setting would they study? How could Jews become integrated French citizens without diminishing their dedication to being Jewish?

Emancipation and Education

In their initial efforts to establish a modern Jewish school system, French Jewish leaders sought to link Jewish education to both the specific process of regeneration and the general French goal of national unification. Modern education stood at the center of their plans for promoting the regeneration and integration of French Jewry. According to this vision, Jewish schools and schoolmasters would produce Jewish youths versed in both their religious heritage and the basic academic skills required for citizenship in the developing French state.[20] Jewish primary schools would also prepare their students to take up manual trades and artisan crafts that would theoretically enable them to integrate into the French economy.[21]

This focus, however, placed Jewish schools at odds with government educational priorities. In the early years of the nineteenth century, the regenerative mission compelled Jewish instructional aims to diverge from the goals of the general French public school system. Both the Napoleonic and Restoration regimes directed their educational resources toward the improvement of secondary education for the first third of the nineteenth century.[22] Such an emphasis made sense: the Napoleonic bureaucracy (which the Restoration regime inherited and, to some extent, maintained) required the creation of a class of mid-level civil servants trained at French secondary institutions, the *collèges* and *lycées*. While the Restoration government issued decrees encouraging primary education beginning in February of 1816, it failed to back these directives in the national budget. Consequently, significant growth of the French primary school system did not begin until the 1820s.[23]

Jewish education, by contrast, needed to concentrate upon primary schooling. In the eyes of both Jewish and non-Jewish educators, most Jewish children lacked the knowledge necessary to attend French secondary schools. Jewish pupils therefore needed to learn elementary subjects such as the French language and basic arithmetic in order to participate successfully in French social and economic life. As a result, while the French school system concerned itself with polishing the abilities of more advanced students to serve state needs, consistorial educators worked to create a Jewish student pool equipped with rudimentary scholastic skills.[24] In their initial negotiations with state authorities, consistorial leaders needed to demonstrate the utility of Jewish institutions to government officials pursuing a different educational agenda.

The concern with utility begged a fundamental question: namely, Jewish educators had to explain why Jewish integration required separate schools. No matter which incarnation of the French government held power, state officials consistently held that the establishment of communal schools negated the need for specifically Jewish institutions. In order to make a utilitarian case for separate Jewish schools, the Consistory needed to demonstrate that its institutions made a unique contribution to the missions of integration and regeneration.

Accomplishing this task in turn meant formulating a notion of minority distinction within an official context geared toward engendering conformity. The push toward conformity and integration emerged early in Napoleon's regime. In 1801, for example, his government tried to consolidate the small communes into larger administrative entities. Although this effort did not fully succeed, it indicated the Napoleonic impulse toward greater government uniformity and authority.[25] The Assembly of Notables and the Sanhedrin were products of this political atmosphere, their decisions offering a synthesis between Frenchness and Jewishness. Both bodies obliged up to a point. As Paula Hyman notes, their decisions "split the religious and ethnic elements subsumed within traditional Jewish identity . . . [and] theoretically limited [their Jewishness] to voluntary membership in a religious community alone."[26]

Debates over Jewish education, however, demonstrate that this synthesis was never completely defined. While consistorial leaders certainly favored an educational system geared toward integration, their lobbying tactics suggest that they also perceived limits to how far that process would reach. Justifying separate schools on the basis of equal treatment under the law meant an assertion of French Jewish legitimacy, even as it involved submission to the French system. A role for Jewish education in integrating France implied the validity of Jewish existence and continuity, since integration would take place within a specifically Jewish context. Utilitarian arguments therefore sought to show that, far from undermining the goals of emancipation, maintaining a degree of Jewish distinction would actually promote Jewish integration.

Jewish continuity thus remained consistent with, and could even facilitate, both integration and French national development. The Notables and Sanhedrin had asserted the basic moral and religious compatibility between Judaism and French citizenship. By linking equality and utility, the Consistory reinforced this idea, uniting Judaism with Frenchness while simultaneously preserving and strengthening both. An acculturated Judaism conforming to general social and cultural norms—what Pierre Birnbaum has called "Franco-Judaism"[27]—thus represented a legitimate option for being French.

Utility became the most powerful idea linking Jewish education to this sense of legitimacy. One could most effectively argue the necessity of separate schools by emphasizing their benefits for France. In developing this position, consistorial leaders drew upon the reasoning proffered by advocates of French moral education. According to this school of thought, the formation of loyal and productive citizens depended upon a healthy moral and ethical structure. A sound French education therefore could not entirely ignore those religious teachings that promoted moral advancement.[28] This position represented a middle ground between those who favored complete secularization of education and those disposed toward deepening the involvement of religious personnel in French schools.[29]

The consistorial leadership applied this thinking to the Jewish situation. Any proper education, they argued, had to attend to the moral formation of its pupils. If religion formed the basis for human morality, then Jewish children needed a healthy dose of Jewish religious instruction in order to become moral and productive citizens. Because consistorial schools served large numbers of poorer Jewish children, the emphasis upon moral development and economic functions assumed added importance.[30] According to moral education advocates, poverty resulted from—and contributed to—a severe moral malaise for which religion offered a powerful antidote. By preserving Jewish religious teachings in an era of rapidly advancing disbelief, Jewish schools would address both the economic and cultural development of French Jewry while simultaneously reinforcing the moral underpinnings of French society.

The Consistory's devotion to this argument, however, masked ongoing polarization within French Jewry regarding the function and content of Jewish education. One party—led by the writer and vocal proponent of Jewish reform, Olry Terquem[31]— objected to the contradictory goals of integration and separate Jewish education. This group wished to accelerate Jewish integration and echoed government concern that separate schooling would only impede Jewish entry into French society.[32] More traditionalist Jewish factions, meanwhile, saw the secular components of consistorial education as a danger to Jewish tradition and a pathway to religious indifference. They feared that a school curriculum bifurcated between secular and religious studies would produce students with less knowledge of—and weaker ties to—Jewish tradition.

Distrust of the consistorial program encouraged the persistence of traditional *hadarim*, especially in the Upper Rhine. These "clandestine" schools in Alsace and Lorraine operated in defiance of both consistorial authority and government decree, but with the approval and support of local populations.[33] The traditionalist segment of French Jewry would also support the oppositional tactics of the Alsatian *grand rabbin* Salomon Klein, who later in the century rejected what he perceived as the integrationist approach of consistorial education and set up his own religious academy outside the rubric of the authorized Jewish administration.[34] Within this volatile context, consistorial leaders attempted to balance both state objectives and the poles of educational thinking within French Jewry.

The terms of the school debate between the Consistory and the state took shape even before the Consistory existed. In February of 1805, Napoleon's Minister of Religions, Jean-Etienne Portalis, convened a commission of Jewish notables to formulate an administrative model for French Judaism under Imperial rule. The commission's report, titled the *Plan d'organisation du culte juif en France,* contained a detailed proposal for rabbinical education, yet made no mention of Jewish elementary schools. This omission demonstrates a clear division in the thinking of the Jewish leadership: rabbinical education constituted a religious activity, while elementary schooling did not. Only later on would the idea of separate elementary schools enter Jewish educational schemes.

Nevertheless, the *Plan* raised several issues pertinent to subsequent Jewish educational endeavors. Most significantly, the notables pointed to questions of equality (the state's obligation to treat all of its citizens equally under the law) and utility (the most efficient method by which Jews could attain state goals of integration and loyalty). The report took care to acknowledge the state's need to supervise its authorized religions and their personnel to ensure that their teachings did not undermine state authority. But the notables also stressed that the state's supervisory role obligated it to protect "liberty of conscience," which they termed "the essence of a sage and equitable government." For this reason, they called for a religious administration comparable to that of the other state religions: "the principles that rule the Catholic and Protestant religions ought therefore to govern the Jewish religion, and a legal organization should place it, like the others, under the supervision of the government."[35]

The notables, however, also pursued their own agenda. They had convened in response to a government summons, to be sure, but that summons stemmed from factors other than Napoleon's goals of administrative hegemony. Nearly fifteen years after emancipation, French Judaism teetered on the brink of institutional collapse. The old Jewish communal structure had disappeared, and nothing had arisen to replace it. French Jews had, in fact, petitioned the Empire to intervene financially to head off impending disaster. Utility, then, rested on two basic criteria: the survival of French Judaism and the achievement of integration and regeneration. These two goals became intricately connected for the notables. Enlightenment and integration marked the path to Jewish survival as well as to a strong France.

As the Consistory's leaders took up the cause of Jewish education, their notions of utility and regeneration began to take a more defined form. In February of 1810, the Central Consistory submitted a detailed school plan to the Minister of Religions, Préameneu.[36] The proposal advocated the creation of a vertically integrated Jewish school system, in which each Jewish community would strive to establish its own primary school. These local institutions would provide instruction in French language and basic arithmetic, skills seen as essential to both cultural integration and economic productivity.[37] They also called for the best elementary students to advance to the Jewish theological schools envisioned for each of the seven consistorial districts. These secondary institutions would train Jewish educators, or identify and prepare young men for the highest tier of Jewish education: rabbinical training and ordination.[38]

The schools' curriculum accentuated Jewish utilitarian goals while seeking to assure Préameneu that instruction in the Jewish schools would not distinguish them markedly from their non-Jewish counterparts. Jewish pupils would study secular and religious subjects, devoting ample attention to both French and arithmetic. Religious teaching would focus on "a precise knowledge of principles, religious duties and morals," designed to form loyal Jewish citizens. These lessons would be limited to Hebrew reading and writing, the basic skills necessary for Jewish worship and biblical study. Probably owing to the lack of qualified Jewish schoolteachers, a Christian master would conduct the secular lessons during the first part of the day, with a Jewish teacher administering religious instruction in the afternoon.[39] Jewish primary schools thus assumed a two-pronged mission: to equip Jewish pupils with the skills necessary to become productive citizens of the developing French state, and to inculcate the moral values necessary for good citizenship.

This moral mission, in fact, made the founding of Jewish schools even more urgent. All over France, the consistorial leaders wrote, Christian schoolmasters excluded Jewish children from their lessons. Prejudice therefore deprived Jews of primary instruction, hindering regeneration and integration. Those lacking religious instruction risked becoming "immoral men, dangerous to society and to the state."[40] Morality also linked Jewish primary schooling to the proposed theological academies by creating a civic pedagogical function for the French rabbinate. Rabbis would oversee religious instruction in the primary schools, even conducting the lessons themselves in the absence of other qualified Jewish teachers. To assure that these schools achieved the intended goals of integration and regeneration, however, French rabbis themselves needed proper education.[41] Their training in modern theological schools would prepare them not only for spiritual leadership, but also "render them capable of enlightening their coreligionists in [their] religious and social duties" and cultivating loyalty to Napoleon and to France.[42]

This line of argument made little progress with the Imperial administration, which appeared reluctant to acknowledge any utility for separate Jewish schools. Matters came to a head in September of 1811 when the Central Consistory sent its aforementioned, forcefully worded petition to Préameneu. The letter stressed that the school issue held "the highest importance for the Jews of the Empire," for "the Jewish youth rots in ignorance and risks tumbling into corruption [due to the lack of] the establishment where it could receive religious instruction."[43] Préameneu's curtly worded reply, however, once again questioned the concept of separate Jewish education. He asked the Consistory whether establishing Jewish schools, a Jewish seminary, or a *faculté théologique* for the Jews merited the government's attention at all. Préameneu pointed out that specifically Christian primary schools represented "establishments of religion and of charity" targeting the poor.[44] Usually, Protestant pastors and parish priests directed these institutions. In many towns, in fact, schools operated under the auspices of local charity boards (*bureaux de bienfaisance*). Christian schools often taught children of all creeds, except for classes in religious instruction intended only for the Catholic and Protestant children.[45]

Since existing establishments offered sufficient educational opportunities for children of all faiths, French Jews had no right to demand special schools for themselves. Instead, Préameneu wrote, they should be permitted to participate equally in the existing system so that "their children should in no way be excluded from the schools opened by the *bureaux de bienfaisance*."[46] If a commune lacked public schools—or if religious considerations made Jewish parents reluctant to send their children to such schools—then local rabbis should emulate the Catholic and Protestant clergy and offer religious lessons outside of the schools. Rabbis could also open religious schools as extensions of their synagogues, providing poorer children with religious learning and "the instruction necessary to all of their class": reading, writing, and basic arithmetic. In any case, the Minister emphasized that if the Jews still deemed it necessary to establish their own schools, those schools would be subject to the same regulations as all other educational institutions.[47]

Beyond its educational implications, Préameneu's reply called into question Judaism's civic function. His suggestion that rabbis move religious lessons to the synagogue demarcated a specific, moral sphere in which Judaism could become involved in French education. The municipal, or "common," schools represented distinctively French space because they received public funding and political authorization. Their overwhelmingly Catholic character, in Préameneu's opinion, reinforced their French quality; Judaism, however, did not possess an equal claim to that space. Even though Judaism was an authorized state religion by this time, the scope of its legitimate activity remained ambiguous. The Consistory's organizing legislation certainly prescribed regeneration as a basic consistorial responsibility, but parochial education was not understood to be part of that equation.[48] Préameneu clearly classified Jewish education alongside charity and poor relief, which was administered by religious boards and within specifically Jewish locations such as synagogues.

Instead of discouraging the Consistory's leaders, though, Préameneu's response emboldened them. They chose to overlook his scolding tone while seizing upon a rhetorical opening. From their perspective, Préameneu had implied that Jews *could* open their own schools as long as they adhered to official educational guidelines.

The Central Consistory's leaders moved quickly. Less than two weeks later, they informed Préameneu that they agreed to his conditions and that departmental consistories would seek to build their own educational institutions according to government guidelines.[49] Faithfulness to the regeneration mission remained central to the plan. Jewish children would receive elementary instruction in both Hebrew and French, basic arithmetic, religious and moral practices, translation of the Five Books of Moses, "as much Rashi as possible," and teachings from the Prophets. This combination would connect "the knowledge necessary [for] each *israélite* for the practice of the [Jewish] religion" to "the duties of the subject toward the Sovereign and of the citizen toward the country."[50] The Consistory also called for all French Jewish communities to establish schools wherever possible so that poor children might receive the same education as those from wealthier families.[51] While the government did not guarantee any material support, Préameneu had inadvertently cleared the way for the establishment of a system of officially sanctioned Jewish primary schools.

The grand consistorial vision, however, faced a number of practical obstacles. Most seriously, the cost of running a school strained the resources of the departmental consistories, making them more amenable to state involvement. The Consistory of Wintzenheim, for example, operated seven schools during 1811–12 at a cost of nearly 10,000f.[52] While the community wanted to open six additional primary schools within its district, it could not meet all the costs itself. Drawing upon the premise of regeneration as a national responsibility, the Wintzenheim leaders naturally turned to the central government for financial assistance. Their petition echoed the general consistorial plan, invoking notions of social utility and tying successful regeneration to proper religious instruction.[53] New primary schools would prepare their students for the prospective Jewish theological schools, which would include both religious study and advanced instruction in the French language. The student body at these more specialized schools would not exceed eighteen students, and at no time would more than eight students attend at consistorial expense.[54] This arrangement would yield a small, select group that would subsequently carry regeneration throughout the region as teachers and community leaders. The Consistory intended to fund the theological schools through a combination of its own funds and a sliding scale of student fees, but the project would still require some government help.[55]

Unfortunately, actual material conditions pared this plan down considerably. Most seriously, the Wintzenheim leaders overestimated the number of students that the schools would attract. They assumed, for example, that children from wealthier Jewish families would attend Jewish schools in proportion to their presence in the population. Such participation was, in fact, rare if it occurred at all. Families concerned with beginning or continuing an upward economic climb had less incentive to send their children to schools that stood outside of the French educational mainstream.

As the French University began to establish its authority in the second decade of the century, ambitious French citizens of all religions began to view the French educational system as their passport to social and economic advancement. Even Isidore Cahen, whose father Samuel was a driving force in the French regeneration movement, did not attend the consistorial Jewish schools in Paris. A gifted student, Cahen opted instead for a more elite track that took him to the prestigious École Normale Supérieure, where he graduated with honors and placed third in the *agrégation* examinations.[56] As for the theological schools, they appealed only to those seeking more specialized religious training, and never really moved beyond the planning stage. The recruitment pattern at the central rabbinical school—where French rabbinical students tended to come from the lower rungs of the economic ladder—underlines the preference of middle-class and wealthier Jews for the French system in matters of secondary education.[57] A budget built upon student fees therefore seemed to ensure ongoing financial shortfalls.

At this early juncture, however, such contradictions had not yet become apparent. The emphasis on regeneration colored consistorial plans and attracted sympathetic government officials. The Prefect of the Upper

Rhine drew liberally upon regeneration vocabulary in recommending the Wintzenheim proposal to his superiors. Above all, he wrote to Préameneu, the "principal motive" behind Jewish schooling at all levels was "to pull the *israélites* who make up this district out of the ignorance" in which they lived. Expanding the reach of consistorial schooling would also weaken the Jews' attachment to "certain Talmudic traditions unfamiliar to Jews living in the interior of France."[58]

The most effective solution, the Prefect concluded, remained government control over Jewish schooling. Under existing circumstances, the state could not entrust Jewish education to "country rabbis" (*rabbins du pays*), when instructors in the Jewish schools needed a strong command of French. Jewish teachers who lacked mastery of French would, he feared, teach only Hebrew while neglecting the secular subjects taught in the Catholic and Protestant schools.[59] The Prefect recommended the establishment of a Jewish theological school at Surentz under the direction of a rabbi with a strong knowledge of French, chosen by Préameneu himself. The rabbi would receive a salary from the consistorial budget and would have to file regular progress reports with the University administration.[60]

Although the Wintzenheim project never came to fruition, it helped outline the template for future school negotiations between the Consistory and the state. First, all parties accepted the central government's tutelary role as the supervisor of Jewish education. Control, however, also implied a degree of commitment. As many scholars have noted, emancipation carried with it a bounty of privileges for French Jews, but also the weighty obligations of citizenship.[61] The notables and Sanhedrin had outlined Jewish obligations to France, but the consistorial leaders believed that these obligations ran in two directions. Because the state's responsibility included providing primary education for its citizens, government control over Jewish schools implied an obligation to grant them meaningful support.

Obligations, though, proved no match for a shortage of resources. The Restoration regime inherited a budget crisis that had necessitated cuts in the civil service and the army.[62] Unable to assist every school, French officials repeatedly rejected consistorial attempts to transform the state from policy-maker to funding source. The Restoration government instead selectively supported those institutions it found most useful in advancing civic goals. Consequently, Jewish schools seeking funds had to move their programs closer to general French guidelines. Satisfying utilitarian criteria thus became essential to promoting specifically Jewish education to government officials who did not immediately acknowledge the need for separate Jewish schools.

The goal of utility functioned as an effective government "carrot," drawing Jewish parochial education toward the French mainstream. In October of 1819—in the first years of the Restoration regime—a consistorial official named Gerson-Lévy addressed an awards assembly for students in Metz's Jewish schools. His remarks outlined the prevailing historical narrative of French Jewish history while defining the parameters of utility within which Jewish schools operated.[63] According to Gerson-Lévy, the Jewish schools of Metz focused primarily upon the formation of loyal and productive citizens. The historical isolation of the Jews had contributed to their oppressed state, and education represented the best means of ameliorating their situation. By combining moral formation with book learning, Jewish schools strove to "rescue the [Jewish] youth from idleness, to ennoble its moral state, to substitute useful inclinations for dangerous ones, to replace routine with method, to inculcate a happy medium between superstition and non-belief, to render the children attentive to their duties toward God, toward the King, toward the nation and toward the future."[64]

Gerson-Lévy extolled the nature of elementary schooling in Metz, where the schools were "open to children of different creeds" including the Jews. But, he continued, "if one considers that part of education which creates human happiness[—]that is to say Religion[—]if one considers that it is important for society that each person worships the Supreme Being according to the movement of his choice, one cannot disregard the utility of establishing schools particular to each faith."[65] Existing French public schools did not provide adequate religious instruction to Jewish children. The regeneration of Jews through moral education therefore required specifically Jewish institutions.

Acceptance of Judaism's specific educational mission had generated significant local financial support in Metz, which was admittedly among the more prosperous Jewish communities in France. Metz's Jews had supplied much of the funding, assisted by the local chapter of the non-sectarian Société pour l'Encouragement de l'Instruction Primaire. Civil authorities also played key roles in opening the school, with both the mayor's office and the municipal council providing political and financial support. The municipal council of Metz, for example, had voted an annual subsidy of 600f every year since the school's inception in 1819, while the Interior Ministry allocated 500f in 1819 and 1820, and 300f in 1821. The departmental council (*conseil général*) also allotted 500f for both 1823 and 1824.[66]

These generous yearly subventions helped the Metz schools gain a firm footing at the earliest stage. By 1830—when French regimes changed again, this time to the constitutional Orleanist monarchy—the Metz Jewish schools had a budget of 1200f per year, half of which came from the town council.[67] The friendly environment had enabled the Metz Consistory to open a supplementary Jewish school in March of 1819 to serve more advanced students, and to plan for a primary school for Jewish girls.[68]

Such an amiable climate did not exist, however, throughout France. Without the presence of willing local authorities and Jewish populations, Jewish schools faced significant financial obstacles. Weak local support consistently translated into material problems that prevented the establishment of a broadly based Jewish school system. The lukewarm response of municipal governments to Jewish school proposals resulted at least in part from the interaction of two sets of factors. First, local prejudice against Jews could doom consistorial appeals.[69] Equally important, the added expense of separate Jewish schools lay beyond the means of many municipalities whose financial burdens increased steadily throughout the nineteenth century.

Napoleon had sought to centralize education under the auspices of his University. The growth of this bureaucracy, however, occurred within the context of the Emperor's military campaigns, which sapped the nation's resources. As a result, the responsibility for funding and supervising primary education (as well as other public services) increasingly fell to local authorities while national policy guidelines emanated from Paris. At the same time, the state restricted the communes' abilities to raise additional revenues.[70] Jewish schools thus competed against both communal schools and other public services for municipal funding. Even after the end of Napoleonic rule, the quest for financial assistance remained an uphill battle, especially in the smaller communes, as state assistance targeted Jewish schools that promised the best chance for success rather than encouraging the opening of new institutions.

Under the later Orleanist regime (1830–48), this unwritten practice eventually became official policy. A report issued by the Conseil Royale de l'Instruction Publique in 1830 noted that, "In the propositions of aid that have been made up until now to the council in favor of the Jewish schools, we have felt duty bound to encourage a nearly exclusive preference toward those [Jewish] schools which were already the object of some subventions on the part of the communes or the departments."[71] Jewish schools already receiving meaningful local funding would receive money from the central government; weakly supported schools would not. This strategy intended to encourage communities to support their own schools while "stimulat[ing] similar sacrifices [among] the indifferent communes." Local authorities would more likely aid Jewish schools if they saw that the central government would respond in kind.[72]

While this principle helped those schools with friendly local governments, it also conferred a veto power on less accommodating communal officials who could now thwart Jewish school plans by refusing to support them. Jewish populations saddled with hostile or apathetic municipal councils therefore found it extremely difficult to establish their own communal schools. Weak local support translated into equally inadequate help from the central government, leaving the brunt of financial responsibility upon the Jews themselves. Consequently, only larger or more affluent Jewish populations could hope to operate separate schools. Ironically, these larger Jewish communities—for example, Metz, Paris, Bordeaux, and Marseille—were those most likely to receive assistance.

Even within these communities, no guarantees existed. In 1830, for example, the Jewish community of Marseille operated a boys' school and a girls' school, both of which relied almost exclusively upon a small group of Jewish benefactors. Of their combined 3,600f budgets, 3,000f came in a lump sum donated by eleven local Jewish merchants. Neither the municipal nor the departmental authorities contributed any money to the institutions. In keeping with its stated criterion of rewarding communal involvement, the Ministry of Education approved a grant of 300f toward the remaining 600f balance.[73] The last 300f was left for the schools themselves to raise, probably from among the original Jewish benefactors.

The Parisian Jewish schools faced a similar predicament. The Paris Consistory also operated both a boys' school and a girls' school in 1830. The boys' school had a budget of 4,758f of which 3,800f came from consistorial funds. The girls' school had a budget of 5,059f, all of which had been raised through private donations. As in Marseille, neither the department nor the municipal authorities offered any aid, leaving a deficit of 958f.[74] The recently installed Minister of Education, Joseph Mérilou, allotted 500f in hopes that his grant would attract "the attention and benevolence of the department and the commune."[75]

As belts tightened and attitudes hardened, Jewish communities across France faced growing intransigence. In the Alsatian community of Brumaltz, described by one observer as "one of the richest communes of the department," the Jewish schools could not obtain any aid.[76] The president of the Jewish school committee in Strasbourg complained to the Rector of the Academy that the department contained more than 100 communes where the Jews should have "indisputable rights for obtaining aid for Jewish primary instruction." Only five of these towns, however, had extended any funding to Jewish schools, and even these five had refused to provide the suitable locale required by law.[77]

Even when the local authorities did lend a hand, their help often proved grossly inadequate. The Jewish schoolmaster of Haguenau, for example, reported his school's total expenses as 1,060f: 370f for the building and heat, 600f for the salary of his primary assistant and 90f for a second assistant. So oppressive were the circumstances, the schoolmaster lamented, that he found it necessary to divide the puny revenues produced by small tuition fees with his assistant "to keep him from dying of hunger." He had even devoted a portion of his own small salary to help cover the school's maintenance costs. The school had received no help from the town except for a grant of 600f from the mayor and an allotment of firewood. The communal council, though, had declined to include a permanent allocation in the town budget.[78]

Melodrama notwithstanding, early Jewish schools stood upon mostly unsteady foundations. While national policy makers placed a high priority on educational utility, local officials often held the power to define that utility to suit their own interests. As regimes changed and the century moved forward, these interests and definitions came to be expressed increasingly through financial decisions. Interestingly, while funding seemed to rest upon integration and utility, few had to do with the academic performance of the schools. In practice, the civic emphasis on utility linked the fate of Jewish schooling to the political, social, and economic conditions of local communities. Larger, more prosperous, and more willing Jewish populations therefore had better prospects for establishing schools and keeping them open. Meanwhile, the political and financial direction of French education ensured that Préameneu's initial skepticism about Jewish schooling would not dissipate over time.

In the longer term, the link between utility and regeneration presented a further danger for Jewish leaders. If they argued that separate Jewish schools were useful tools for regeneration, they had to admit that not all French Jews had integrated. Seeking a wide-ranging Jewish school system implied that integration would be an extensive process, and that many French Jews needed to be convinced to fulfill their obligations as citizens. Consequently, consistorial leaders needed to strike a careful balance between their enthusiasm for Jewish schools and any political indiscretion that would undermine the case for schools or worse, reflect badly upon French Judaism as a whole.

2

Roadblocks to Regeneration

In January 1832, Louis Cottard sent a passionate letter to the Minister of Education on behalf of the Jewish schools within his jurisdiction. As Rector of the Academy of Strasbourg, Cottard was the top educational official in the district and hoped to win government financial support for Jewish schooling. Cottard brought to his work a strong belief in the moral value of modern education, and viewed Jewish communal schools as vital tools for the social and economic regeneration of French Jews. Without them, Jewish children would fall prey to "ignorant and dangerous Talmudists" who would ignore arithmetic and the French language in favor of religious obscurantism, emphasizing a messianic return to Jerusalem that would encourage disloyalty to France.[1]

Despite their utility in Cottard's eyes, Jewish schools faced enormous obstacles in the northeast. First, most Jewish communities were too small to support their own schools. In addition, only two communes within his jurisdiction—Haguenau and the larger community at Strasbourg—provided money for Jewish schooling. Indeed, the financial condition of most Jewish schools remained precarious, and some of these institutions had even closed.[2] By withholding money, Cottard argued, local officials undermined national policies encouraging Jewish integration and regeneration.

Cottard had reason for disappointment. At first glance, the early years of the July Monarchy seemed to usher in a new era of greater religious equality. Most significant, in February 1831 the National Assembly voted to include a permanent fixed appropriation for French Judaism in the national budget. The Jewish Consistories now enjoyed the political legitimacy accompanying a line in the budget, as well as a more regularized financial situation. Historians of French Jewry generally consider this act the final step in achieving full religious equality. Berkovitz argues that the new law emboldened Jewish leaders to pursue state financial aid more vigorously and openly from their more legal secure position.[3]

Equal status, however, did not necessarily entail equal treatment, and the inclusion of Judaism in the state budget did not solve all of the Consistory's problems. Even though the law now provided a fiscal foundation for French Judaism, it proved grossly inadequate in meeting consistorial expenses. Equally important, the terms of the new law did little to ease the problem of justifying separate Jewish education. In fact, subsequent legislation undermined those very educational institutions that Cottard considered so vital to Jewish regeneration. Ultimately, while civic funding did pull some Jewish schools into the French system, it proved just as effective at keeping others out.

Cottard's letter also points out the larger contradictory forces impeding Jewish educational plans. With the passage of the Guizot school law in 1833, the French government called for a stronger, more uniform local commitment to primary education. The new law, however, did not necessarily shower benefits upon Jewish schools. Local authorities continued to control educational funding decisions, yet remained reluctant to support separate schools for a small, politically weak segment of the population. In this context, the demands of utility and equality collided: the Jews deserved equal treatment under the law, but only insofar as that equality proved useful. Centralization further compounded the difficulty of proving the utility of Jewish schools. Consequently, a strategy based solely on either utility or equality could not succeed. As we will see below, joining the two concepts enabled Jewish leaders to demonstrate the unity of Jewish and French interests, and to attract the support of government officials.

The slippery understanding of utility and equality complicated their task. Defining the utility of French Judaism, for example, involved sensitive issues. Even a self-proclaimed philosemite like Cottard expressed negative attitudes toward Jewish traditionalism that echoed the views of many non-Jews both inside and outside the government bureaucracy. The question of how best to integrate the Jews of Alsace was certainly far from resolved during the 1820s, and doubts regarding Jewish business practices and political loyalty found their way into educational debates.[4] Persistent skepticism toward Jewish integration again raised the apparent paradox of separate Jewish education: how *could* Jews hope to integrate by schooling their children separately from everyone else? Cottard himself considered their progress meager. His solution called for changing the priorities of French education to encourage the growth of Jewish schools designed to mediate between French culture and traditional Jewish life.

While hardly a novel approach, Cottard's position maintained the tutelary function of the state that had proved so compelling to French *régénérateurs* like the Abbé Grégoire and to Jewish *maskilim* in Central Europe.[5] Yet the situation in France during the 1830s remained distinct from those other contexts. Outside of France, the *maskilim* and their allies did not have the weight of emancipation behind them. Without that political and legal foundation, state responsibility remained largely theoretical and undefined. Shmuel Feiner argues that the cognizance of emancipation, and the initiation of efforts to attain it, stimulated a reorientation in the Berlin *haskalah* at the end of the eighteenth century. A wider embrace of German culture replaced its original emphasis on a revitalized Jewish culture, and a revamped political discourse centered on emancipation and citizenship.[6] This new direction, as Feiner describes it, was largely unilateral: Jews had to embrace German cultural models as a means for achieving the universal rights of liberty and equality (not to mention fraternity) symbolized by the French Revolution. While they could request government intervention on their behalf, they had no inherent expectation of material or political assistance.

In France, on the other hand, emancipation created a two-way obligation. Jews had to integrate, but the state had to provide financial as well as political support for integration to occur. Simply put, Jewish leaders and sympathizers like Cottard believed that the tutelary state had to back up its ideological obligations with money. As the consistorial leadership would later argue in 1847, *qui veut la fin veut les moyens*—desiring certain goals meant a commitment to supplying the means to achieve them.[7] Government financial aid represented a concrete, tangible expression of this commitment, while withholding it implied indifference to the terms of emancipation.

Such an argument, however, was effective only to the degree that one accepted the basic premise of the state's responsibility to educate Jews. Unfortunately for French Jewry, for the first third of the nineteenth century French school policy did not firmly demonstrate a commitment to educating anyone unable to reach the secondary level. While the central government did devote some money and energy to primary schooling, French officials generally shied away from direct financial involvement in the school system. Indeed, inconsistent local support for Jewish primary education mirrored general trends in French primary schooling during this period. Some communes provided more support for primary schools, others less.

This haphazard atmosphere constituted a main impetus for the Guizot school legislation in 1833. As Grew and Harrigan point out, the Guizot Law marked the midpoint—rather than the beginning—of a rapid period of expansion in the number of French schools. School growth gained momentum largely from an improvement in local circumstances that occurred independent of the central government. The law's provisions, they conclude, reflected the prior growth of the French school system in addition to encouraging the expansion that followed its passage.[8] Consequently, one may interpret the Guizot Law as an attempt to rein in a system whose demands had exceeded the central government's administrative capacities.

The Guizot Law also advanced the general movement toward centralized political control that characterized the early July Monarchy. The law standardized the spheres of responsibility for primary education, asserting ministerial control over the content of primary schooling and the certification of its personnel. Through the University and the Ministry of Education, the central government formulated curricular guidelines for all French schools. A decree of 1834, for example, outlined a uniform class schedule for all primary schools to follow.[9] The Guizot Law also attempted to override the educational influence of the Catholic church through state-regulated teacher certification and compensation requirements. François Furet claims that this goal was in fact "crucial" to Guizot's agenda, in which reasoned learning would lead to moral and peaceable personal behavior.[10]

Like Rome, however, a completely centralized France could not be built in a day, or even in a decade. Despite the work of Guizot and his bureaucrats in Paris, responsibility for working out the practical details of primary schooling still fell to local authorities. The Guizot Law charged the communal councils with organizing primary schools and providing the necessary material resources. Communes also had to supply teachers with lodgings, a salary, and suitable locales in which to conduct their lessons. While the central government continued to subsidize individual educational institutions, the law heaped greater fiscal responsibilities upon communal authorities. As a result, local factors weighed even more heavily in the expansion of public education. The outcome produced an uneven mix of religious and secular schools with large disparities in resources between different communities, or even institutions in the same community. Students were often separated by gender, with a greater emphasis on the education of boys in communal primary schools.[11] The secondary level remained elitist, accessible to the bourgeoisie but not to those from lower economic classes.[12]

Under these conditions, local civic support for Jewish schools remained inconsistent. In fact, the Guizot Law seemed to place Jewish institutions at an even greater political—and thus practical—disadvantage. True, Article 9 of the law allowed for the establishment of more than one sectarian public school in a single commune. Permission to open such an institution, however, depended upon the consent of municipal authorities who would also bear the ensuing fiscal responsibility. By requiring each commune to establish a primary school, the Guizot Law created a rationale for communes either to ignore requests for confessional schools or to favor one religious group over another. Teaching orders such as the Christian Brothers established a strong presence in a number of communes that opted to turn over their schools to clerical personnel. During this period, Catholic educational institutions in general began to make deeper inroads throughout France.[13]

The Guizot Law's objectives also stood at odds with the development of a Jewish educational system. Above all, the law sought to establish greater uniformity of curriculum and instruction. Any steps toward standardization were likely to hamper institutions serving specific minority populations. Curricular guidelines issued by the government in April 1834, for example, contained provisions that at first glance seemed problematic for French Jews. New standards now mandated three stages of moral instruction. Children would learn "prayers and pious studies" between the ages of six and eight years. From the ages of eight to ten, they would study "religious history," concentrating upon "Christian teaching" thereafter.[14] Jewish students in French communal schools would have to sit through these lessons on a regular basis or face exclusion from the public education system.

Jewish arguments for educational fairness alluded repeatedly to this inequitable situation, but with little effect. Even if Jewish leaders could persuade Ministry officials, the central government exercised only moderate influence in local affairs. Enforcement of the Guizot Law therefore proved erratic at best. Despite legislative proclamations from Paris, local interpretations of the law could justify unequal financial support for Jewish education projects or block them altogether. Consequently, while the French school system experienced an enormous expansion of its institutions and clientele after 1833, Jewish schools became more specialized in their activities and the population they served. The Guizot Law thus affected Jewish primary education in much the same manner as the earlier policies of the Restoration regime: government policy officially sanctioned the existence of separate Jewish education, but money and politics impeded the establishment of Jewish schools.

At the time of the Guizot Law's enactment, state-authorized consistorial schools existed on a very limited scale. In 1831, the Central Consistory reported twenty-one Jewish primary schools operating under its auspices.[15] By contrast, estimates of the number of French primary schools during the same period range from between 28,000[16] to as many as 36,000.[17] This relatively small number of Jewish schools lay scattered among seventeen towns. Only the larger communities—Metz (three), Strasbourg, Paris, Bordeaux, and Marseille (two each)—operated more than one Jewish school. The remaining schools served different Alsatian communities.[18]

Consistorial officials attributed the modest number of Jewish schools to a clear lack of cooperation on the part of municipal authorities. The Jewish school supervisory committee of the Lower Rhine complained that even Cottard's enthusiastic support for Jewish schools had not generated any assistance from the department's municipal councils.[19] Their inaction left the Jewish committee to search for funds on its own, generally with minimal success. Of the 110 communes in the Lower Rhine where Jews resided, only seven had government authorized Jewish primary schools. Of these seven, only four communal governments aided Jewish education: Haguenau, Wissembourg, Soultz, and Bischeim. The other three schools were relegated to an "ephemeral existence" that did not bode well for the future growth of Jewish primary schooling.[20]

Larger Jewish communities also had trouble obtaining civic funding, even when public officials supported their efforts. Cottard reported in 1831 that even in Strasbourg, which had a relatively large Jewish population, the well-run Jewish school faced certain closure without government aid. The school received 600f from the town of Strasbourg, but it had lost the 2,400f that it used to draw from the consistorial budget when the state established the *budget du culte israélite*.[21] Local officials also took direct action to undercut Jewish schooling. In 1834, for example, the Nancy Consistory petitioned the Ministry of Education for financial aid to keep its school open. Guizot himself responded by authorizing a grant of 400f, but also ordered the town to assume complete responsibility for supporting the school thereafter.[22] The following year the Rector of the Academy of Nancy, Armand, forwarded another aid request in light of the municipal council's repeated rejection of consistorial petitions for assistance. The council had concluded that because Nancy's Jews constituted about one-thirtieth of the town's total population—approximately 800–1,000 people—their school could claim no more than one-thirtieth of the town's education budget.[23] The communal schools operated by Catholic teaching orders received a total of 1,700f or 1,800f per year from the town, while the Jewish school got 600f. As a result, the council held that the present allotment already represented three times the proportionate size of the Jewish population.

Armand, however, questioned the council's reasoning. He observed that its refusal of assistance resulted from an erroneous interpretation of its obligations under the Guizot Law. Nancy operated three communal schools that accepted students free of charge and directed their efforts toward the children of "less fortunate families." Fueled by the city's approximately 28,000 Catholic residents, these schools had grown rapidly. In addition to the material costs of the three schools, the commune paid each schoolmaster a salary of between 1,200f to 1,500f each year. The council had mistakenly assumed that communalizing the Jewish school would entail similar expenses—approximately 1,700–1,800f annually—that it felt lay beyond its means.[24] Armand had tried in vain to clarify the council's actual obligations, pointing out that the law required only a 200f minimum salary for a teacher. Given the small Jewish population, the existence of a suitable locale in the local synagogue, and the fact that a number of the Jewish students already paid a monthly fee, Armand argued that the council could meet its obligations simply by paying the Jewish teacher about 500f per year.[25] Treating the Jews equally need not have conflicted with fiscal responsibility.

Even so, Armand found it necessary to conjoin the goals of equal treatment and educational utility. He wrote that if the Minister concurred with his interpretation, the municipal council would likely allocate the necessary funds and confer communal status upon the Jewish school. This assistance would serve as a vital investment in an institution that had performed well and that was "directed in a superior manner." Armand's comments in this case went beyond mere local boosterism. His efforts to help the Jewish school contrasted sharply with his opinion of Nancy's Protestant school, which he described as "useless [*inutile*]" and whose closure he strongly recommended.[26] The Prefect of the Meurthe echoed Armand's call for fairness, and advised the maintenance of Nancy's Jewish school "for the security of families who profess the *culte Israëlite* [sic], in regard to the freedom of religious education."[27] Equal treatment, the Prefect concluded, ought to form the primary goal of administrative action in the case.

Despite these arguments, Guizot declined to intervene any further. In November 1835, he informed both the Prefect and Armand that he would not extend any more financial aid to the Jewish school at Nancy. The law, he wrote, called for the communes "to provide for the normal expenses of their public schools." The Ministry could provide assistance only after the commune had exhausted all other sources of revenue. He therefore remanded the consistorial request to the Nancy municipal council, leaving the fate of the school in the hands of local officials who had already proven at best apathetic toward the project.[28]

None of these officials addressed the broader meaning of the municipal council's decision. The council had not just mathematically miscalculated the amount of its financial obligations to the Jewish school; it had rejected the utility of public schools divided along confessional lines. Certainly, a significant portion of the council's argument rested upon its professed inability to pay for more than one set of schools. It had also maintained, though, that dividing Nancy's children into confessional schools would impede the integration of the local population. Continued segregation would only hurt the Jews by "perpetuat[ing] [those] characteristic nuances that render [them] a separate nation."[29]

This line of argument extended the thread begun during the Empire and Restoration. Stressing integration as the ultimate utilitarian goal continued to form a fundamental component of the educational dialogue during the July Monarchy. When in November 1830 the Paris Consistory made its yearly request for school aid to the departmental authorities, the Prefect of the Seine replied that schools separated by religion were the product of a "system of intolerance" that the July Monarchy had ended. If the Consistory wanted to retain its "special schools," it would have to pay for them itself. Léon Kahn, an early historian of French Jewish education, saw in this attitude the seeds of destruction of the existing educational system. The Napoleonic and Restoration regimes, he wrote, had divided schools and schoolchildren by religious confession. The Consistory, "confident in the laws," had planned its schools according to this principle. The establishment of the Jewish religious budget in 1831, though, had delegitimized separate Jewish schooling for all but the poorest French Jews. The budget also actively assailed those schools by restricting their access to public funding.[30]

Changes in the French school system during the 1830s thus undercut both utilitarian and egalitarian strategies for promoting Jewish education. While regeneration remained a common goal for both the government and the Consistory, local authorities did not necessarily see separate Jewish schools as the most suitable vehicles for attaining that goal. As the French system expanded, Jewish schools faced increasing competition for funding and political support. The Jewish petitions in these cases suffered from their emphasis of equality over utility. Whereas concepts of fairness might hold an ideological appeal, utilitarian realities proved far more potent where public money was concerned. These problems became more difficult to avoid as the concept of educational *utilité* became even more closely identified with overcoming the perceived reluctance of French Jews toward integration. For many French officials—even for self-proclaimed philosemites like

35

Cottard—Jews and Judaism in their present state were incompatible with French citizenship. If one accepted the common view that education represented the best road to Jewish integration, arguments for segregated school systems became even weaker.

The individual pratfalls of both negotiating strategies compelled Jewish leaders to attempt to unite them whenever possible. Appeals for fairness *could* appear as seeking special treatment if not properly grounded in utilitarian logic. Similarly, utilitarian reasoning alone made little impact. Jewish schools, small in both size and number, often escaped the attention of ministerial officials. Consistorial lobbying therefore had to balance notions of special consideration with fairness on the basis of utility. While the consistorial leaders—who considered themselves fully patriotic Frenchmen—certainly felt a personal attachment to egalitarian ideals, the appeal to fairness also added weight to their utilitarian positions. The utility of Jewish education came to rest in the state's moral interest in meeting its obligations to treat all its citizens equally, as well as in the unique ability of Jewish schools to advance the cause of integration.

As Jewish leaders tried to communalize their schools, these factors became more entangled. In 1842, for example, a group calling itself the Comité Communal d'Instruction Primaire Israélite appealed for the communalization of the local private Jewish school in Sarrebourg. Communalization would render the municipality responsible for providing both a suitable locale for the school and a salary for its faculty.[31]

Above all, the Sarrebourg petitioners sought to establish the school's utility. The school served more than fifty Jewish boys and girls who received instruction in both secular and religious subjects from a certified teacher and his assistant. The religious component of the curriculum, they wrote, played a crucial role in the school's program. The Jewish environment made the school accessible to pupils from traditional families, opening a door to general knowledge for children whose parents would not have permitted them to study with the non-Jewish schoolmaster at the local communal school. Despite the vital service it provided and the void that it filled, the school had received no municipal support. Its only funding came from the students' parents, who paid both the teachers' salaries and the school's material expenses.[32] Certainly, the petitioners concluded, the equal status of French Judaism under the law obligated the commune to support a Jewish equivalent to the instruction provided for Christian children.

Sarrebourg's municipal council, however, disagreed. In rejecting the request, its members questioned the logic of maintaining a separate Jewish school. The town, they argued, already operated a communal school open to children of all religions and respectful of the beliefs of its Jewish pupils. The presence of twenty Jewish children within the total student body of 160 offered proof of the communal school's suitability. Furthermore, the council held that funding a specifically Jewish institution would detract from the education it provided to the children of other religions.[33] Like their non-Jewish counterparts, the Jewish children of Sarrebourg could receive a "complete education" in the public school while exercising "a perfect liberty of belief." Several of the communal school's Jewish students, they noted, had won academic prizes and had even received municipal aid toward their expenses at the *école supérieure*. Finally, attendance at the communal school could only prove "advantageous" to the Jews in "ending [their] isolation and enabling their children to absorb the mores of French society."[34] The council's understanding of utility thus trumped Jewish claims for fairness. Indeed, for the Sarrebourg council, the most equitable course of action was also the most sensible and efficient.

The fairness argument rang hollow elsewhere within the local administration. The Comité Communal d'Instruction Primaire of Sarrebourg, which supervised primary education in the town, also rejected the Jewish petition. It agreed with the municipal council that the existing communal school adequately accommodated all religions, and the municipal authorities had never received any complaints about the instruction of Jewish children. Equally important, the town lacked the resources to operate an additional primary school.[35] A separate Jewish school would therefore not serve enough of the town's inhabitants to justify the expenses it would generate.

Concerns regarding the integration process reinforced the committee's ideological objection. The committee argued that if the Jews established their own public school, only Jewish children would attend it. A Jewish communal school would therefore create "a point of separation" that would damage civic efforts to combat the prejudices "that unfortunately subsist even now in this district." The participation of Jewish children in the common educational system with non-Jewish children, by contrast, would redound to the Jews' benefit by accelerating their integration. Lastly, the committee did not detect any great demand among Sarrebourg's Jews for a specifically Jewish communal school. Despite the existence of the Jewish private school, "a great number of families" sent their children to the communal schools, even to the girls' school operated by a Catholic teaching order.[36] Admittedly, the committee's assessment contained some strikingly convoluted logic: namely that the failure of the Jews of Sarrebourg to utilize a separate communal school that did not exist rendered such an alternative unnecessary. Still, its report employed utilitarian arguments to refute the petitioners' arguments for equal treatment.

The committee's recommendations received wide acceptance within the civil administration. The Comité d'Instruction Primaire of the Strasbourg district and the *sous-préfet* of Sarrebourg both agreed that the small number of Jewish school-age children—which they estimated as only about forty boys and girls—hardly justified a separate school. Their attendance at the existing communal schools encouraged contact between children of different religions, created a spirit of "tolerance and union" in the town and thereby advanced the progress both of primary education and Jewish integration.[37] Both the Rector of the Nancy Academy and the Prefect of the Meurthe echoed these opinions and advised the Minister to refuse the request.[38] The Minister concurred and soundly rejected the Sarrebourg petition.[39]

In Sarrebourg, political and material forces intersected to impede consistorial school plans. While advocates of separate Jewish schools grounded their arguments in principles of equality, government officials adhered to more utilitarian standards. In order to receive official sanction—and thereby civic financial support—a school had to serve a Jewish population of some size that would otherwise have gone without primary schooling altogether. Hamstrung by small numbers and insufficient resources, very few Jewish communities could satisfy these criteria.

Local Jewish populations also proved to be insufficient and unreliable sources of financial support for Jewish schools. Ideological opposition to Jewish primary schooling emanated from within French Jewry as well as from external sources. One of the most difficult problems involved the credibility of the schools and their teachers among the populations they sought to serve. More than one staunch Jewish traditionalist distrusted the French public schools, which they saw as havens for Catholic proselytizing and Jewish apostasy. Consequently, unauthorized or "clandestine" Jewish schools sprouted in areas where Jewish traditionalism had strong roots.[40] These institutions usually offered a more traditional Jewish education, eschewing much of the secular curriculum of the public schools. The observation that half the school-age Jewish children of Sarrebourg availed themselves of the publicly supported primary schools, for example, meant that half the Jewish children did not. Whether they sent their children to clandestine schools, public schools, or no school at all, half the Jewish families in Sarrebourg refrained from sending their children to the consistorial school.

This general absence of enthusiasm suggests that even Jewish communities with the means to expand the Consistory's educational network often lacked the will to do so. A fundamental problem lay in the students targeted by Jewish educators. While the Jews of Alsace did have their grandees, the schools' clientele consisted mostly of children whose families occupied the lower end of the economic scale.[41] As a result, Jewish educators had trouble raising money from the people most likely to use their services, which forced them to look to traditional sources of philanthropy. French Jewish schools consequently became earmarked by financial necessity, identified as charitable institutions whose utility lay in their value to poor Jews.

This perception hemmed in consistorial negotiators. Arguing for an expansion of consistorial schooling within this context meant that French Jews had not adequately integrated, that they remained indigent, backward, and of possibly questionable loyalty. The correspondence in both the Nancy and Sarrebourg cases indicates the persistence of this view among French civic officials. In response, consistorial leaders struck a delicate balance between expanding their school operations and shoring up existing institutions.

An additional obstacle arose with the inclusion of Judaism in the national religious budget in 1831. The *budget du culte israélite* addressed only religious expenses, disrupting the flow of money from the Central Consistory to the Jewish schools. While the consistories could still designate funds for schools, the fixed amount they received from the budget limited their financial flexibility. Moreover, the new system placed Jewish schools under the jurisdiction of an Education Ministry intent upon shifting the main financial responsibility for primary schooling to the communes. Jewish educational institutions could therefore not expect any great measure of future aid from the central government. For their part, local authorities remained indifferent toward separate Jewish schooling.

The new budget regulations increased the financial pressure upon Jewish schools, even as the government sought to regularize the Jewish religious administration. Shortly after the Guizot Law's passage, the president of the Jewish school committee in Nancy complained that his school would suffer enormously from this change. Prior to 1831, the school had received 1,500f of its total expenses of approximately 2,200f directly from the consistorial budget. The municipal government had also contributed an annual sum of 160f, with the remaining balance coming from donations and a small number of student fees.[42] These new procedures, though, deprived institutions such as the Nancy school of consistorial funding.[43] Nancy's school committee petitioned the departmental administration for help, but the Prefect perfunctorily responded that the school remained the responsibility of the commune, not the department. The commune of Nancy, though, had allotted only 120f per year, hardly enough to meet the costs of running the school. Even after the commune raised the allocation to the previous level of 160f, the school's situation remained precarious. The president finally appealed to the Ministry of Education, warning that the Jewish school might have to close its doors in the absence of financial assistance.[44]

By weakening the financial ties between Jewish schools and the consistorial administration, the *budget du culte israélite* circumscribed the perceived boundaries of Jewish education. Many French Jews began to view Jewish primary schooling as a non-religious activity, raising questions over its proper form and function. After February 1831, Jewish officials all over France noted a considerable drop in voluntary contributions to Jewish schools. Leaders of the Marseille Consistory, for example, complained that the establishment of the *budget du culte* had created the false impression that the state would now provide for all of French Judaism's material needs: "Our coreligionists, who had never before refused the tribute of their zeal and generosity . . . [now believe] that we ought to apply to the Government . . . which will not hesitate to lighten their burdens by tossing to Jewish primary education some scraps of the nourishment of which the other schools of the realm partake."[45]

The Bordeaux Consistory's school committee reported similar problems. While the Jewish school at St. Esprit served only about twenty students, consistorial officials believed that it could easily have accommodated sixty-five or seventy-five if supplied with the necessary funds. The new state of financial affairs, however, had cut off traditional funding sources while hindering the establishment of new ones. Before 1831, the Bordeaux Consistory had regularly raised approximately 1,500f among its constituents to help pay the school's expenses.[46] The municipal council had extended 300f of aid in 1830 after the Christian Brothers had taken over the communal school, which thereafter no longer admitted Jewish children.[47] Between the communal allocation and donations from the Jewish community, the Jews of St. Esprit had managed to pay a teacher. Following the state's assumption of the Jewish religious budget, however, "voluntary donations promptly exhausted [either] the good will or the abilities of the Jews of St. Esprit and Bayonne." The resulting shortage of funds prevented the St. Esprit school from expanding its operations.[48]

Consistorial goals for a national system of Jewish primary schools crashed upon the rocks of these practical limitations. As the educational demands of the central government placed greater financial burdens upon communal budgets, questions of utility superseded questions of fairness. When Isaac Weille, the commissioner of the Toulouse synagogue, petitioned the Prefect of the Haute Garonne for financial help, he lamented that more than forty of Toulouse's Jewish children went without education due to the synagogue's inability to pay a Jewish teacher. The children's families were reluctant to send them to one of the new communal schools that did not provide any instruction in Jewish religious principles. This lacuna, Weille argued, left a portion of his congregants "deprived of the benefit of public education."[49]

Weille's arguments for equal treatment proved no match for the utilitarian assessments of the civil authorities. The departmental council rejected Weille's petition, as did Guizot, both asserting that primary education was a communal affair over which the department had no jurisdiction. Both parties also echoed the views of Toulouse's mayor, who argued that the town's small Jewish population did not warrant such an expenditure, especially when the majority of Jewish children already attended the existing communal school.[50] In May 1834, the Toulouse municipal council concurred, rejecting Weille's petition on the grounds that not enough Jews lived in town to justify the expense of a separate school. Jewish children, the council maintained, suffered no prejudice at the communal schools where they received "all the elements of instruction with regards to the present knowledge of society and the religion that they profess."[51]

While general ambivalence toward separate Jewish schooling did not completely erase Jewish education in France, Jewish officials had to adapt their plans to the available resources. As the central government's commitment to public education expanded, both Jewish and civic officials devised alternative means for providing religious instruction to Jewish children. The Toulouse council, for example, offered a compromise: the commune would pay for religious lessons conducted outside the school in order to avoid the expense of a separate institution for a small number of children. Consequently, the council raised its annual allocation to the local synagogue from 300f to 500f in 1835, designating the extra money for the communal rabbi "under the condition that he teach the Hebrew language to the poor [Jewish] children."[52] This supplemental line remained in the municipal budget at the end of the decade.[53]

The Toulouse case reveals a growing awareness of the impracticality of Jewish schooling on a wide institutional basis. Changes in levels and sources of funding either put Jewish education on the track of general philanthropy or restricted its scope to moral and religious lessons. Slowly, the very concept of Jewish education began to evolve from one of separate schools and schoolmasters into one of supplemental programs of religious instruction. The growth of French public education thus limited the possibilities for the establishment of a separate system of Jewish schools. As the century wore on, local governments had to assume greater financial responsibility for primary education. Local authorities in turn often lacked either the financial means or the ideological commitment to support separate Jewish education.

As the French educational system began to absorb French Jews in greater numbers, the concepts of utility and equality took on new significance. Separate Jewish schooling became more difficult to justify, since dividing Jewish children from non-Jews contradicted the ultimate goal of integration. Nor did equal treatment under the law necessarily assume the option of separate education; rather, it connoted the wider accessibility of French education. By the end of the July Monarchy in 1848, consistorial concerns over fairness had begun to focus less on the establishment of separate institutions and more on the treatment of Jewish students within the French system. The bureaucratic definition of utility, meanwhile, began to stress the best use of available resources toward an expanded goal. If Jewish education's *raison d'être* had heretofore consisted of facilitating integration, it now added the goal of protecting Jewish children from Christian proselytism and prejudice in the classroom. This expanded idea of utility gave new urgency to Jewish pedagogical efforts after the 1850s.

The redefinition of equality also indicated a shift in the interpretation of Jewishness and Frenchness. While early consistorial petitions called for separate and equal treatment for Jewish schools, the goal of national integration implied a community of values and goals. From this perspective, "equal treatment" connoted the equal application of the state's utilitarian criteria in the general national interest. From the government's standpoint, withholding support from Jewish schools did not constitute anti-Jewish discrimination, but rather a policy decision based on the most efficient use of limited financial resources. The principle of fairness, meanwhile, affirmed the compatibility of Jewishness and Frenchness. For Jewish education advocates, Frenchness and Jewishness became intertwined and mutually reinforcing, so that being Jewish became a valid way of being French. Jewish leaders opposed government utilitarianism to the extent that it threatened this delicate balance. As the French school system grew, however, it became increasingly clear that the Consistory would need to reconsider the relationship between French Jews, Jewish schools, and the state.

3

REDEFINITION AND CONSOLIDATION

On March 2, 1869, the leaders of the Jewish Consistory in Strasbourg sent a report to the Central Consistory in Paris detailing the state of Jewish education within their jurisdiction. At first glance, the report glowed with satisfaction. The Strasbourg leadership pointed proudly to strong Jewish participation in the educational system. In all, 2,671 Jewish students attended either French public schools or private "free schools" (*écoles libres*) in 1868, including six Jewish "special schools" (*écoles spéciales*) for boys, five *écoles spéciales* for girls, and one "pre-school" (*salle d'asile*) for children below school age. The Strasbourg leaders pledged to press on, "following the path marked by the law and encouraged by the benevolent dispositions of the departmental administration." Their consistory, they promised, would "continue to propagate the benefit of education in our communities, either by the conversion of *écoles libres* into communal schools (*écoles communales*), or by the construction of new schoolhouses, or finally by opening classrooms whose location is the responsibility of the communes."[1]

Achieving these goals, however, meant overcoming significant obstacles. The Consistory's educational work had encountered "plenty of difficulties, notably . . . the ill will of the municipal councils [who have pleaded] the insufficiency of local resources and the needs of the majority religion." Local officials had not been forthcoming with financial assistance, and only five of the Strasbourg Jewish schools received any aid.[2] Shortages of money and a dearth of students hindered the establishment of Jewish schools in other communities. Fifty-four communities had no hope of opening a

Jewish school, but the Consistory was working toward establishing schools in twenty-seven others. The greatest need existed in rural areas, where "the [Jewish] children frequent the Christian schools and the cantor (*ministre-officiant*) or his delegate provides religious instruction." To address the situation, the Strasbourg leaders had sought to foster cooperation between different Jewish communities, but this task had proven difficult, if not impossible.[3]

The conflicting themes of the Strasbourg report—pride, optimism, wariness of Catholic influence in the schools, and *kvetching* about the communal authorities—reflected the general situation of French Jewish schooling during the Second Empire (1851–71). As in earlier years, the fate of Jewish schools depended upon the desire of local Jewish communities and the good will of civic officials. Faced with an expanding French school system, unsympathetic municipal leaders, competition from the Catholic church, inadequate material resources, and a limited clientele, Jewish educators gradually narrowed the focus of their activities.

Although the consistories had struggled against all these forces from the beginning of their educational work, new school legislation in 1850— known as the Falloux Law, after the Bonapartist Catholic deputy who championed it in the National Assembly—eventually forced a reassessment of their plans. Like the Guizot Law before it, the Falloux Law was the product of a new French political regime. Ostensibly, it represented a means of returning the Catholic church to the forefront of moral and political leadership in France. In practice, however, Louis-Napoleon Bonaparte, Napoleon's ambitious nephew, used the law and subsequent measures to enlist the Catholic clergy in his struggle to reestablish his uncle's Empire (a goal he accomplished via a coup d'état in December 1851). In January 1852, he issued a new constitution that installed him at the head of what François Furet poignantly calls a "Caesarean democracy"; by December, through a popular referendum, Louis-Napoleon became the Emperor Napoleon III. The Second Empire, which would last until the military debacle of the Franco-Prussian War in 1871, imitated its predecessor through an intensive effort to centralize political power in the Emperor's hands. It also united the Emperor with the forces of religion and political conservatism as a means of maintaining civil order.[4]

Patrick Harrigan, however, disagrees that the Falloux Law pitted religious schools (specifically those run by a reactionary Catholic church) against more secularly oriented public schools. The bulk of this struggle, he holds, occurred at the ideological and rhetorical level. In terms of educational practice, Harrigan sees the three decades between the Falloux

Law and the Ferry Laws of the late 1870s as an era of cooperation between church and state that resulted in the construction of a national school system. During this period, school enrollments boomed, suggesting that the idea of education as a necessity of life had made significant inroads. Competition between Catholic and public schools, he concludes, resulted from the dovetailing of school goals and clientele as the two systems became more similar toward the end of the 1860s.[5]

The history of Jewish schools under the Falloux Law indicates divergence from the general pattern that Harrigan describes. As we have seen, the religious and philanthropic character of Jewish schools limited their potential clientele. Their financial and political need for utilitarian justification based upon the mission of regeneration and integration in turn necessitated an earlier alignment of their curricula with French standards. The Catholic schools undertook a similar alignment, but they were not as completely beholden to strict conformity. Consequently, if the Falloux Law eased the rivalry between Catholic and public schools, it exacerbated the competition between Jewish schools and the public school system.

From a Jewish perspective, the Falloux Law threatened to alter an educational structure in which Jewish schools already stood on the margins. Its best-known measures expanded the teaching privileges and supervisory powers of the Catholic clergy, simultaneously calling for all French teachers to place greater emphasis on morality and the maintenance of social order. In pursuit of these goals, the law weakened the power of University officials while augmenting the authority of the departmental prefects and Catholic clergy. The number of administrative districts (*académies*) in the University grew from twenty-two to eighty-six, but the size of each district shrank; the responsibilities and influence of the rectors who headed each *académie* both diminished proportionally. In some areas, the rector became something of a figurehead, "a departmental functionary without authority in comparison to the bishop and the prefect."[6]

The new rules further undermined the University's authority by creating alternative paths to teacher certification. Prior to 1850, communal schoolteachers needed to possess the *brevet,* an official certification requiring the successful completion of University examinations. The Falloux Law, however, allowed individuals with either three years of teaching experience in an authorized school or a letter of obedience from a religious order to receive relatively automatic authorization. While the law required that each commune establish and maintain at least one primary school, it freed municipalities to turn their schools over entirely to clerical teaching personnel.[7] Equally important, the law placed responsibility for school supervision in the hands of departmental academic councils, whose members included the Rector, a primary school inspector named by the Minister of Education, the Prefect, a bishop and a priest named by him, a Protestant minister, and a rabbi.[8] The bishops tended to dominate these councils, especially in areas with large Catholic majorities. From these authoritative positions, they facilitated the activities of clerical teachers, sometimes at the expense of non-Catholics.

The Falloux Law thus opened the door for the Catholic clergy to reinforce and expand its presence in French education during the Second Empire. The number of schools affiliated with religious orders (*écoles congréganistes*) tripled between 1850 and 1863, topping out at approximately 3,000. While this number represented less than 10 percent of the approximately 36,000 secular schools (*écoles laïques*) in France, municipal councils often preferred to hire instructors belonging to religious orders. This clerical teaching corps headed primary schools and conducted elementary education throughout France, becoming a significant force in the educational system.[9] The variety and availability of different Catholic instructors made it easier for communes to match their resources with a specific teaching order. Furthermore, opting for schools run by clergy usually translated into lower school costs for communal councils.[10] These measures created the potential for French primary schools to become extensions of Catholic clerical authority, while deemphasizing the importance of the minority Protestant and Jewish religions within the school system.

In many respects, Jewish education suffered under the Falloux Law. New economic mandates further reduced civic financial resources, compelling existing schools to consolidate their positions. Equally important, resurgent Catholic domination of the public school system—especially on the secondary level—fanned Jewish fears that French schools would turn into new venues for Catholic proselytism. Some Jewish schools achieved communal status during this period, gaining regular financial support from their communes. The communalization of Jewish schools tapered off rather early during the 1850s, however, indicating an end to any meaningful growth of Jewish primary education.

At the same time, uneasiness about religious apathy among French Jews fermented within the consistories. Several high profile conversions and incidents of clerical interference in educational matters spurred fears about general weaknesses in French Judaism that might imperil its future. Consistorial leaders responded with a renewed commitment to educating young Jews, hoping to reinforce Judaism against Catholic proselytizing.

Jewish schooling, however, lacked the institutional strength of Catholic education. In addition to its demographic dominance and political influence, French Catholicism enjoyed other, more subtle advantages. Through the first half of the nineteenth century, Catholic clerical orders arose to open and direct religious schools in communes all over France. These groups established their own internal hierarchy based on status and prosperity. Teaching orders such as the Christian Brothers and Frères Maristes tended to serve larger institutions with more resources, while less prominent orders such as the Clercs de St. Viateur served smaller, poorer communities. As Sarah Curtis has noted, this tiered system allowed communities to establish schools according to their available resources while enabling Catholic personnel to ensconce themselves in the communal education system.[11]

Minority status and fiscal constraints, by contrast, limited the flexibility and accessibility of Jewish education. Whereas Catholic teaching orders often fulfilled the legally mandated educational requirements for a commune, Jewish leaders needed to justify their schools as additional expenses. With extra money in short supply, Jewish schools paralleled the lower ranks of the Catholic system: as mentioned earlier, they tended to attract mostly needy pupils, and lacked prestige. Inadequate resources thus compartmentalized Jewish schools as philanthropic institutions whose students were destined mostly for vocational training instead of higher learning. Even the Parisian consistorial schools—supported by patrons that included the Rothschild family—directed their lessons toward poorer children who were not expected to go on to secondary education. In order to serve as a bulwark against Catholic conversionary pressure, Jewish education needed a new set of priorities. In response, the Consistory gradually began to focus on providing classes in religious instruction for all Jewish children. While consistorial leaders did not immediately abandon the idea of a separate Jewish school system, the Second Empire set the stage for a later transformation of Jewish educational strategy.

The shift in consistorial approach also signaled changes in the relationship between Judaism and state in France. In the first half of the nineteenth century, Jewish educators had pressed the case for Jewish schools by demanding equal application of the state's tutelary functions and fiscal responsibilities. By the 1860s, however, the French bureaucracy had become less responsive to arguments for equal treatment on behalf of Jewish institutions it considered redundant, divisive, and therefore *inutile*. While consistorial leaders remained reluctant to give up the dream of a national Jewish school system, conditions on the ground forced a reformulation of educational priorities and a redefinition of "equal" and "useful."

Determining just what those concepts meant framed the Jewish school issue during the 1850s and 1860s. Disagreement over the utility of a minority religion was not unique to Judaism. Protestant officials, in fact, often faced many of the same problems. In 1861, for example, Protestant parents in the commune of Castetarbe petitioned for the communalization of their private school, arguing that the present subvention of 150f was too little to maintain the school and pay the teacher. While the municipal council eventually raised the teacher's salary from 150f to 400f, it refused to communalize a Protestant school where a communal Catholic school already existed. The Protestant school in Orthez, meanwhile, achieved communal status based on the commune's large Protestant contingent.[12] By creating a gateway for greater Catholic influence in the schools, the Falloux Law thus weakened minority claims on public educational space.

The Consistory's revised school plans therefore became deeply intertwined with ideas of Jewish legitimacy in France. Educational bias in favor of Catholicism rendered Judaism more of a "private" entity, in the sense that it had less of a presence in the French public school system. This exclusion in turn left less civic money available for Jewish schooling. While civic funding was never overly abundant, inclusion in the budget meant inclusion in the concept of the civic. So long as the French authorities had an obligation to facilitate Jewish schooling, French Judaism would remain part of the public realm. For consistorial leaders, marginalized Jewish education stood only a few steps short of a marginalized French Judaism. Striving for equal educational treatment under the law—even as hopes for a broad Jewish school system faded—enabled Jewish leaders to continue assigning meaning and mission to French Judaism on their own terms.

The tapering off of Jewish school growth contrasted sharply with other educational trends. Most significant, the Catholic school system doubled its enrollment between 1850 and 1863.[13] As Antoine Prost has observed, Catholic schools gained momentum from two main factors: "favorable municipalities" where local populations welcomed a Catholic educational presence; and wealthy local notables who could help them financially and convince—or compel—locals to enroll their children.[14] While Jewish leaders lacked the coercive powers of their Catholic counterparts, the same basic elements proved essential to the success or failure of Jewish schools: acquiescent local authorities and sufficient clientele. The difference in the Catholic situation lay in its larger and more receptive audience, among both the populace at large and the civil authorities.

The growth of Catholic schooling—or at least communal schooling run by Catholic clerics—did not single-handedly push Jewish schools to the sidelines. Indeed, the two sets of schools hardly competed for the same students. But the availability and affordability of Catholic schooling placed

Jewish educators at a great disadvantage when it came to competing for financial support, especially considering the tendency of municipal councils to seek the cheapest possible school option. Even Catholic clergy experienced problems in obtaining educational funds from communal officials, and often had to turn to private donors. Most Catholic schools relied on local philanthropy, small alms, and student fees for daily expenses.[15] Catholic schools, though, possessed significant advantages in this regard, from the institutional fundraising structure of the church to the sheer number of faithful who might contribute. Jewish schools relied on much smaller pools of potential donors; their concentration on poorer children also tended to negate student fees as a significant source of income. By giving communal officials greater control over primary education, the Falloux Law rendered Jewish schooling more vulnerable to local attitudes. Not surprisingly, the spread of Jewish educational institutions came to a decisive end in the years following the law's passage.

In light of these difficulties, Jewish education advocates began to pursue the communalization of their schools in greater numbers. Petitions for communalization usually required the assent of the communal council and mayor, and success depended upon the endorsements of municipal, departmental, University, and ministerial officials. While legislative mandates for local school funding and leniency toward confessional education helped Jewish schools in friendly municipalities, the communalization system empowered less accommodating officials to derail Jewish educational projects.

The process of obtaining communalization held to the established utilitarian pattern: successful Jewish schools had a better chance to receive financial support than those that struggled to attract students. Shortages of money and students compelled smaller communities to treat Jewish education as a supplement to the communal schools rather than as an institutional alternative. For example, a consistorial survey of 1851 reported that all three Jewish schools in Paris—a boys' school, a girls' school, and a *salle d'asile*—were communalized, due mostly to the size of their student bodies. The two primary schools served approximately 250 students while about 164 children attended the *salle d'asile*. Surrounding Jewish communities, by contrast, lacked sufficient numbers to support their own schools or to merit any assistance from their communes. Some offered courses in religious instruction, but no Jewish alternative to the local communal school existed.[16]

Likewise, of the five Jewish schools in the Bordeaux Consistory, the two largest—a boys' school and a girls' school that served over 150 students combined—received communal subsidies, while the other three schools—one for boys, two for girls—were private and served approximately 130 total students.[17] Other communes in the district, however, had fewer resources and thus offered fewer educational options. Unlike Bordeaux, the smaller communities of Libourne and Clermont-Ferrand had too few children to justify separate schools. Instead, Jewish students attended the local communal schools and received religious instruction from the local cantor as they approached the age of thirteen.[18]

Similar patterns held elsewhere in France. The Nancy Consistory, for example, reported that in most of its communities Jewish children attended "mixed schools" operated by the commune and open to all religions. Far from lamenting this state of affairs, the Nancy leadership did not perceive "any inconvenience" because of it.[19] To the contrary, the district's Jews, the civil authorities, and the general populace of the department all appeared perfectly content with the arrangement. In one of his inspection reports, the head of the departmental academic council remarked that "the *israélites* appear to be in less of a hurry to demand special schools than the Catholics and Protestants. In Nancy, they have abolished the communal school that had been earmarked for them. Their children frequent the other public schools."[20]

Only five communes within the Nancy district had separate Jewish schools. These tended to be rather modest institutions, serving approximately twenty to thirty students apiece. In Sarrebourg, thirty-three Jewish children attended a Jewish school while twenty-one attended the town's communal schools. Only the Jewish school in Phalsbourg had a larger student body, reporting its attendance as fifty boys and girls.[21] In these places, Jewish opinion regarding the utility of separate schools remained divided and Jewish families often voted with their feet. The case of Nancy, though, indicates that the growth of the French system reduced incentives for smaller Jewish communities to undertake the expenses of separate schools.

At this stage, however, Jewish leaders remained unwilling to admit publicly that a significant portion of French Jewry remained opposed or ambivalent to separate Jewish schools. Instead, consistorial documents from the 1860s deflected responsibility onto municipal administrators: educational difficulties were the fault of uncooperative civic officials, while success was directly related to civic support. Hostile municipal officials received most of the blame for the inadequate level of Jewish schooling in the Colmar district in the northeast, where the consistorial leadership complained that none of their schools enjoyed the full benefits of communalization. Some Jewish schools received small subventions from their communal councils; others only an allotment of firewood. The prejudicial attitudes of the municipal council also confined Jewish schooling to unsuitable accommodations. While the Jewish teachers received adequate salaries from the town, the consistorial leaders lamented the "deplorable" state of the school buildings. The Christian schools, they wrote, occupied "newly built, monumental constructions," while the Jewish schools found themselves "relegated to an old cottage" pieced together out of "a former barracks," lacking even the necessary hygienic space prescribed by law. The Prefect himself had protested this state of affairs to the communal authorities, as had the Consistory, both without success.[22]

These difficulties suggest that the pattern established before the Second Empire persisted through the 1860s: Jewish schools required a combination of Jewish and civic support in order to succeed. Civic help was more likely available to larger Jewish communities with established schools. Five Jewish schools within the Marseille consistorial district, for example, received public funds: the boys and girls schools in Marseille and Nîmes, and the school for boys in Lyon. Each of these institutions served between thirty and forty students (with the exception of the Marseille boys' school that had sixty students) and each received between 600f and 1,200f from their respective communes. Marseille's Jews had also opened a *salle d'asile* that served approximately forty Jewish children of both genders, a project to which the Prefect had accorded 1,000f in 1851 and 1852.[23] In the late 1860s, the Jews of Carpentras opened a private boarding school (*pensionnat*) for young girls directed by a Mlle Milhaud, who held a *brevet élémentaire*.[24] As in Metz twenty years earlier, this combination of Jewish and civic financial support bred greater activism in Jewish education. Over time, the economic stratification of Jewish schooling pulled more successful schools toward the French system while marginalizing smaller, poorer ones.

Communalization also demanded educational conformity. The Falloux Law had mandated a primary curriculum teaching "religious and moral instruction, reading, writing, French grammar, arithmetic, and the system of weights and measures." Optional subjects included "applied arithmetic, history and geography, physical sciences and natural history applied to practical purposes," agriculture, industry, and hygiene; carpentry, "surveying and linear design"; and "singing and *la gymnastique*."[25] In addition, communal schools could operate only under the direction of certified teachers.

Jewish educators did their best to meet these requirements, installing at least the basic curriculum in consistorial schools and seeking out certified instructors. Certified teachers headed all of the communalized Jewish schools in the Marseille district, for example.[26] The need for certified instructors created an interesting situation in St. Esprit, where the teacher at the Jewish girls' school held a *brevet de capacité* and was assisted by a Catholic *institutrice* who also possessed a *brevet*.[27] While this situation may or may not have been unique among Jewish schools—at least, no other consistory reported employing non-Jewish elementary schoolteachers—it indicates that proper certification of a schoolteacher could outweigh his or her religion where public money was concerned.

To address the need for instructors, Jewish leaders took advantage of the Falloux Law to expand the Jewish teaching corps. Like members of the Catholic orders, Jewish clergy automatically qualified for the *brevet*. This provision facilitated the opening of Jewish schools in smaller communities that lacked University-trained Jewish teachers and the means to support them. The Nancy Consistory reported such circumstances in several schools within its jurisdiction. The only sources of Jewish education in the communes of Insming and Dienze, for example, were private parochial schools directed by local *ministres-officiants* who possessed *brévets du degré élémentaire*.[28] By enlarging the elementary teaching pool, the Falloux Law enabled Jewish schools to operate in communes that might otherwise have gone without them.

Despite this hidden benefit, the demands of complying with the law limited the number of Jewish communal schools and pushed Jewish education largely into the private, parochial realm. Jewish religious learning thus came to occupy a dual state in the elementary system: technically inside the officially mandated French curriculum, but physically outside the schoolhouse walls. Private Jewish schools did little to address the problem, since middle-class Jews were reluctant to send them their children. Jewish commentators worried that this situation could weaken Jewish continuity at a time when Jewish religious laxity seemed to be rising. The attempt to establish equality for Jewish education therefore constituted a struggle against the marginalization of Judaism.

These fears were not unfounded. According to available documentation, Jewish public schooling ceased its period of modest expansion during the decade following the passage of the Falloux Law. The Ministry of Education authorized the establishment of eleven different Jewish schools between 1835 and 1848.[29] In March of 1850—the month of the Falloux Law's passage—it issued two additional decrees.[30] From that point forward, the Ministry handed down decisions regarding subventions and charitable donations to existing Jewish schools, but did not authorize the establishment of any new institutions. While individuals like Rabbi Salomon Klein continued to engage in unauthorized educational activities,[31] no new establishments opened under official auspices.

Even the stamp of communalization did not guarantee financial security. A Jewish communal school received a regular subvention from its municipality, and perhaps extra help from the departmental or national government, but this level of financial support usually proved insufficient. Jewish schools generally lacked public support and thus depended upon charitable donations and student fees for a large portion of their expenses. The local consistory often served as the medium for charitable donations made to these institutions, either directly or via the local charity board (*bureau de bienfaisance*).

Charitable donations, though, produced inconsistent and irregular income for communalized Jewish schools. Donations often came in the form of gifts and bequests (*dons et legs*), which generally passed rather easily to private Jewish schools, but more slowly to communal ones (which needed government approval before accepting them). The same requirement applied to contributions made to the Jewish private schools operated by the consistories, which needed government authorization for any donation or legacy.[32] Protocol usually called for the local mayor to accept the funds, either alone or in conjunction with the departmental consistory. The law also required various municipal and departmental authorities to submit testimonial documents to the Ministry of Education. Final authorization came by imperial decree following a review by both the Minister and the Conseil d'État. This bureaucratic maze was hardly practical for addressing the immediate daily needs of a Jewish school considering that the entire process could, in some cases, take more than a year. For example, the 300f bequeathed by Esther Peixotto of Bordeaux reached the Bordeaux Jewish communal schools nearly eighteen months after her death in 1860.[33]

Communalization thus proved to be a two-edged sword. While Jewish communal schools received civic aid, the money often proved inadequate. At the same time, accepting public money made receiving private donations more difficult. While the Falloux Law expanded the playing field for Catholic schools, it limited the Consistory's educational reach and forced it to narrow its operations. The shift resulted from more than simple supply and demand. Battered by social, economic, and political realities, the ideal of regeneration gave way to concerns about Jewish survival.

By the later years of the Second Empire, these forces combined to coax consistorial leaders away from their fixation on formal schools and prod them toward a more program-oriented approach to Jewish education. In December of 1868, the Central Consistory asked each departmental consistory to report on Jewish education within its jurisdiction. The questionnaire asked which communes had schools specifically for Jewish boys and girls (*écoles spéciales*), the number of students attending these schools, and the level of financial aid provided by the civil authorities. The Consistory also wanted to know how communities without Jewish schools provided religious instruction, and an assessment of the chances of establishing new Jewish schools within the various districts.[34]

Responses to the questionnaire painted a picture of loosely managed and poorly funded schools serving an ever narrowing clientele. Increased specialization produced educational segregation according to class, level of religious observance, or both. Maintaining the consistorial focus on separate schools meant catering to the poor while leaving many Jewish children without access to religious education. An absence of religious learning would also leave Jewish children more susceptible to proselytism within a school system dominated by Catholic clergy.

The 1868 survey demonstrated that time had not moderated the problems of the past: availability of and participation in Jewish education varied according to locality, as did the level of financial support that individual programs and institutions received. Typical reports came from the southern consistories of Bordeaux and Bayonne. Each operated Jewish schools in their consistorial seat (*chef lieu*) with civic financial aid, while more remote locations generally lacked any organized Jewish schooling. In Bordeaux, the boys' school had 120 students, while the girls' school served eighty and the *salle d'asile* seventy. No other community in the district, however, held any promise for founding a new school. In Clermont-Ferrand, Jewish children attended the Catholic schools and received supplementary religious instruction from the local *ministre officiant*.[35] Bayonne also had two Jewish schools, one each for boys and girls. Each of these establishments served approximately twenty-five students and, like the Bordeaux schools, received municipal financial subsidies.[36] Still, the commune's contribution of 2500f to the two schools fell far short of the total school budget, leaving the Consistory to make up the difference. The Bayonne leadership complained that the situation remained unsatisfactory even though they had stretched their financial resources to their limit, and the small number of students involved precluded additional help from the commune.[37]

Meanwhile, the growing French school system continued to muscle Jewish education to the sidelines. The Colmar Consistory, for example, reported that the sizeable Jewish population of Mulhouse offered its best prospects for establishing a Jewish school. The commune, however, operated only non-confessional schools.[38] Apparently, this arrangement satisfied many Jewish parents: 289 Jewish children—162 boys, 127 girls—attended these schools.[39] With such a large contingent of Jewish children already attending the public schools, Jewish institutions had little chance of attracting enough students to stay open.

In the eyes of many observers, the inconsistency in French Jewish education posed a latent threat to French Judaism. Although the Falloux Law did not specifically rescind Jewish educational rights or privileges, neither did it specifically affirm them. In fact, the law's original draft in 1850 had not assured equal supervisory access to the schools for Jewish officials, an omission that struck some Jews as a sign of nefarious motives. Isidore Cahen, for one, protested that, "The consequences of the new education law have sadly already made themselves felt upon our religion; everywhere religious equality is found unraveled, everywhere minorities—and ours especially—see themselves excluded, or nearly so, from the benefit of public education."[40] The Falloux Law, he observed, placed control over communal schooling in the hands of the municipal authorities, who in turn would likely cede "the exclusive and absolute direction" of their educational institutions to ecclesiastical personnel. Catholic clergy would "close [their schools] *de facto* to all non-Catholics, since in place of having the State—protector of all religions—as tutor and supervisor, the students [would] be submitted to the intolerant direction of one exclusive religion." Such abuses, Cahen warned, would occur not only in predominantly Catholic communities but throughout France.[41]

Cahen also railed against the additional supervisory powers the new law granted to the Catholic clergy. He noted that the eighty-six examining juries charged with certifying secondary school instructors counted only one Jew among their 516 members. School committees seeking to promote Catholic educational goals could therefore easily discriminate against Jewish teachers.[42] Article 10 of the proposed law also excluded Jews from proportional representation on the departmental academic councils that would oversee school operations. These councils consisted of delegates chosen by the Minister of Education from among the civil administration and the Catholic and Protestant clergy. The councils would form in any department where "there exists a legally established church [*où il existe une église légalement établie*]." The Minister would also designate Jewish representatives "in each department where there exists a legally established consistory."[43] Cahen reasoned that, because some consistorial districts included several departments, the law could result in the absence of Jewish members from many of the local academic councils. He therefore urged the Central Consistory to lobby to change the word *consistoire* to *synagogue*. This modification would establish a legal basis both for proportional representation on the academic councils, and for the opening of Jewish schools "wherever our religion is organized, wherever there is a *ministre du culte* salaried by the State, a temple, [or] a regularly organized community."[44]

55

Although the wording of the law remained intact, Cahen's reasoning represented an important departure from existing Jewish thinking. His argument for proportional representation dismissed the criterion of utility based on communal size; instead, Cahen affirmed the equal status of French Judaism in the French religious structure, arguing for Judaism's relevance no matter how dispersed or small its pockets of adherents.

Cahen had personal reasons to distrust the intentions of Catholic authorities. Following his graduation from the École Normale Supérieure and his successful completion of the *agrégation* exam in 1849, he had received an appointment to a chair in philosophy at the Lycée-Napoléon at Vendée. The bishop of Luçon, however, opposed the appointment of a Jewish philosophy professor at the predominantly Catholic *lycée* and promptly closed the school's chapel. The Ministry subsequently withdrew the appointment and offered Cahen an alternative position in literature. Cahen refused the new post, effectively ending his academic career.[45] The experience left him with a deep suspicion of Catholic involvement in public education.

This sentiment resonated in his numerous writings in the *Archives israélites,* whose editorship he inherited from his father, Samuel, in 1862. Cahen linked the Catholic intolerance that he saw as the Falloux Law's inevitable consequence with his own bitter experience at Vendée. In his view, the dismissal of Jerome Aron from a chair in history in Strasbourg solely on account of his Jewish faith reinforced his interpretation of events.[46] Henri Martin, a prominent attorney for the Conseil d'État, also discerned a pattern of discrimination against Jewish teachers. The Ministry of Education, in his opinion, had undertaken a systematic effort to drive Jews from the ranks of history and philosophy instruction.[47]

The apprehension created by the Cahen and Aron affairs generated suspicion about the ultimate objectives of Catholic educational domination. In response to Cahen's dismissal, Simon Bloch—editor of the other significant French Jewish periodical of the time, the *Univers israélite*—warned that Catholic instructors posed a serious threat to members of minority religions, and that Cahen's termination had resulted from the conversionary objectives of Catholic educators. Jewish instructors, after all, "do not imitate the maneuvers of certain professors who . . . seek to draw [their] Jewish listeners to the desertion of [their] beliefs. . . . Could this be why the bishop of Luçon rejects the Israelite professor who . . . would not lend himself to serving as an instrument of apostasy and corruption against his coreligionists and against the Protestants?"[48]

Jewish wariness of Catholic proselytizing from the teaching lectern represented a specific manifestation of a broader fear of Jewish conversions. Decades earlier, the conversions of notable Jews such as the Ratisbonne brothers cast a shadow upon the striving for social, economic, and educational advancement. Théodore and Alphonse Ratisbonne came from a wealthy, prominent family in Strasbourg, where their father, Auguste, served on the consistorial board. Having attended elite schools, Théodore converted in 1827 and studied for the priesthood; Alphonse became a Catholic in 1842 and joined the Jesuit order.[49] Although the reform-minded writer Olry Terquem dismissed Jewish misgivings in an essay of January 1858—arguing that "these converted Jews over whom we make so much noise have no numerical importance and . . . our *communion* will hardly be affected by them"[50]—the threat remained real among many Jewish thinkers. Further uneasiness resulted from the well-publicized case of Edgard Mortara, the son of an Italian Jewish family. As an infant, Mortara had fallen gravely ill and had been secretly baptized by his Catholic nursemaid. In 1858, he was abducted by church authorities and taken to a convent. Pope Pius IX ignored numerous calls by both Jews and non-Jews for the child's return, and the Mortara Affair became an international issue.[51]

In light of these events, the relative weakness of Jewish religious education struck an alarming chord with the consistorial leadership. In a typical comment, the Colmar Consistory expressed few doubts as to how the Catholic clergy would employ its new power in the classroom. In Bolleviller, for example, Jewish boys had to attend the local Catholic schools since the commune lacked a Jewish school. "As in all communes deprived of Jewish schools," the report bitingly observed, "there they acquire perfect knowledge of the dogmas of Christianity."[52] In the consistorial view, the situation especially threatened Jewish children in smaller towns, due to the absence of a strong Jewish educational alternative. Neither the commune of Uffholtz nor that of Cernay—with nearly fifty Jewish schoolchildren between them—had a Jewish school due to a lack of financial resources. At Uffholtz, the *ministre officiant* conducted religious lessons; in Cernay a retired merchant led the classes, though his teaching left "much to be desired." This arrangement troubled the local Jewish leadership; but how else could one "combat the contrary tendencies of which the Jewish children are the earwitnesses [*les temoins auriculaires*] in the Catholic schools that they are obliged to frequent [?]"[53]

The rabbi of Uffholtz, whose report deeply influenced the Colmar Consistory's assessment, had strongly voiced his own apprehension regarding the dangers of Catholic proselytizing. From the "tenderest age," he wrote, Jewish children found themselves "initiated into the practices [and] ceremonies of the predominant religion." As a member of a school inspection delegation, he had seen Jewish boys and girls using elementary schoolbooks depicting Christian religious ceremonies. Jewish parents regularly complained to him that certain Christian teachers had even required their Jewish students to read New Testament passages for their reading lessons.[54] The municipal authorities, however, had turned a deaf ear to his protest that, according to the principle of Jewish legal equality, "it is not essential to drill the children in reading by placing between their hands Catholic works such as books of prayers [and] gospels." The local council had replied that it would require the teachers to dismiss Jewish children from the classroom during religious instruction and that any "shocking allusion" that could engender prejudice toward Jews would be omitted from the lessons.[55]

These promises, however, rang hollow in the end, and in the rabbi's opinion the situation remained unsatisfactory. Without the cooperation of the civil authorities, the rabbi had little leverage in his "battle against the obsessions, the honey-coated words, the menaces, the mockeries of a *curé*, of an *abbé*, of more than one nun who have such an easy time with the poor little ones of five or six who frequent our [communal] *salles d'asile*." Only the establishment of Jewish communal schools, the rabbi concluded, could remedy "this evil."[56] The Colmar leadership agreed, warning that without communalization Jewish religious education would eventually erode so severely that within "ten years the Jews will do no more in the synagogues than listen to the cantors [*ministres-officiants*]."[57]

Even as consistorial leaders fretted over the dimming prospects for communalization, they did not give up on Jewish education completely. In fact, a more viable long-term solution to the problem showed up all over the 1868 survey responses. As mentioned above, French school legislation named only the required components of elementary studies, not the venue or manner in which they should be administered. Hemmed in by the strong Catholic presence in communal schools, Jewish educators moved their lessons outside of the communal schoolroom. The Paris Consistory reported that smaller Jewish communities such as Le Hâvre could not open their own schools, but had opted to provide religious instruction as a supplement.[58] The same situation existed in Laferté, where the town's fourteen Jewish children received individual private lessons from the local cantor.[59] In St. Etienne, where the prospects for opening a Jewish school remained remote, Jewish children attended Christian schools and received their religious lessons on Thursdays and Sundays from the cantor and the local rabbi. Indicative of the resonance the dream of a national Jewish school system still held, the Lyon consistorial leaders reluctantly clung to the old vision. While the St. Etienne courses served only seventeen students, they believed the classes would grow if the municipality extended the financial aid necessary to found a Jewish school.[60]

The new strategy appealed to Jews in both the north and south. In Toulouse, for example, the local rabbi conducted "a course in Hebrew and religious instruction" for which he received 400f from the municipal authorities. Classes met each day of the week except Saturday and were attended by twenty to twenty-five Jewish boys and girls.[61] In Mulhouse, too, Jewish children received religious lessons in tightly organized courses conducted by the rabbi and two tutors.[62] Students were divided into six classes according to aptitude and gender, with the classes split equally between boys and girls. In contrast to the situation elsewhere, Mulhouse's courses kept regular hours with four different sessions between eleven o'clock in the morning and six o'clock in the evening. This arrangement satisfied even the disgruntled leaders of the Colmar Consistory, providing equal opportunities for Jewish and Christian students.[63]

These conditions, however, reflected special circumstances. In Mulhouse, political and commercial interaction between the town's Jews and the predominantly Protestant population created a tradition of cooperation that carried over into the schools. As one historian has pointed out, religious prejudice hindered Catholic economic success in Mulhouse while leaving the activities of Jewish businessmen relatively unaffected. Cultural issues such as mastery of the French language and economic productivity posed greater hurdles to Jewish social and economic advancement in Mulhouse than any religious considerations. By the 1860s, the town's Protestant elite had constructed an education system aimed toward promoting French language and culture. Their schools welcomed all segments of the population and created no special disabilities for Jewish children based upon religious belief.[64] Mulhouse thus constituted a somewhat unique situation in which Jewish religious education occupied relative equality with Christian instruction. Jewish schooling stood on shakier ground in less cooperative communes elsewhere in the department.[65] Nevertheless, the burgeoning success of the Mulhouse program and others like it made Jewish supplementary religious instruction an increasingly attractive, practical option for shoring up French Judaism at mid-century.

The Falloux Law thus stimulated a period of consolidation and redirection for Jewish schools by painting the initial consistorial vision out of the national definition of French education. By emphasizing local support for schools, the law discouraged any meaningful expansion of Jewish communal schooling on a national scale. Jewish educators found themselves pitted against their Catholic counterparts in a competition for limited municipal school funding that they could not hope to win. Squeezed financially, politically, and geographically, Jewish education began to assume a more specialized role, narrowing its mission from the complete regeneration of French Jewry into a largely philanthropic operation aimed at the Jewish poor.

The economic and curricular separation of Jewish schooling pointed to an evolving sense of acceptable Jewish space in France, which in turn influenced visions of Jewish education. Earlier in the nineteenth century, the concept of utility had focused on goals of acculturation and national integration: Jewish schools were useful, their supporters argued, because they facilitated the process of becoming an *israélite française*. At the same time, equality had justified civic financial and political support for separate schools. By the end of the 1860s, however, Jewish leaders had linked utility and equality: Judaism's utility now derived from its equality; the state's authorization of Judaism and the creation of the Jewish religious budget should have been the last word on Judaism's civic suitability and moral value. That value lay in Judaism's continued moral significance as an agent of integration: Jewish educators believed that poor Jews should become French, but within a distinctly Jewish context. But what of those Jews in less need of integration? Concerns over Catholic proselytizing, conversion, and general Jewish religious laxity reinforced the notion that French Judaism's moral relevance was not limited to the children of the poor. To fulfill its moral mission, Jewish education had to seek a new space within French society, to move beyond the Consistory's original integrationist goals.

The Consistory staked out that space by establishing supplementary programs of religious instruction that would appeal to wider groups of Jews. The growth of these programs spoke to a perceived need to perpetuate Judaism, to search for new venues in which to pass on religious learning. The logistics of schooling in France, however, pushed this search out of the schoolhouse and out of the "public" arena. At the same time, squeezing Judaism out of communal schooling allowed a greater potential for flexibility in delivering religious education as a supplement, with minimal state or municipal involvement.

The shift to programs in religious instruction therefore constituted more than just a defensive step against conversionary pressure: it also signified an assertion of French Judaism's importance despite its more private definition. If the withholding of civic money had closed the door to the communal school system, it had simultaneously left open a broad, private playing field in which the consistories could exert greater influence. Freed from the burdens of state regulation, classes in Jewish religious instruction began to benefit from a reallocation of consistorial resources. The Third Republic's campaign to remove religious teaching from the communal schools accelerated this transformation of French Jewish education; but the seeds of change had already been sown by both the Falloux Law and local dynamics.

II
Rabbinical Education and the State, 1808–1906

4

How Much Latin Should a Rabbi Know?

In September 1864, the Bordeaux Consistory installed Simon Lévy as its chief rabbi (*grand rabbin*). The public ceremony took place with appropriate degrees of pomp and solemnity. At precisely 2:15 in the afternoon, Lévy entered the sanctuary of the synagogue on the rue Causserouge. Garbed in his rabbinical vestments, he strode in at the end of a lengthy *cortège* comprised of the members of the Bordeaux Consistory and other local Jewish dignitaries. The procession moved deliberately, accompanied by songs "at once of a simple and grandiose character." When all had taken their seats, the president of the Bordeaux Consistory, Alfred Léon, welcomed the new *grand rabbin* with a speech trumpeting the virtues of Bordelais Jewry:

> [T]he rich are willing to let themselves be won over when you go to solicit charity, and the poor will accept the offering of your discreet hands with respectful humility; both will listen with pleasure to your pastoral lessons that will incline their hearts to practice the prescriptions of our divine law with exactitude. . . . In Bordeaux . . . you will have occasion to recognize how great is the respect for liberty of religion; you will become aware of it through the consideration that your religious character will attract on the part of men of all religions and all ranks; and . . . I have full confidence that through your spirit adorned with so much solid and varied knowledge, and your gentle and sociable character, you will not take long to form noble and sympathetic relations [with them].[1]

Léon's remarks contained more, though, than simple flattery and boosterism. In listing the benefits of Lévy's new post, Léon delineated what had become the common description of the French rabbinical office. As *grand rabbin,* Lévy would not only see to the proper performance of Jewish religious rituals: he would administer poor relief, oversee religious education, and serve as a liaison with non-Jewish notables and public officials. These functions represented a transformation of French rabbinical duties. Rabbis had traditionally been involved in many of these tasks; now, they were expected to do so within a French context, as figures with standing beyond their religious community.[2] Léon's use of the phrase "solid and varied knowledge" in particular points to a significant change in French rabbinical expectations. In the eyes of the Jewish establishment, an authentic *grand rabbin* needed strong secular learning in order to fulfill his religious duties.

This rabbinical prototype had not emerged overnight, nor had it generated spontaneously. Disagreement over the relationship between religious and secular instruction had caused ongoing friction among French Jewish leaders and between the Consistory and the government as well. Debate over the content, quality, and quantity of rabbinical education raised specific issues of control and finance, as well as larger questions regarding the nature of the rabbinate and French Judaism. In this respect, state attitudes toward rabbinical education provide a useful contrast to the situation of Jewish elementary education. While the central government—in its various nineteenth-century incarnations—paid only cursory attention to the problems of Jewish primary schools, it took far greater interest in the fate of the central rabbinical academy. If the forces of utility, equality, and money nudged Jewish primary education out of French civic space, the same factors pulled rabbinical training more fully into the civic arena. Once there, rabbinical education became subject to the policies of the French University and the influences of French politics.

The transformation of rabbinical training was also linked to general French educational expectations. Because its charter bound it to emulate French University standards, the rabbinical school had to conform to developments within that wider system. In many respects, conflicts over rabbinical studies reflected broader tensions within French higher education. The issue of classical languages brings this relationship into stark relief. Traditional nineteenth-century French educators saw the integration of French and classical studies as a means of linking modern French society and culture with a glorious ancient past. Studying classical literature, they believed, also bolstered a student's intellectual abilities and personal morality. Latin and Greek authors exposed French youths to high ideals, while translation exercises developed stronger grammatical skills and composition style. The Napoleonic University reinforced the traditional emphasis on classical subjects, and during the 1830s and beyond, Latin and Greek remained the primary distinction between elementary and secondary schooling.[3]

French reformers, on the other hand, considered the University's curriculum stagnant and too removed from the intellectual movements of the day. Their influence, however, varied according to the priorities of the ruling regime. The Napoleonic University stressed classical subjects as a means of training a loyal and productive pool of public servants, while the weaker years of the Restoration opened the door for curricular revision. In the late 1820s the liberal Minister of Education, Antoine Vatimesnil, led a concerted effort to deemphasize classical studies in favor of mathematics, science, and modern languages.[4] While a government collapse derailed his program, Vatimesnil's reform proposals presaged later battles over the content of French schooling.

Amid this ongoing struggle, the Consistory struggled to formulate an appropriate course of rabbinical instruction in which the status of Latin and Greek became a central point of contention.[5] Berkovitz and Albert have each argued that the impetus for expanding the secular components of French rabbinical training originated within the government rather than within the consistorial system.[6] Secular learning, however, was not necessarily at odds with rabbinical education. In other European Jewish communities, rabbis had employed classical knowledge to reinforce Jewish traditionalism. Rabbis in seventeenth-century Amsterdam, for example, used sermons to convey Jewish tradition to Sephardic immigrants with limited knowledge of these concepts and practices. Their sermons drew upon conventional forms of rabbinical discourse, but also upon the rhetorical forms of Aristotle, Cicero, and other classical orators.[7] By the beginning of the nineteenth century, the Talmud Torah of Hamburg—a Jewish parochial school—offered a curriculum that combined secular and traditional religious learning.[8] Secular knowledge, particularly of modern languages, also began to show up in rabbinical job descriptions in other parts of Prussia.[9] The *Plan d'organisation* adopted this approach by favoring greater secular learning for French rabbis.

Its authors also grasped the need to establish a utilitarian basis for rabbinical education in order to win government approval. Consequently, they stressed the program's benefits both for French Jewry and for France as a whole, and the logical implications of the government's stated desire to treat all three religions equally. Fairness and utility therefore intersected for both Jewish and civil officials. While many of these Jewish leaders sincerely

CHAPTER 4

wished to create a more modern rabbinate, they understood that emphasizing secular training could also enhance rabbinical prestige among the civil authorities. In this sense, the government acted as a stimulator, but not as a dictator: the Consistory needed to operate within a predetermined set of principles in order to gain state support, although at the outset no one directly ordered them to do so.

Charting the status of classical subjects, and rabbinical proficiency in them, measures the degree to which the consistorial rabbinate internalized French civic standards of education and culture. The curricular history of classical studies also demonstrates the financial role played by state officials in effecting changes in the rabbinate and the degree to which French Jews might have resisted the process. Although consistorial leaders presented a general air of consensus to government authorities, disagreement over the utility of classical studies—and thus of the modernization of French rabbis—divided their ranks. Even as Latin and Greek became ensconced in the rabbinic curriculum, the school's leaders and their critics continued to debate the merits of these subjects. State bureaucrats also weighed in, constantly pressuring the Consistory to improve the rabbinical school's classical curriculum. Assessing the results of these courses provides insight beyond the rhetoric that the issue generated, opening a window into the way that state policy influenced one of the main public faces of French Jewish culture.

Among its main supervisory responsibilities, the Jewish Consistory assumed a mission to remake the French rabbinate.[10] While the Consistory's charter did not specifically mandate this function, proponents of a "modern" French rabbinate saw rabbis as agents of the Jewish integration to which the Notables had agreed and sought to train them accordingly. Indeed, the Portalis commission had argued in 1805 that properly trained French rabbis could "edify their listeners in the French language."[11] Toward this end, it recommended training rabbis in both secular and religious subjects at two rabbinical schools: one in northern France ("Nancy, Strasbourg, or Metz") and one in the Midi ("at Bordeaux or Bayonne"). Although the government never approved this plan, its main components echoed clearly in subsequent consistorial proposals.[12]

The consistorial leadership prioritized rabbinical changes shortly after it settled into place. While one author has asserted that the Consistory refrained from requesting authorization for a rabbinical school until 1816,[13] archival documents reveal that the Central Consistory petitioned the French University for permission to open a rabbinical school as early as 1809.[14] This initial appeal held that by recognizing Judaism as an official religion, the state had implicitly authorized the Consistory to educate its own clergy. Because the other state religions operated their own clerical training institutions, the principle of equal treatment under the law should have allowed for an official Jewish rabbinical academy. Consistorial leaders also questioned the logic of authorizing a religion and placing certain obligations upon it while simultaneously restricting its ability to meet those obligations. They therefore proposed a modified version of the *Plan d'organisation,* advocating the establishment of a central rabbinical academy and two theological schools to advance the process of regeneration.[15]

The government's tepid response elicited a more detailed consistorial plan emphasizing an updated vision of the rabbinate. Rabbinical studies would digress from the "medieval" past, conforming more closely to University standards. Rabbinical students would learn French, and they would have to become versed not only in theology, but also in the humanities—specifically, Latin, logic, and rhetoric—to obtain ordination. Religious education would include traditional Jewish texts ranging from the Bible to the commentaries and legal codes of Maimonides and Joseph Karo. Ordination would depend on an examination administered by the seminary faculty, presumably demonstrating competence in the entire course of study.[16]

This scheme once again generated little enthusiasm within the Ministry of Religions, compelling Jewish leaders to adjust their proposal. Twice more in 1810, the Central Consistory renewed its request, but with a greater utilitarian focus. In addition to maintaining Jewish equality with Christianity, the Consistory's leaders stressed the necessity of rabbinical educational institutions for the promotion of Jewish integration.[17] This approach portrayed Judaism as both distinct (and thus equal) and integrated (and thus useful). A revised plan announced in March 1812 expanded the role of the theological schools, which would be established in each consistorial district. Their curricula would merge talmudic and theological subjects with secular French secondary studies.[18] Aspiring rabbinical candidates would have to pass examinations in basic French and arithmetic; those who excelled in both theological studies and "the culture of human sciences and *belles lettres*" would receive preference for the office of *grand rabbin*.[19] For better or worse, the consistorial plan linked the expectation of equal treatment to the utility of secular learning for French rabbis.

Utilitarian principles continued to crystallize around the rabbinical role in advancing French Jewish integration, and the secular knowledge necessary to do so. In July 1812, a bureaucrat in the Upper Rhine recommended that the Minister of Religions, Préameneu, appoint rabbis with a command of the French language to lead Jewish theological schools. These rabbis should come from the "interior" of France (as opposed to the northeast), and should file regular progress reports with the University.[20] While Préameneu took no action, these recommendations foreshadowed official policies yet to come. For their part, Jewish leaders understood the requirements for authorization: French rabbis had to expand their secular knowledge in order to facilitate the integration of their fellow Jews.

Unfortunately, the Napoleonic government's march toward war and eventual collapse pushed the *Plan d'organisation* aside. The return of the Bourbons to the French throne after 1815 sparked new consistorial efforts. At first, the political climate seemed more favorable to education. A royal order of February 29, 1816, for example, called for the expansion of public primary schooling and for improvements in secondary education. A supplemental order of June 14, 1816 outlined specific guidelines for teacher certification.[21] These acts failed to create any administrative momentum for a rabbinical school, especially since the fall of the Empire left the economy in a shambles, and the Restoration regime faced an uphill struggle for political credibility.[22] Still, in the autumn of 1816, the Minister of the Interior and Religions, Joseph Laine, posed the question of the rabbinical school to the Commission de l'Instruction Publique.[23] The commission agreed that academically integrated rabbis would speed the progress of enlightenment among French Jews. Toward this end, it advised requiring rabbinical candidates to complete the *bachélier-ès lettres* degree in advance of pursuing their calling.[24] The monarchy's inherent weakness, however, precluded any concrete political or financial support for such a scheme.

Jewish officials appropriated this utilitarian language into their subsequent lobbying, combining it with the goal of Jewish survival. When asking for permission to open a theological school in 1822, for example, the leaders of the Metz Consistory asserted that all *grands rabbins* should possess the *bachélier-ès lettres* degree. Secular training, they wrote, would steep *grand rabbins* in the French language and enable them to model French culture for their fellow Jews. It would also prepare them to combat the dangerous "spirit of indifference which would [otherwise] propagate among our coreligionists."[25] The Metz leaders linked this notion of utility to the absence of a rabbinical school, observing that only nine *grand rabbins* existed for all of France, and two of them resided in Paris.[26] So few rabbis, they lamented, could not effectively promote Jewish integration. Jewish integration and Jewish continuity had, in this case, melded into a single goal.

With the rhetorical alignment out of the way, the Consistory needed to work out the school's budgetary logistics before gaining final approval. In the years before the establishment of the Jewish religious budget in 1831, neither the Ministry of Religions nor the Consistory had the resources to open and operate a rabbinical school. The situation changed in 1826 when the *grand rabbin* of the Central Consistory, Abraham de Cologna, resigned to become head of the Jewish community in Trieste. The Consistory applied his 6,000f salary to the projected rabbinical school budget of 9,000f, with the remaining money to be collected from among the Jewish communities.²⁷ Although the estimated budget ultimately proved insufficient, the assurance of self-support with minimal public assistance tipped the scales within the religious administration. The school's final curriculum would not be formulated, though, until late in 1828, and only in April 1829 did it receive official approval. Finally, in September 1829, the École Central Rabbinique de France opened its doors in Metz.

Initially, the departmental consistories applauded the news of the school's authorization, taking care to cite its utilitarian advantages. The Paris Consistory gushed that rabbis trained there would "one day become men capable . . . of serving as an example, through their piety and their enlightenment to those whom they are called to guide in their religious and moral duties."²⁸ The Marseille Consistory agreed on the necessity of both religious and "profane" education. Secular learning, they affirmed, would enable the rabbis "to represent the nation and to earn its respect." Since rabbis acted as role models for the laity, their training would enhance "the piety" and political status of French Jews.²⁹ The modern French rabbinate now represented both the symbols and the instruments of successful Jewish integration.

The united front of elation over the school's establishment, however, did not heal internal Jewish strife over rabbinical learning. Most notably, disagreement over the school's location produced discord that festered for the first three decades of its existence. In September 1827, the Consistory of the Lower Rhine—seated in Strasbourg—argued that the school should be located within its circumscription in the Alsatian provinces. A royal order of 1819 had decreed that either the host departmental consistory or the general consistorial budget should absorb the costs of Jewish religious education. Since the majority of French Jews lived in Alsace, they would in one way or another shoulder the majority of the financial burden for the rabbinical school and should therefore have the honor of hosting it. The Strasbourg leaders also argued that the traditional Jewish environment of Alsace would assure better talmudic instruction.³⁰

On the other side stood more reform-minded Jews who wished to see a new French rabbinate trained in Paris. Paris, in their eyes, represented the country's cultural and intellectual center and thus offered better educational opportunities for French rabbinical students. If rabbis were to serve as agents of Jewish integration, they needed to become imbued with French culture themselves. Rabbinical students could best attain this goal in Paris, which also offered more than adequate Jewish educational resources. The Paris camp remained a small faction in those early years, supported mostly by advocates of religious reform such as the writer Olry Terquem and the educator and journalist Samuel Cahen.[31] These two poles of thought would not disappear; as the following chapter shows, when the time came to address problems at the École Rabbinique, the Paris and Metz factions formed all over again.

The competition between Metz and Paris reflected a broader conflict between Paris and the provinces. Some historians paint this as a political tension, dating back to Jacobin attempts at centralization in the wake of the Revolution and continued by the Napoleonic Empire.[32] Others see additional economic motivations. The conservative Legitimists of the Second Empire, for example, hoped to convince rural notables and peasants to remain in the countryside and revitalize the rural economy.[33] Both interpretations imply a cultural division that pitted more cosmopolitan and politically radical Paris urbanites against provincial peasants and grandees not eager for change. At the time of the Revolution Jewish society followed this general pattern: a more urbane and acculturated Parisian population versus a more culturally isolated and religiously traditional rural one. In the following decades, and throughout the 1820s, Jewish leaders in the provinces repeatedly clashed with those in Paris over religious and educational reforms.[34]

Despite the political influence of Parisian Jewry, practical reasoning favored opening the rabbinical school in Metz. First, accommodations in Metz were cheaper than in Paris. The Jewish community of Metz had offered to close its existing private rabbinical academy and house the new institution in that building. In addition, Metz's prestigious French *lycée* meant that the rabbinical school could recruit its secular faculty locally.[35] Metz also held symbolic significance as the site of a famous medieval talmudic academy and as the residence of the great medieval rabbinic scholar Rashi.[36] Finally, Metz's proximity to the majority of French Jewry in the northeast would mean closer contact between rabbinical students and the population among whom they would carry out their integrationist mission.

Founding the École Rabbinique in Metz also allowed consistorial leaders to connect utility and equality in a much more effective way than they could for Jewish primary schools. The rabbinical school would combine religious and secular education, reconciling Judaism and Frenchness. French rabbis would then convey this new sensibility within a specifically Jewish context, engendering a distinctly Jewish process of integration. The portrayal of the French rabbinate as a useful tool for integration opened the door for affirmations of Jewish equality and continuity. The Central Consistory's final plan for the rabbinical school emphasized these egalitarian themes, asserting that to fulfill its integrationist mission, "a special establishment . . . for the youth who wish to deliver themselves to *la science théologique* [has become] a pressing and incontestable necessity."[37]

The Consistory built this affirmation of equality into its proposal by stressing the school's plans for financial independence. The rabbinical school would fall under the "immediate direction" of the Strasbourg Consistory with "special oversight" by the Central Consistory. Each departmental consistory would sponsor a specified number of *boursiers,* students who would attend free of charge and receive stipends from the school budget. The school would also accept an unspecified number of paying resident and day students. Institutional expenses would come directly from the annual budget of the Central Consistory.[38] Rabbinical education would thus unite French Jewry financially as well as religiously, strengthening the consistorial system through the attention and support the school would attract. Just as money solidified the bonds between Judaism and state, it would also connect all French Jews through the rabbinical school. Because the budget would mix communal and government funds, new rabbis would represent products of both French Jewry and the French nation.

The school's curriculum reinforced this image in intellectual terms. The Consistory required that rabbinical candidates be French citizens at least eighteen years old; they would also need to possess certificates of good conduct from their local consistorial leaders, who would test their knowledge of Hebrew, the Bible, and the Talmud, but also of French language, history, and geography. Admission would depend upon passing another set of examinations upon enrollment to ensure student abilities in all subjects.[39] The curriculum, of course, combined religious studies in Hebrew, biblical exegesis, Talmud, and rabbinical commentary with secular requirements: Latin, logic, oration (*l'éloquence française*), French history, and mathematics. Instructors in the secular subjects would employ only those books approved by the Conseil Royal de l'Instruction Publique and the University. Finally, the Talmud professor would use the decisions of the Napoleonic Sanhedrin to demonstrate "the harmony . . . between our religious beliefs and the laws of the State and obedience to the King."[40] French rabbinical training thus became a model of Jewish integration as well as a tool for furthering the process.

The effectiveness of the consistorial approach became apparent when the Minister of the Interior, La Bourdannaye, inserted this same dual mandate into the rabbinical school's initial charter. His order authorizing the school emphasized state authority over the new institution and stressed its integrationist mission. He also affirmed the government's right to remove any faculty member whose teachings it deemed contrary to state law or to the decisions of the Sanhedrin.[41] Administratively, the school would have to please two different masters. Technically, it operated under the jurisdiction of the Ministry of Religions, but its educational function demanded conformity to the curricular norms of the French University: an emphasis on classical learning mixed with the legacy of Napoleon's technocratic focus upon military, social, economic, and political goals.[42] Herein lay the school's ultimate claim to utility: the École Rabbinique united its practical religious function with the broader ideals that the University represented. In doing so, French rabbis would work not just for the good of French Judaism, but for the general welfare of France.

This formulation allowed Jewish leaders to assume a unity of purpose with the government with which they tried to mitigate interference. In May 1828, for example, the Minister of Religions asked why the proposed admission requirements did not include a certain level of classical knowledge. In his view, this branch of learning represented fundamental preparation for the specialized studies that rabbinical students would undertake.[43] The Central Consistory answered that rabbinical candidates tended to come mostly from poorer families unable to afford Latin tutors.[44] In addition, acquiring the knowledge already prescribed for admission demanded a great deal of time. A Latin prerequisite made no sense when students could learn the subject just as easily after enrollment. If the school hoped to attract strong candidates, it could not overburden its incoming students with excessive preparatory requirements.[45] Linking civic and religious interest assumed that hurting one meant hurting the other. This view of utility—that impeding recruitment of students to a modern rabbinical school would impede the modernizing mission of the rabbinate—temporarily defused a potential conflict.

Attempts to relax classical requirements, however, raised delicate issues for the Jewish leadership. As we have seen, post-Revolutionary French administrations had come to view the French school system as one of the primary agents of national integration, and no division of the clergy was exempted from scrutiny of its intellectual credentials. The Catholic church, for example, experienced its own controversies regarding the quality of clerical education and the intellectual level of priests.[46] In the preamble to its deliberation of July 23, 1828, the Conseil d'État reaffirmed its commitment to regenerating French Jews by providing proper social and intellectual formation through public education.⁴⁷ This statement implied that French Jews had not made suitable progress toward regeneration. Consistorial leaders understandably bristled at this insinuation and remained sensitive to it afterward. Within this context, rabbinical proficiency in classical languages came to symbolize not only the school's academic quality but—in some quarters—the fidelity of French Jewry to the terms of emancipation.

Finances ultimately proved to be the most effective source of political leverage, enabling state officials to give teeth to their policies regarding French rabbinical education. For the first two years of its existence, the École Rabbinique received only isolated government subsidies that did little to ameliorate its precarious financial condition. When the National Assembly instituted the Jewish religious budget in January 1831, it provided annual funding for the École Rabbinique and attached state salaries to consistorial rabbinic posts. Jewish leaders welcomed this measure as an affirmation of the school's usefulness and of the government's commitment to the survival of French Judaism.⁴⁸

That commitment proved important, as the government became the school's main source of funding during the nineteenth century. The school's founding guidelines had called for the Central Consistory to contribute 13,500f from its own budget.⁴⁹ While the consistories ostensibly distributed these funds, the French Treasury represented the actual financial source. After the establishment of the Jewish religious budget, however, a royal decree officially fixed the subvention at 8,500f, all of which came from the Treasury.⁵⁰ From then on, the government directly supplied the bulk of the budget for training the French rabbinate.

Even with this help, the school soon ran into budgetary problems. As early as 1831, it reported a deficit of 1,200f, a debt that compounded each year. The Ministry of Religions allowed the Central Consistory to help cover these deficits in 1831 and 1832 and issued supplemental allocations of 1,000f for the following three years. Still, by the end of 1837 the deficit had grown to roughly 1,800f.⁵¹ In 1838, the Ministry agreed to raise its fixed allocation from 8,500f to 9,000f.⁵² The debt continued to mount, however, even after the state increased its allocation to 22,000f.⁵³ The budget proposal of 1867, for example, projected a shortfall of 4,550f.⁵⁴ Such debts continued to accumulate over the ensuing decades.

The consistorial leadership also faced legal hurdles in addressing the crisis. Prior to 1831, both the Central Consistory and its departmental branches had generated the bulk of their revenue from communal taxes and assessments on Jewish households. When the National Assembly assumed Jewish religious expenses in 1831, however, it abolished these powers and

CHAPTER 4

limited consistorial fundraising to appeals for voluntary contributions.[55] Without sufficient communal funds, the rabbinical school became even more dependent upon state support.

Struggles over the rabbinate took place largely against this backdrop of financial uncertainty. With the French Treasury providing the school budget and rabbinical salaries, government officials exercised greater oversight to assure compliance with state regulations and the proper use of public funds. One might therefore read consistorial concessions to state demands as a mixture of ideological affinity and political realism. Financial dynamics also undermined the rabbinate's ability to resist lay incursions upon its communal authority. Dependent upon the state for their salaries, French rabbis found it difficult to raise strong objections to their diminishing influence in the consistorial administration. The fiscal connection between Judaism and state provided traction for those who wished to tailor rabbinical studies to French standards, while it weakened those who struggled to preserve traditional rabbinical learning.

Long after the school opened in 1829, the prioritization of secular studies remained problematic. In 1841, the school's administration still lamented that "the students of the less advanced divisions are . . . in a state of inferiority [in secular studies which is] completely elementary; that which resembles more a school for the instruction of the younger ages than an establishment of advanced religious instruction; and among . . . those who are nearly at the moment of seeing their course of studies come to an end, there are still several who leave much to be desired."[56] This "embarrassing" weakness left French rabbinical students inferior to their colleagues educated abroad, particularly those who had studied in Prussia. Improving the curriculum, though, required a parallel improvement in the school's "pecuniary and educational conditions."[57] Both processes promised to be difficult and slow.

This report precipitated a new, more open debate. Some of the most publicized Jewish commentary flowed from the pen of Adolphe Franck, a staunch advocate of secular learning. Franck was a respected educator in the French University, having taught philosophy at the *collège royal* of Nancy and at the Paris *faculté*. He also sat on the Central Consistory and helped to conduct rabbinic ordination exams. In the *Archives israélites* of February 1841, Franck issued a scathing indictment of the search for a philosophy teacher for a Jewish school in Nancy. The skills of the candidates—three of whom had attended the École Rabbinique—had deeply disappointed the search committee. Its members had subsequently complained to the Consistory of Nancy that both "the national tongue and the holy language of our fathers [apparently] are barely taught in the only establishment devoted to furnishing rabbis for France."[58]

Franck's article prompted forceful reactions from government officials. The Prefect of the Moselle—who had departmental jurisdiction over the École Rabbinique—recommended significantly stricter entry requirements and higher academic standards.[59] The Minister of Religions believed that Franck's report pointed out serious deficiencies at the rabbinical school, where students secretly received "frivolous and even dangerous" readings and followed a grossly inadequate curriculum. He instructed the Central Consistory to investigate the allegations, reminding its leaders of their responsibilities both to the school and to the government.[60] Although the Minister mentioned no specific punishments or rewards, he adopted a much bolder tone than in previous communications.

This new attitude derived in part from a different understanding of the financial relationship between the government and the rabbinical school. In June 1841, an unsigned internal memorandum to the Minister clearly articulated the implications of this relationship for both parties.[61] When the state had authorized the École Rabbinique in 1829, rabbis did not yet receive government salaries. Their inclusion on the civil payroll, however, enabled—and in fact obligated—the Ministry to make greater demands of the institution, and to intervene as it saw fit: "Now that the Rabbis [*sic*] are salaried by the State, [the State] has the interest and the right to require that they be provided with the knowledge necessary to exercise their functions in a useful manner."[62] Only after rabbis began to draw state salaries, in the author's view, had rabbinical education become a civic affair. State money thus drew the secular and Jewish realms closer together, injecting civic authority into traditional Jewish space.

While this interpretation of events did not necessarily match the historical record, the author's assessment reveals the central principles of government involvement in religious life generally and with Judaism in particular. As always, the government wanted French rabbis to have a solid moral foundation from which to exercise "a salutary influence" upon their fellow Jews. State financial participation in rabbinical training also required the administration "to neglect nothing" in order to achieve the desired results.[63] In effect, public money transformed an internal religious matter over which the government had exercised only general supervision into a civic issue requiring a more active state role.

In this respect, government attitudes toward Judaism reflected general administrative trends within the French regime. A wider goal of national unification, for example, colored much of the July Monarchy's legislative program. The Orleanist government attempted to move the country toward a more centralized administration, with initiatives designed to promote cultural and economic integration on a national scale. These programs became increasingly rooted in Paris, attempting to draw provincial institutions into a closer relationship with the French civil authorities.[64]

Not surprisingly, centralization did not occur within a pluralistic framework. As Steven Kale has argued, French cultural conservatives of the 1850s saw Catholicism and French society as inextricably bound together. "Moral order," he writes, "was equivalent to [the] Christian culture . . . purveyed by the church through its pedagogical, social, and evangelical foundations."[65] Although writing a decade before the period that Kale studies, the author of the June memorandum articulated views consistent with later French conservatism. Clearly, he expected French Jews to conform to French standards of culture and education. Like Kale's Legitimists of the 1850s, his definition of "French" incorporated Christianity; he then used this amalgamation as both a template and yardstick for Jewish integration. In contrast to their Christian counterparts, he wrote, rabbinical students—"like the Jews generally"—persistently avoided French public schools where "the Christian populations draw upon the knowledge that makes the sciences and letters flourish, and which each day causes the progress of civilization."[66] Rabbinical students chose instead to confine their studies almost exclusively to the Talmud, neglecting essential subjects like the French language. The Christian clergy had "always" spread knowledge among their flocks, in addition to serving as "the unique keepers of the sacred flame." They now prepared their future clergy "through the study of the sciences and letters, and in the establishments of higher religious instruction they learn . . . Philosophy as well as French Literature, Greek, and Latin." By contrast, the French rabbinate's continued indifference toward secular education undermined its ability to "exercise a moral influence" upon French Jewry.[67]

Extending the logic of centralization, the author blamed these problems on inadequate civil supervision of rabbinical training. The Conseil d'État, for example, had failed to recognize the implications of not requiring more extensive secular learning at the École Rabbinique upon its creation. The author understood this oversight: because at that time Jewish clergymen did not receive state salaries, the Conseil d'État could not strongly object to a situation unrelated to the public interest.[68] Public funding for Judaism, however, had changed matters entirely. The permanent allocation of civil money created a direct link between the state and the École Rabbinique that deepened the government's obligation to ensure the school's success. This relationship also required greater Jewish responsiveness to government demands.

Although no concrete action resulted from this episode, Franck's article had given voice to a growing number of criticisms. Dissatisfaction with the rabbinical school's performance continued to grow in both government and Jewish quarters throughout the 1840s. Another unfavorable report, published in the summer of 1847, initiated a strong push for reforms.[69] The report followed an inspection of the school by two highly respected members of the Central Consistory: Franck, who had become one of its vice-presidents; and Salomon Munk, who served as secretary. Like Franck, Munk possessed considerable academic credibility in both Jewish and secular circles. A well-known Orientalist, he had also served as an aide to the prominent Jewish lawyer and politician Adolphe Crémieux. The appointment of Franck and Munk signaled the gravity of the school's situation and the need to make a credible case for change to both concerned Jews and government officials.

Franck and Munk called for extensive curricular improvements, especially in secular studies. They agreed with the school's administrators, though, that insufficient resources severely impeded effective reorganization and reform. These obstacles went far beyond the ability to offer courses. Funding shortages jeopardized the personal welfare of both students and teachers, further weakening the quality of instruction. Franck and Munk described a school building in a dangerous state of disrepair: rotting staircases, buckling floors, and poorly furnished rooms with drapes that had not been replaced for sixteen years and that threatened to crumble at the slightest touch.[70] The library lacked copies of classic literary collections and basic theological texts published in France and Prussia over the previous three decades.[71]

Equally important, faculty salaries and student scholarships—both supplied by the French Treasury—stood well below acceptable levels. Frank and Munk also pointed out the weakness of the analogy between the Christian and Jewish situations. The school's scholarship students each received only 400f from the government, compared to the 600f received by the vastly larger number of students attending the Catholic and Protestant seminaries.[72] Money worries eroded the morale of students and teachers and distracted them from their work. The oppressive atmosphere adversely affected not only the retention of faculty for secular courses, but also the ability of students to concentrate fully on their studies.

The school's leaders responded to the report by focusing on its financial aspects. Their appeal for a budget increase invoked the fiscal relationship between Judaism and state, citing the "impartial justice" expressed through the government's assumption of rabbinical salaries. That same sense of equality should apply to the "institution destined to form religious leaders" worthy of government remuneration.⁷³ By charging the École Rabbinique with attaining certain goals, the state had accepted the responsibility for enabling it to do so. "The [financial] question," they concluded, seriously threatened the provision of "a rabbinical education worthy of our noble country, worthy of a religion that has allied itself so well with the principles of a sound philosophy."⁷⁴ The Central Consistory seconded this request, asking for an additional 5,000f on top of the present 10,000f allocation.⁷⁵ Both petitions held that the government's responsibility toward its funded institutions compelled it to help ameliorate the present state of affairs.

The financial relationship between Judaism and state, however, mandated that any successful argument for fair treatment depended on the school's utility. This requirement once again forced Jewish leaders to address perceived deficiencies in secular learning as part of their request for more money. Even before Franck and Munk visited the school, its administration had tried to improve classical instruction. The former instructor of classical subjects, Rabbi Louis Morhange, had taken over the courses in Hebrew literature, exegesis, and Jewish history.⁷⁶ M. Bonnieux, a more qualified instructor who also taught at the *collège royal* of Metz, now conducted the Latin and Greek classes.⁷⁷ As a further step, the Central Consistory suggested requiring French citizenship and a minimum age of sixteen for incoming students. These measures would ensure that rabbinical candidates possessed the equivalent of a completed secondary education (a prerequisite first proposed by the government several years earlier). The new rules would require candidates to read Hebrew with the Sephardic pronunciation (as opposed to the Ashkenazic pronunciation common to the Alsatian boys who made up the bulk of the student body) and to demonstrate an ability to translate the Talmud into French.⁷⁸ Coursework would also become more demanding, requiring a classical curriculum consistent with University standards. Religious learning would continue to focus on Talmud and Hebrew, exegesis, biblical history, and homiletics.⁷⁹

Both the academic and financial prongs of these proposals intersected at the hub of Jewish integration, and thus, of utility. Above all, Jewish leaders reiterated their commitment to the creation of a modern French rabbinate. Despite their material hardships, both rabbinical students and teachers remained infused with "the most ardent love of France and its institutions," retaining "a true comprehension of the needs of our times, of the resulting obligations for the religious minister, and the profound conviction—because it rests upon the same principles as our belief—that the duties of the man and of the citizen cannot be separated from those of the *israélite*."⁸⁰

The École Rabbinique intended to nurture among its students the skills necessary for the promotion of integration. Achieving this end required the state's fulfillment of its material obligations.

Jewish calls to strengthen classical studies, however, did not meet with universal approval. For some critics, the secular emphasis resembled the thinking of the recent reform rabbinical conferences in Brunswick, Frankfurt am Main, and Bresslau between 1844 and 1846. At these meetings, proponents of radical reform had clashed with their more moderate colleagues over questions such as interfaith marriage, Hebrew prayer, messianic belief, and Sabbath observance.[81] Many French Jews followed these deliberations closely, among them radicals such as Olry Terquem and moderates like Samuel Cahen. In 1856, the *grand rabbins* heading each consistorial district held their own conference at which they instituted moderate changes to consistorial Judaism without enormous controversy.[82]

During the 1840s, however, conservative voices within French Jewry also remained loud and defiant. Benjamin Gradis, a Jewish businessman in Bordeaux and an influential member of its consistory, sent a lengthy protest to the Central Consistory in which he specifically targeted the increased attention to secular subjects.[83] Gradis warned that in such a climate, the school's library would soon include works by such "licentious and immoral" authors as Lucretius, Horace, and Aristophanes. Jewish youths should receive this sort of literature, he wrote, only "in small pieces."[84] Gradis also attacked the presence of instructors from the *collège royale* of Metz in the chairs in philosophy and literature. "Philosophy," he wrote, "is a vague science, badly defined [and] easily susceptible to receiving an antireligious direction." A religious institution should therefore permit only instructors of unquestionable "principles and piety" to conduct such courses. Even then, their activities should be limited to "proving definitively that the doctrine of the Bible is superior to all the systems of Philosophy [*sic*]."[85]

Gradis did not stand alone. In a separate letter, the Consistory of Bordeaux agreed that if the curriculum had to include philosophy, direction of the course ought to be entrusted to "a Hebrew theologian." The theological schools of other religions, the Consistory noted, followed this procedure: "Not one of them exists in which philosophy is taught by a layman or a theologian foreign to the religion of these same schools."[86] On a more general note, the Strasbourg Consistory worried that the increased emphasis upon secular studies distracted rabbinical students from the most important aspect of their training. Secular requirements had become so extensive that the study of theology had become "an accessory, when it ought to be the principal object of instruction."[87]

CHAPTER 4

Unfortunately for the reformers, their momentum coincided with the turbulent final months of the July Monarchy. Within less than a year, revolution erupted on the streets of Paris, reaching a head in the bloody conflicts of June 1848. From the rubble of the June Days emerged an unsteady republican government at whose head would soon sit Louis-Napoleon Bonaparte, who would declare himself Emperor Napoleon III after a *coup d'état* in 1851. The political whirlwind understandably swept aside minor issues such as rabbinical curricular reform.

Napoleon III's rise established the legitimism outlined by Kale as the prevailing political authority in France. Yet that authority was not incontestable, and the cultural conflicts that it produced indirectly encouraged a renewed emphasis upon secular learning—and especially classical studies—at the École Rabbinique. The unintentional agent for this policy was Hippolyte Fortoul, Minister of Education from 1851 to 1856. By pushing for greater centralized control of the education system, Fortoul sought to purge the Empire's opponents from the University ranks and to assert its authority over primary schooling.[88] His efforts were hampered, however, by the surge of church influence under the Falloux Law, backed by a significant contingent of the French elite. Fortoul achieved even less success in secondary education, where his attempts to increase scientific instruction at the expense of classical studies met with stiff resistance from the educational establishment and the University's traditional clientele. Ultimately the ascendant Catholic teaching clergy, sanctioned by the Falloux law, reinforced the secondary curriculum that had sunk deep institutional and cultural roots.[89] Proponents of classical studies emerged from this conflict newly empowered, with Latin and Greek firmly entrenched in French higher education and—by extension—at the École Rabbinique.

In this atmosphere, the conflict over classical studies at the École Rabbinique created odd intellectual bedfellows. Dismissing the importance of classical learning for rabbis meant that Jewish traditionalists had potentially aligned themselves with the more liberal, progressive scientists of the French context; those who supported classical studies had adopted the more conservative position of French educational thinking, one in fact supported by the Catholic church. Even these divisions did not always firmly apply. Conservative thinkers bent on reconstructing French royalism, for example, thought classical training inappropriate for teachers who would be assigned to rural posts where they would need to educate peasants in more efficient agricultural techniques.[90]

Such tangled intellectual alliances add nuance to historical depictions of French educational struggles as Manichean battles between "religion" and "science."[91] The Jewish case suggests that the problem lay more in an inherent tension between tradition and modernity, and the ways in which the perceived demands of modern education affected the function and content of traditional religious and cultural institutions. Classical study had a different connotation at the École Rabbinique than it did at other schools and seminaries. The rabbi who learned Latin and Greek became decidedly "modern," while any other French citizen who did so remained decidedly "traditional." Herein lay an essential paradox for the Jewish leadership: rabbis considered modern within Jewish circles might be considered too traditionally educated in the non-Jewish world. Of greater significance, deemphasizing Latin and Greek study for rabbinical students meant severing Judaism from the very intellectual tradition to which many French Jews wished to lay claim.

Addressing this conundrum meant that Jewish leaders once again had to convince government bureaucrats of the rabbinical curriculum's relevance and the status of classical study in it. In December 1849, the *Univers israélite* published a letter from an unnamed government official to a "Journalist en Provence." The author espoused the virtues and advantages of the classical curriculum, and outlined the importance that the educational administration attached to classical studies. He particularly defended the study of Latin and Greek, citing the standard opinion that "the knowledge of these two languages . . . constitutes the foundation . . . of all good education." Studying Latin, the author wrote, taught grammar and style, as well as "poetry, morality and history."[92] Any responsible institution of higher education with a moral mission could not easily justify excluding this essential element of instruction.

Given their legal relationship to and fiscal dependence upon the government, the leaders of the École Rabbinique had little choice but to try to adhere to prevailing views. Latin and Greek remained in the school's secular curriculum in the years that followed, and served as selling points to the civic authorities. In 1850, for example, the Metz Consistory suggested adding "sacred and profane knowledge" to a revised version of the school's admission requirements.[93] New faculty appointments also demonstrated the school's efforts to strengthen its secular program. In 1854, the school hired Maurice Salomon—a recent graduate of the École Normale Supérieure in Paris, who also taught at the Metz *lycée*—to teach Latin and Greek.[94] School administrators offered Salomon's unassailable credentials as proof of their commitment to improving classical instruction, which had undergone "a notable amelioration" generally. The study of classical languages had progressed and translations of Latin and Greek authors "of the first rank . . . [are] fully understood."[95] According to this glowing report,

CHAPTER 4

French rabbis (and by extension French Judaism) had fully embraced the French vision of educational utility.

How much conditions actually improved, however, remains questionable. At best, classical instruction experienced high and low periods, often for reasons unrelated to the wishes of either the government or the school administration. The same report announcing the advances of 1854 also noted that the entry of a significant number of new students had necessitated a reorganization of the secular curriculum. Six students now attended the "philosophical lectures; the others still follow the courses in French, Latin, and Greek."[96] Despite the purported improvement, only slightly more than half the student body possessed sufficient classical knowledge and none of them apparently had those skills upon admission. The situation did not progress rapidly. In 1856, consistorial inspectors reported that rabbinical students were translating Plutarch from the Greek and Salluste from the Latin, but they could not describe any of them as strong in either subject.[97]

As the 1856 report illustrates, curricular guidelines meant little unless enforced in practice. Exploring the application of the rabbinical school's classical curriculum sheds important light on how much control government officials actually exercised over the school, the French rabbinate, and the education of clergy in general. This influence is harder to discern in the Christian seminaries since Latin and Greek were already central to their curricula. Among rabbis, though, the vocational relevance of classical languages was less clear. Accordingly, documentary evidence indicates that the school administration did not always strictly adhere to prescribed regulations. While defined standards existed, instructors could—and often did—exercise considerable flexibility in applying them. Consequently, the school managed to satisfy civil demands for change while simultaneously preserving the traditional religious focus of rabbinical training. This assertion should in no way suggest a condemnation of the school or its faculty; rather, it illustrates the delicacy of balancing religious and secular education under trying conditions. The question remains, though, as to how closely classical studies at the École Rabbinique resembled the picture its leaders painted for government officials.

Rabbinical ordination examinations provide the most accurate measure of the weight of classical subjects in a French rabbi's expected base of knowledge. Between 1860 and 1905, the vast majority of the tests included sections in Latin and Greek, but the importance assigned to these subjects varied considerably over time. The earliest record in the file tells of Abraham Cahen, a student who had all but completed his studies at the École Rabbinique at Metz prior to the school's relocation to Paris in 1859.[98] Though

Cahen's academic file contains only vague details, it explicitly states that the secular section of his examination involved only a composition in philosophy submitted to Adolphe Franck. As for classical studies ("the translation of Greek and Latin authors"), the jury reported that Cahen had "regularly attended the courses in ancient literature . . . at the École Centrale Rabbinique." The examination board deemed these studies sufficient—given the "exceptional position" in which the move to Paris had placed Cahen—and passed him. Apparently, the secular requirement did not play a central role in the committee's decision, since Cahen received only an average grade (*assez bien*) in philosophy and was not even examined in Latin or Greek.[99]

A similar judgment seems to have applied in the case of Jacques Auscher. Auscher had graduated from the École Rabbinique in Metz in 1859 with the *premier* degree of communal rabbi, but had applied for the more prestigious degree of *grand rabbin*. As in the case of Cahen, the examining committee took into consideration "the quite exceptional position of the aspirant" and waived his examinations in secular subjects.[100] The 1864 minutes also demonstrate a less than stringent application of classical requirements. Though all five candidates completed the classical section of the examination, the results proved mediocre at best. None of the students scored higher than *bien,* indicating above average but not outstanding results. Three of the five—Simon Lévy, Emile Cahen, and Isaac Weil—were permitted to pursue the degree of *grand rabbin*. A student named Rosenthal was ordained as a communal rabbi while the fifth, Néphthali Lévy, failed.[101] Obviously, in this instance the Latin and Greek sections did not carry sufficient weight to derail the careers of otherwise qualified students.

By 1866, however, classical studies had assumed greater importance. In March of that year, three students—Emmanuel Weill, Samuel Lehmann, and the returning Néphthali Lévy—applied for ordination. Weill and Lehmann received only the degree of communal rabbi, despite considerable success in the religious sections of the examination. As the jury noted, the students' poor performance in philosophy, Latin, Greek, and French literature constituted the deciding factor.[102] Weill and Lehmann had not adequately demonstrated their capabilities in the secular fields, which had become the apparent dividing line between the communal and the *grand rabbin*.

This shift in ordination criteria reflected changes in the school's status. As discussed in the following chapter, the École Rabbinique had moved from Metz in 1859 and reopened in Paris in 1860 as the Séminaire Israélite. In seeking authorization for the move, the Central Consistory had argued that the intellectual atmosphere of the capital would produce higher levels of secular learning among French rabbis. As the first class to have studied exclusively at Paris, the 1866 candidates represented the first fruits of the promised curricular improvements. Consequently, the examining committee likely held these students to the higher secular standards through which the school administration, the Central Consistory, and even the government had justified abandoning the old school at Metz.

Changing rabbinical roles also encouraged stronger enforcement of the secular guidelines. Under the Second Empire, the French rabbinate took on numerous public duties in addition to its ceremonial and educational functions. The Falloux Law of 1850 empowered *grands rabbins* to sit on departmental academic councils alongside prominent Christian clergy. In order to meet their Christian counterparts on as equal a footing as possible, *grands rabbins* needed at least a working knowledge of the basic French curriculum. At the same time, rabbinical training had begun to emphasize homiletics, a change intended to add to Judaism's public prestige while educating French Jews in the tenets of their faith. The pedagogical thinking of the period drew a direct line between knowledge of the great Roman and Greek orators and the development of public speaking skills. As the public representatives of French Judaism, *grands rabbins* needed a solid grounding in the classics in order to perform their public duties, particularly the delivery of sermons. These considerations had formed the basis of the restructured curriculum.[103]

The examinations of 1867 bear out the tighter classical requirements. All six students who applied for ordination that year took written tests in philosophy, French literature, and ancient literature (Latin and Greek) as well as Hebrew. In the Latin section, out of a possible twenty points, only Heymann Beckert (fifteen) and Joseph Lehman (thirteen) received more than nine points. These two, however, also scored only ten points on the French section. All the students did better in the religious sections, with Lehman, Beckert, and Marc Lévy receiving the degree of *grand rabbin*. Benjamin Wahl obtained the degree of communal rabbi; Emile Hirsch and Néphtali Bloch failed, but both earned the first degree the following year.[104] In this case, the secular sections did not prevent ordination, but once again differentiated the communal rabbis from the *grand rabbins*. School records show that Beckert and Lehman (who would later become the seminary's director) had excelled in their studies. While the school registry characterized Lévy as no better than an average student (*assez satisfaisant*), he nevertheless attained the higher rank by scoring just well enough on all sections of the examination.[105] Religious subjects still carried considerably more importance, while inadequate secular knowledge could block a candidate from the higher degree.

This shift in standards, however, also owed much to wider trends in French secondary education. During the 1850s, proficiency in classical studies represented the intellectual currency necessary for entry into the elite levels of the University.[106] By the 1860s, though, a growing group of liberal educators favored reorienting the French educational system toward the technical and scientific expertise necessary for industrial and economic development. The rise of reformers like Victor Duruy—who served as Minister of Education from 1863 until 1869—threatened to reduce the curricular significance of classical languages and the influence of those who taught them. Not surprisingly, Duruy's efforts met with the same dogged resistance as those of his predecessors. One biographer has concluded that Duruy's restructuring of the French school system eventually failed largely because it threatened the curricular sanctity of Greek and Latin.[107] Though Duruy could only implement partial changes, his program prepared the way for the later deemphasis of classical subjects under the Third Republic. Educational reform became a central project of the Radical Republican regimes of the late 1870s, notably driven by the Minister of Education (and later Prime Minister) Jules Ferry. While the Ferry Laws of 1878–82 mainly targeted primary schooling, secondary educational reform stood on the horizon and with it, a reconsideration of the utility of learning classical languages.

In this more volatile political atmosphere, the rabbinical school's administration enjoyed greater freedom to navigate a course more amenable to its practical and educational goals. Ironically, the atmosphere of reform in the general system enabled the school to reinforce its more traditional curricular elements. Ordination examinations of the late 1870s indicate a gradual decrease in the importance of secular subjects. Candidates took oral and written tests in Talmud, Hebrew, philosophy, French literature, Latin, and Greek. The distribution of points clearly favored the religious subjects, which meant that a student could perform poorly in the secular sections but still pass the examination. While secular and classical studies remained integral components of the rabbinical curriculum, Latin and Greek had lost significance as ordination criteria.

As the Third Republic asserted more control over the schools in the late 1870s and 1880s, the deemphasis of Latin and Greek continued. In September 1883, Abraham Bloch sat for tests in ten different subjects. The secular section included only compositions in philosophy and French, and a test in Syriac and Arabic.[108] The same three subjects comprised the secular elements of the ordination examination of Félix Meyer in 1888.[109] Five years later, three more students—Sylvain Bénédict, Salomon Karpe, and Edgard

Sêches—took the same examinations.¹¹⁰ In 1893, the test again included only these three secular evaluations, omitting Latin and Greek.¹¹¹

While the documents offer no explicit rationale for this change, the evidence suggests that more students may have fulfilled their classical prerequisites prior to enrollment. As discussed above, the school's leaders had for some time expressed the desire to require the *bachélier-ès-lettres* of incoming rabbinical candidates. In addition, most of the students who took no Latin examination had attended the consistorial Talmud Torah of Paris, a preparatory school for rabbinical candidates and Jewish religious teachers that the rabbinical school annexed in 1880. Records of the Talmud Torah for this period show that several students each year passed at least the first section of the *baccalauréat,* the qualifying examination for university study. At least some rabbinical students learned the basics of Latin and Greek either independently or from their secondary schooling. Better preparation at the secondary level diminished the need for strict classical training at the seminary.

By the turn of the century, though, classical languages had returned to the ordination requirements. The results of the examinations of April 6, 1903, indicate that all three candidates sat for tests in philosophy, French, Latin, and Greek.¹¹² Classical subjects continued to appear on ordination exams as late as 1930.¹¹³ This reemphasis appears to have resulted from a combination of factors. In part, increased Jewish immigration produced a growing number of applications from foreign-born students. In 1904, for example, Rabbi Joseph Lehman, the school's director, interviewed an applicant for admission, a Hungarian immigrant named Samuel Danilef. Lehman reported that he had been "struck" by Samuel's "inarguable erudition." "He knows," the director wrote, "or purports to know German [and] classical German literature, and to have studied arithmetic, geometry, history and the physical and natural sciences on his own." He had also studied Hebrew literature and claimed knowledge of "a number of talmudic tracts." While impressed with Samuel, Lehman recommended admitting him first to the Talmud Torah so that he could fill in the "lacunae of his secular knowledge," including Latin and Greek. If he performed well, Samuel could then enroll at the seminary.¹¹⁴ In this case, classical requirements provided a means of imposing standards upon students educated outside of France and maintaining the French character of the seminary. This role also suggests that the school's leaders had by then internalized Latin and Greek as essential components of a French rabbi's education.

As at the school's founding, though, money issues also encouraged this academic path. The ascent of the Radical Republicans in the later 1880s lent greater force to the burgeoning anticlerical campaign. Among other measures, the Radicals proposed doing away with the entire religious budget. With the tide turning toward a complete separation of religion and state, the seminary felt a considerable financial pinch. On March 10, 1885, the Chamber of Deputies eliminated 10,000f in stipends for rabbinical students, reducing the school's budget to 22,000f.[115] From then on, the National Assembly began to decrease the Jewish religious budget, just as it did with the Catholic and Protestant budgets. Funding cuts exacerbated the rabbinical school's deficit, which rose to 50,000f by 1899. After an appeal from the Central Consistory to its departmental branches yielded only 2,310f, the House of Rothschild apparently intervened, extending the school's line of credit to rescue it from fiscal disaster.[116]

Facing financial uncertainty, the school's leaders sought new sources of revenue. The seminary administration eventually undertook its own fundraising activities, appealing directly to individual French Jews. In 1902, for example, Joseph Lehman read the school's annual report at the prize ceremony for the Parisian Jewish schools. Complete with an attached contribution form, the published pamphlet offered an overview of the rabbinical program and a list of the school's individual benefactors. An introduction by the Chief Rabbi of the Central Consistory, Zadoc Kahn, echoed the appeal for aid. A separate section listed the seminary's budget, underlining the inadequacy of its existing material resources.[117]

Like any good advertisement, these appeals portrayed the school in the most flattering light, highlighting the seminary's consistency with what had become the accepted French rabbinical model. In amalgamating the traditional and the contemporary, the school sought

> to endow [its] students not only with the most necessary and most precise professional knowledge, but also with an infinite number of ideas, notions, [and] facts drawn from the contemplation of that which classical antiquity and Jewish antiquity, as well as modern thought . . . have produced . . . in seeking to resolve the problem of life and of eternity; to enlarge indefinitely the circle of their ideas [and] the field of their moral vision; to train them to think powerfully by arranging their thought according to the clearest, most lucid, most luminous form, and to act scientifically, with wisdom and with courage; in a word, to render them as capable as possible of accomplishing their holy mission.[118]

This description of the French rabbinate strongly resembled that formulated by the seminary's original founders. Shrinking civil support, though, had changed the school's target audience. Instead of attempting to persuade the French government of the school's necessity and utility, the seminary administration turned to French Jewry itself. The fundraisers expected their terminology to resonate with their potential supporters, suggesting the perceived resonance of these values among French Jews.

The evolution of the French rabbinical curriculum during the nineteenth century thus documents the Consistory's attempts to reconcile Jewish needs with the expectations of citizenship. Jewish attention to French educational policy acted as a driving force behind the continuing presence of classical studies in French rabbinical training. Meanwhile, intellectual currents emanating from both inside and outside the Jewish administration sharpened the focus upon the study of Greek and Latin by prospective French rabbis. French Jewish leaders had to balance these secular demands with traditional rabbinical studies, melding Judaism and Frenchness. The resulting curriculum thus embodied a utopian vision of consistorial Judaism, in which Jewishness and Frenchness worked interactively to fashion a cultured Judaism. Ideally, French rabbis would acquire secular knowledge and promote loyalty to France through the lens of traditional Jewish learning, while simultaneously fusing traditional Jewish practice with that secular world.

Balancing secular and religious knowledge, though, meant accounting for practical as well as ideological considerations during a turbulent century. French Judaism needed a school to train its rabbis, but the Consistory needed government assistance to keep that school open. Consistorial leaders and school administrators both understood that state financial aid depended upon adherence to the mission of regeneration and integration. Obtaining and maintaining civic funding for the rabbinical school meant acceding to the government's curricular demands. No matter which regime held power, state authorities repeatedly focused upon the quality of classical instruction in their periodic assessments of the school. Despite shifting standards and contentious points of view, the continuous return to classical studies suggests a continuity of expectations for French Jews that transcended the different political eras of the *longue durée*. This combination of forces produced an ironic result: though not central to rabbinical training, Latin and Greek eventually became standard components of rabbinical education. Even after the law separating church and state in 1905 ended the government's financial support of the rabbinical school, ordination examinations continued to include classical subjects. The continuing emphasis on Latin and Greek had, in three quarters of a century, created a tradition of classical learning among French rabbis. Within the confines of rabbinical curriculum, at least, integration had been achieved.

5

A Tale of Two Cities:
From Metz to Paris

While the consistorial leadership worked to assure that all Jews in France became cultured *israélites,* the best integration strategy remained a point of contention. French Jewish leaders not only disagreed with government definitions of Judaism; they actively (albeit subtly) sought to tailor them to suit their own conceptions. The process that Ronald Schechter has identified in the eighteenth century thus continued throughout the nineteenth: rather than assimilating themselves into France, French Jews tended to assimilate France into themselves.[1] Where these ideas and government definitions met, conflict often followed.

This description echoes the political historian Sudhir Hazareesingh's analysis of the formation of the idea of citizenship in modern France. Citizenship, he argues, represented not a single concept, but the amalgamation of different notions emanating from separate political factions. The final definition of "citizen of France," he concludes, sprung from the accumulation of these ideas, a swirl of formulations that coalesced around a common core of principles. The doctrinal building blocks of French citizenship were not imposed from "above" but grew up gradually from "below."[2] Similarly, the concept of *Jewish* citizenship in France formed first among the Jews themselves, a group whom its leaders portrayed as united despite serious internal divisions. Evolving ideas about the relationship between Judaism and France interacted with the expectations and demands that government officials handed down from above to produce Franco-Jewish citizenship.

CHAPTER 5

Here, though, the French Jewish experience diverges from Hazareesingh's model, in that Jewish attitudes did not take shape independent of outside forces. The financial relationship between Judaism and state enabled government officials to influence the development of Jewish self-perceptions by favoring one approach to integration over another. Through the application of political and financial pressure, the French bureaucracy helped to mold consistorial integration strategies, thereby shaping the public image that they expected French Jews to internalize. The protracted controversy over the location of the central rabbinical school demonstrates the state's concrete power to influence Jewish views of the rabbinate and its place in France.

As discussed in the previous chapter, a vocal faction of reform-minded French Jews had opposed locating the École Rabbinique in Metz from the very beginning. By the middle of the nineteenth century, the school's perceived deterioration prompted louder calls for action, and some movement toward substantive change. Although the upheavals of 1848 derailed these plans, Jewish calls for reform resurfaced as the general climate stabilized. With this renewed focus on the school's problems, Jewish leaders and government authorities revisited a question raised publicly by Adolphe Franck in 1841: Should the rabbinical school remain in Metz or should it move to Paris?

The question of moving the École Rabbinique from Metz to Paris gave a physical dimension to preexisting fissures within French Judaism. Arguments over the particular virtues of Metz or Paris became vehicles for broader disputes, such as the proper guidelines for rabbinical training, the growing prominence of Parisian Jewry within the consistorial system, and a general tension between the capital and the provinces. Moving thus presented an opportunity to recalibrate both the official image and internal dynamics of French Judaism through one of its most visible institutions. The rabbinical school also represented a tangible Jewish space within France, where government financial participation legitimated the perpetuation of French Judaism. The relocation question therefore emphasized the civic role in shaping Jewish religious life. Ideological and financial considerations had justified the school's establishment; both criteria would eventually rationalize its transfer to the capital.

The indictment of the Metz location and, by extension, its Jewish community, represented one of the most serious rifts opened by the debate. A common criticism alleged that Metz lacked sufficient secular educational resources, while Paris offered access to the finest institutions and personnel of the French University as well as more than adequate religious instruction. Moreover, the Metz Consistory's influence had declined since the first half of the century. In 1815, Metz had been the second largest consistorial district with approximately 6,600 Jews (more than 14 percent of French Jewry). By 1841, the Metz district retained approximately 8,000 Jews, dropping it behind Colmar (which had grown to approximately 14,000) and Paris (approximately 9,000). Its percentage of the total Jewish population had diminished, however, to 11.63 percent. By 1853, the Metz district's population hovered around the same level, but the Nancy Consistory, with nearly 9,000 Jews, had surpassed it. At the same time, by 1853 the Paris district had become the country's largest, with more than 20,000 Jewish residents (23.25 percent of the total population). Clearly, demographic trends pointed toward the capital as a growing French Jewish center, while Metz appeared to be on the decline.[3]

Material issues compounded the controversy. As the École Rabbinique had fallen into a dangerous state of physical dilapidation, Metz's shrinking Jewish community could not provide a new locale for the school. At the same time, the Central Consistory's national fundraising efforts fell flat. With the situation deteriorating, the Central Consistory turned to the government for help. After lengthy negotiations, the Ministry of Religions agreed to pay for improvements to the school building. While an apparent windfall for the Metz community, this financial arrangement bound the project to the authority and rhythms of the French bureaucracy. Both factors raised considerable obstacles to the renovation of the Metz locale, ultimately resulting in the project's failure and the transfer of the École Rabbinique to Paris in 1859.

As mentioned above, the idea of moving the École Rabbinique to Paris received its first public voicing on the heels of Franck's critical article, in the pages of the *Archives israélites* in 1841. Along with the status of classical studies, the transfer issue found its way into general discussions of reforming the school, only to languish in the wake of 1848. When the dust had settled by January 1849, momentum for reform once again built within the Central Consistory, whose leaders proposed the idea to the government authorities.

The new regime's response, however, posed potential danger for the Jewish leadership. In some quarters, the transfer issue threatened to mushroom into a referendum on the progress of Jewish integration. One ministerial official, for example, interpreted the school's physical troubles as a sign of Jewish "hostility" to French culture. In its efforts to promote "our morals and the laws of our civilization," he wrote, the Jewish Consistory had encountered "great obstacles in the prejudices with which the majority of rabbis[—]to whom the spiritual direction of the Jewish communities is entrusted[—]have shown themselves to be imbued."[4] Moreover, the location of the École Rabbinique in the center of one of the Jewish populations "most hostile" to modern morals and civilization could only perpetuate this "hostile spirit" among the rabbis themselves. Transfer would remove future rabbis from this counterproductive environment, enabling the Central Consistory to train more effective agents of regeneration.[5]

Attaining ideological goals also necessitated revisiting the financial relationship between Judaism and state. Who, for example, would be responsible for procuring a new building in Paris? Would relocation place new, permanent demands upon the Jewish religious budget, in terms of material and personnel, and would the government meet these new costs?[6] Clearly, the Ministry would not write the Consistory a blank check: the goal of invigorating the process of Jewish integration through improved rabbinical training had to be balanced against the costs of pursuing the policy.

The possibility of relocation thus stirred up the same discomfort for consistorial leaders as the curricular debates. Once again, they had to contend with charges that French Jews had not sufficiently regenerated and faced questions about their willingness to do so. While they were cognizant of problems at the school, they sought to portray them in a manner that avoided downgrading the product they wished to sell. Their proposal for transfer therefore emphasized the physical dangers of the school building, focusing on material issues as a means of rejecting any linkage between transfer and a purportedly stunted Jewish integration. They had no effective way, however, to parry the government's economic reservations about moving the school, and eventually had to abandon the idea.

In April of 1850, the Central Consistory changed course, informing the Ministry of Religions that the costs of relocation would exceed its available resources. Instead, they resubmitted Franck and Munk's recommendations from 1847 that asked for government grants to renovate the Metz building and subsidize book purchases for the library. They also requested an increase in the school's annual budget from 10,000f to 15,000f.[7] By December, the decision to keep the school in Metz had won the assent of the religious administration, even though all parties had agreed that this environment impeded Jewish regeneration. Economic considerations thus trumped ideological goals in shaping the immediate future of rabbinical education. Money had also deepened government involvement in rabbinical affairs. If the government's financial relationship with the rabbinical school enabled it to influence what went on in the school's classes, that same power now dictated where those classes would meet.

The attempt to renovate the Metz site demonstrated both the extent and the limits of state authority in Jewish affairs. As haggling over the details of renovation began, the paradoxical nature of the government's role in the project became increasingly clear. No major renovation could take place without financial assistance from the Ministry. At the same time, government regulations and procedures wreaked havoc upon the project, dragging it out for nearly a decade. Ironically, the source behind renovation simultaneously—and unintentionally—derailed it.

Early on, the renovation project followed a pattern that would plague it for the next seven years. The relationship between Judaism and state divided responsibility for the project: the Consistory saw to the quotidian details of planning and execution, while the Ministry exercised the oversight consistent with its financial role. Government involvement subjected the project to the bureaucratic demands of general public works, producing substantial delays. In addition, state funding failed to cover the entire cost of the work. Bureaucratic interference and delays drove costs higher, meaning greater financial liability for both the Metz and the Central Consistories.

Signs of trouble surfaced at the very start with repeated clashes over architectural designs. In April 1851, the Ministry rejected the plans submitted by the Metz Consistory and its architect, M. Dérobe, calling them sloppy, ill conceived, and exorbitant.[8] Protesting this assessment, the Metz Consistory submitted a revised plan.[9] One month later, the Minister, Giraud, informed the Central Consistory that the Commission des Édifices Religieux had unanimously rejected the new proposal as well. Giraud himself concurred with the ruling, spelling out his understanding of his oversight responsibilities: "In intervening . . . in expenses of this nature, the Government should keep essentially to that which makes good use of the funds designated for [the project]; it should only give its consent to spaces conceived with taste and discernment."[10] To meet this standard, Giraud asked for a new plan conceived by a different architect.[11] The cycle repeated itself in July when Giraud rejected the third version of Dérobe's proposal and openly questioned the logic of trying to salvage the original design instead of adopting a completely new one.[12]

The government's financial clout legitimized its architectural opinions. In late November, Giraud informed both the Central and the Metz Consistories that if the renovation had not commenced by the close of the fiscal year, he would have to revoke the 4,000f allocated for the project.[13]

CHAPTER 5

The Metz Consistory, which had assumed a considerable portion of the project's start-up costs, suddenly found its financial safety net imperiled. Construction could not begin, however, without government authorization. The Metz leaders therefore hastily submitted a fourth revised design in the autumn of 1851, modified to respond directly to ministerial reservations.[14] This plan, though, met the same fate as its predecessors when the Commission des Édifices Religieux declared it the least acceptable of all. Weary of delays and wary of the dangerous condition of the school building, the new Minister of Religions, Fortoul, decided to engage the diocesan architect of Metz to create an entirely new design. The new man, Émile Boesvilvald, would make an initial visit to the site in Metz in December.[15] A furious Dérobe protested that he had been treated unfairly and that the government had dismissed his revision without a reasonable explanation. He requested a review of the matter by the Commission des Bâtiments Civiles, an avenue that eventually proved fruitless.[16]

Dérobe's ouster cleared the way forward, yet the renovation continued to sag beneath the weight of bureaucracy. By December 1851, demolition of the old school building began just in time to rescue the 4,000f in government assistance.[17] Although Fortoul approved the allocation the following January, by late August the money still had not found its way to the Metz Consistory and would not arrive until later that winter.[18] The complete demolition of the old building thus ended up taking more than a year, due largely to sluggish government procedures.

Bureaucratic red tape also limited construction to a series of fits and starts. Delays in the initial allocation held up the work until the spring. In the interim, a new problem arose when the budgets designated for the project for 1853 and 1854 proved insufficient to allow work to proceed at a normal pace. To fill the gap, Fortoul approved the appropriation of 6,600f left over from the 1852 budget.[19] From that point, the project seemed to progress somewhat more smoothly. In 1853, the Commission des Édifices approved Boesvilvald's construction plans, and Fortoul quickly authorized the estimated budget of nearly 58,000f.[20] By March, the Prefect of the Moselle had awarded the major construction contracts and arranged for the specialty work to begin that September.[21] In late November, Boesvilvald reported that the renovation was "in full course of execution" and asked Fortoul to release more than 16,000f to pay the contractors for completed work.[22]

The appropriation process, though, continued to thwart significant advancement. Budgetary protocols prohibited allocating a lump sum, necessitating a piecemeal approach to construction. In 1854 and 1855, for example, Boesvilvald had to submit progress reports to the Ministry as a prerequisite for payment at each stage.²³ All expenses also required the final approval of the Conseil d'État. On a number of occasions, work halted while the architect awaited the disbursement of funds. In the autumn of 1853, the Rector of the Academy of Nancy complained to Fortoul that even though the renovation had "begun three years ago . . . it will perhaps end in another three or four years." That year's activity had in fact already ceased while the architect awaited the following year's allocation.²⁴ Winter brought further interruptions, with inclement weather eroding much of the previous year's progress. As a result, by the spring of 1855 Boesvilvald had completed only the demolition of the old school buildings and the pouring of new foundations, some major masonry work, and basic carpentry and roofing on the new principle building.²⁵ The bulk of the work remained undone.

As the project dragged on, concern also mounted over the effects of delays upon the students and faculty. When the demolition of the old building began in 1851, the school had moved to temporary quarters.²⁶ Its new residence, though, did not represent much improvement over the old one. Dispatched by Fortoul to inspect the site in 1853, the Rector of Nancy likened the building's door to that of a "cowshed." Sanitary conditions also appalled him: an overpowering odor had greeted his entry; water dripped into the dormitory rooms; and one student had become ill from the surroundings. The stairways and classrooms were equally dilapidated, with library books stored in a rickety cabinet. Lastly, he noted an "anxiety" among the students and staff attributable to their embarrassment at the state of "nearly ignominious poverty" in which they toiled.²⁷

Meanwhile, the project faced another financial crisis. In the wake of the Rector's embarrassing 1853 report, the Metz leadership pleaded for help from the other consistories of France. Between the work at the École Rabbinique, the cost of their new synagogue, and the relocation of their Jewish primary schools, the Metz Consistory had spent nearly 46,000f. In addition, Boesvilvald had determined that stabilizing the new building required the acquisition of additional land at an estimated cost of approximately 18,000f; without the new property, the project would have to be delayed and possibly scrapped.²⁸ Further cost overruns lay beyond their means.

The Central Consistory responded by organizing a fundraising campaign among the departmental consistories (including Algeria). In three separate circulars in 1854, the national Jewish leadership asked the departmental consistories to solicit funds to ease the burdens of the Metz Consistory. They received a relatively weak response, in part because of economic hardships facing Jews in the eastern departments. Both the Strasbourg and Nancy leadership advised delaying the "ill-timed" appeal for a few months in light of the combination of a food shortage and "the rigors of an exceptionally [hard] winter."²⁹ The Consistories of St. Esprit, Colmar, and Marseille attributed their own modest contributions to the same conditions.³⁰ In the end, the circulars raised a modest 7,100f, with only the Bordeaux, Marseille, Strasbourg, and Algerian communities expressing strong support.³¹

Economic conditions aside, the tepid departmental response to the campaign indicated that not all French Jews had accepted the decision to renovate. Despite consistorial portrayals of unity, a segment of French Jewish leaders remained opposed in principle to keeping the school in Metz. In fact, the ongoing difficulties of renovation rekindled friction over rabbinical training and produced renewed efforts to move the school to Paris. When the Rector of Nancy raised the relocation issue during his 1853 inspection, the school's director, Lazare, asserted a communally oriented vision of the French rabbinate. While conceding that the school might enjoy a better material situation in Paris "under the eyes of the government," Lazare warned that rabbinical students would face the "danger . . . of being transferred to a large city where the Jews, while numerous, often find themselves lost in the crowd."³² By contrast, Lazare emphasized the comfortable environment offered by Metz's "large, dense [Jewish] community," whose "religious spirit forms the sort of atmosphere [that is] indispensable to a rabbinical seminary." Exposure to this spirit connected French rabbis to the historical roots of French Judaism and to the people they sought to lead. This personal bond was essential to the rabbi's ability to communicate with his congregation, especially through homiletics.³³ "In Paris," Lazare lamented, "they will form Hebraists [and] scholars, but not preachers."³⁴

Lazare's depiction fit the general rabbinical model envisioned by the school's founders; but his confidence belied wider disagreement within French Jewry over rabbinical functions. Was the rabbi to be a scholar, concerned with expanding and perpetuating his knowledge at the price of separating himself from his congregants? Or should the rabbi be a communal worker trained to inspire French Jews to acts of charity, religious observance, and good citizenship, a role model for combining "Jewishness" and "Frenchness" while simultaneously convincing Jews to stay in the fold? Lazare's distinction polarized the debate, assuming that one could become either a "scholar" or a "preacher," but not both.

This outlook paralleled the dualist portrayal of the two cities themselves that reflected a broader polarization between Paris and the provinces. Depending on one's point of view, Metz represented either a stronghold of Jewish religious and historical tradition or a provincial backwater isolating the École Rabbinique from the rest of France. Similarly, Paris was either a blossoming metropolitan center that would enhance a rabbinical student's cultural, intellectual, and spiritual development, or a den of iniquity whose temptations would steer young Jews away from their rabbinical calling toward more materialistic pursuits.

The Central Consistory's fundraising appeal brought these opinions into stark relief. Nancy's Jewish leaders called for the school's relocation "in a more suitable place" such as Paris, an opinion held by "a large number of people" within their district. They also predicted that the fundraising campaign would meet stiff resistance, for a successful reconstruction would dash any hopes of moving the school.[35] Even though the Nancy community eventually contributed 600f, its support appeared less than enthusiastic. The reform advocate Olry Terquem reacted more dismissively, declaring that he could not contribute even *la meilleure partie d'un centime* (the French equivalent of "one red cent") toward a rabbinical school located in an "obscure and permanent ghetto."[36] The transfer controversy, like the concurrent question of classical studies, thus became an allegorical vessel into which each side poured its ideals for the French rabbinate and, more broadly, for French Jewry.

As the debates wore on, the school building wore out along with the patience of the French authorities. In 1855, Mardochée Astruc—the father of one of the students—wrote to the Central Consistory that he was alarmed by the "deplorable" state of disrepair into which the École Rabbinique had tumbled. In his estimate, the temporary residence appeared to teeter on the verge of complete collapse.[37] The Metz Consistory passed on his complaints to the Prefect of the Moselle, noting that nothing had improved since the Rector's inspection in 1853. They also pleaded for the Minister to direct the next stage of construction toward the dormitories and study rooms, so that by autumn the students might use at least part of the new building. The present site, they warned, had deteriorated to the point of threatening the health of the faculty and students as well as the quality of instruction.[38] Even though the Prefect endorsed the request, the Ministry took no action and the work proceeded as before.

Meanwhile, the project's budget continued to balloon. In May 1855, Boesvilvald reported that the primary masonry, carpentry, and roofing work for the new building was nearly finished and that he was prepared to begin the painting and woodworking. The cost of the woodworking, though, would have to be adjusted because the price of wood had risen considerably since the calculation of the original estimate.[39] Eventually, this work would require an additional government subvention of 12,000f.[40] Two months later, Boesvilvald wrote that the total budget would have to be raised again, for the material salvaged from the old building had turned out to be useless.[41] In December, Fortoul redirected more than 2,000f from the budget for Jewish religious buildings to help cover these new expenses.[42]

The situation finally reached a head in 1856. That March, the Metz leaders again complained to the Prefect of the Moselle. Taking issue with Boesvilvald's rosy account, they contended that the work had advanced very little during the past year and that a timely completion of the new building seemed unlikely. Protracted construction had compromised the level of studies at the school as well as the health of the students and the director. Linking the project's slow pace to the lack of sufficient funds, the leaders asked for enough money to complete the work as soon as possible.[43] Fortoul responded sympathetically but at arm's length, requesting more exact details about the status of construction.[44] While no concrete gain had resulted from this petition, consistorial frustration with the venture's protraction had spilled into the open where it began to find receptive ears.

Attracting the government's attention, though, did not work out exactly as the Metz leaders had hoped. By the following year, the Ministry of Religions had a new leader in Gustave Rouland (who simultaneously held the Education portfolio), and the project had a new set of problems that eventually proved terminal. In January 1857 Boesvilvald reported the completion of the masonry, carpentry, and roofing while the woodworking and plastering remained in progress.[45] The Catholic authorities of Metz, however, were complaining that the new building stood too close to the neighboring garden of the Convent of the Sacred Heart. At their request, he had altered his original plans to allow for a greater space between the structures.[46] Unfortunately, this arrangement would deprive the adjacent synagogue of much of its natural light. The revised design needed more space, which could be created through the purchase and demolition of some neighboring houses, increasing the budget by more than 3,900f. The Ministry could also expect future overruns in the course of preparing the additional sites for construction.[47]

A ministerial report more clearly detailed the renovation's growing financial demands. According to the architect's estimate, the budget would require a supplementary allocation of over 34,000f in addition to the more than 67,000f approved in 1853, boosting it to over 101,000f. The project had already accrued expenses of more than 66,000f, of which over 16,000f remained outstanding.[48] The report disputed Boesvilvald's assessment of progress, indicating that only the "carcass" of the new building had been completed. Much of the carpentry, metal crafting, woodworking, painting, plumbing, and glasswork remained unfinished, and no furniture had yet been purchased. Combined with the outstanding balance, completing the project would cost the government more than 50,000 additional francs.[49]

As the renovation staggered under the weight of cost overruns, sentiment for moving the school grew stronger within French Jewry. Mardochée Astruc, for one, had suggested such a move in his letter of 1855.[50] The idea also gained support from an increasingly vocal reformist faction within French Judaism that sought to align Judaism more closely to modern life. In 1856, the Chief Rabbi of France, Salomon Ullman, responded to budding calls for reform by convening a conference of consistorial *grands rabbins* in Paris. This assembly implemented various liturgical and ceremonial reforms, heading off a potential schism within French Jewry. Their decisions focused mostly on aesthetics, decorum, and the division of responsibility between laity and clergy. Generally, the conference aimed to unify and standardize French Jewish worship, asserting consistorial control over ritual while avoiding radical religious reform.[51]

These priorities led the conference to endorse the relocation of the École Rabbinique to Paris. On the surface, the decision contains some irony: Ullman himself was born in Alsace and had studied at Metz, as had the majority of consistorial rabbis by that time. Criticizing the school's curriculum thus meant disparaging himself, his colleagues, and by extension consistorial Judaism. While the conference's recommendations contained some self-criticism, its measures laid the bulk of the blame on the school's location in Metz. Most important, it emphasized the need to improve the quality of rabbinic instruction. In Paris, rabbinical students would gain access to secular academic resources that Metz could not match, while simultaneously raising their level of religious study.[52] Educating rabbis in the modern milieu of Paris would expose them to mainstream French culture, solidifying their adherence to consistorial guidelines and enabling them to promote unity along these lines once they assumed their official posts. In short, French rabbis themselves were not inherently inadequate; the school could not equip them to meet their duties in its present location.

If ideological goals represented the carrot of change, economics represented the stick that finally drove that change forward. As criticism of the institution continued to mount, financial issues pushed the government to act. By the second half of the 1850s the renovation project had become a financial black hole for both the Ministry of Religions and the Consistory. The 7,100f netted by the fundraising campaign of 1854 represented less than a third of the 27,000f needed for the purchase of Boesvilvald's additional sites. More seriously, the Metz Consistory was experiencing difficulty meeting its existing expenses.[53] To address the crisis, the Central Consistory launched another appeal in January of 1856.[54] The rabbinical conference's endorsement of relocation, however, derailed this new effort. In June, the Central Consistory took up the issue in a meeting with the Paris Consistory; by autumn, its members decided to seek governmental authorization for moving the rabbinical school.[55]

This decision opened another round of vigorous debate. The Central and Metz Consistories offered competing visions for the rabbinate, each seeking the power to determine the most effective mode of rabbinical education. As the struggle expanded, however, it pulled the rabbinical school into the broader conflict over the general definition and portrayal of French Judaism that had prompted the rabbinical conference of 1856.

In protesting the transfer decision to the Ministry of Religions, the Metz leaders built their case on several familiar planks. First, they pointed out the long tradition of rabbinical education in the city. The authorization of the École Rabbinique in 1829, they argued, had not established a new institution; rather, it had reorganized a rabbinical academy that had already existed for centuries and aligned it with the French state. In Metz the École Rabbinique offered a "complete" education and had succeeded in ordaining the majority of the French rabbinate at that time.[56] Moreover, both state and Jewish authorities had repeatedly affirmed the school's utility by providing financial aid for its daily operations.

This same logic applied to the renovation project. In rejecting transfer in 1849, the Ministry had agreed to finance reconstruction; the Central Consistory had also undertaken the 1854 fundraising campaign to help complete the project.[57] Long-standing financial support demonstrated the government's view of the school's utility. In fact, one of the state's original reasons for choosing reconstruction in the first place was that it had already aided the school in the past. The Metz Consistory had acted upon this precedent in complying with ministerial demands in the course of the renovation, a strategy that had left it with a debt of approximately 54,000f and an unfinished shell of a building.[58]

For its part, the Central Consistory once again produced what had become the standard critique of Metz. The distance between Metz and Paris made proper oversight of the school difficult, if not impossible. In addition, the school's financial woes—the result of an insufficient budget from the outset—had led to its physical deterioration.[59] This decay symbolized the broader problems plaguing the school. From the beginning, the École Rabbinique had suffered from a curriculum "quite insufficient" for "students so poorly prepared" for advanced study. The Parisian setting would help address these cultural shortcomings. Budgetary considerations aside, keeping the school in Metz would relegate it to "a frontier city distinguished neither by the number of its Jewish inhabitants nor by its literary and religious institutions; [a town] which has neither a great library, nor a theological school, nor a faculty of letters or the sciences; finally, in a purely military and industrial city, [the school] is not in an environment favorable to its purpose."[60] Only a move to Paris, the Jewish leaders concluded, could assure French Judaism of "enlightened ministers appropriately prepared for their holy mission."[61]

The relocation controversy had come to embody the struggle between two different conceptions of French Judaism. One, rooted in Alsace, sought to preserve traditional ways and institutions despite consistorial efforts to encourage integration. The second, sprung from the culture that had produced the Consistory, emphasized a mixture of traditionalism and modern life as a French Jew. The definition of "proper" rabbinical education depended upon determining the "proper" rabbinical function within one or the other view of Judaism. Transfer represented one piece of this broader rethinking.

Moving the school thus meant redefining it, its students, and its graduates. Toward this end, consistorial leaders trod upon ground that Ullman's reform conference had meticulously avoided, namely linking the relocation of the school to curricular modifications. At the same time, they limited the extent of acceptable changes, envisioning in Paris a "Jewish seminary, exclusively dedicated to higher religious studies."[62] Because Paris would expand the cultural experience of rabbinical candidates, the school's curriculum could become more specialized. Delicately, they broached the subject of shrinking the secular requirements. The École Rabbinique at Metz, in their view, suffered from the bifurcation of its curriculum between theological and secular learning. This division had been necessary in the past, when French rabbinical candidates were "complete strangers to classical studies." By the 1850s, however, "attendance at the *lycées* and the *collèges* [had] entered the habits of [Jewish] youth everywhere." The Jews of Paris had established a Talmud Torah, "a preparatory school for children destined for the sacred ministry."[63] Revamping the curricular structure would avoid the educational redundancy that impaired rabbinical instruction.

A complete divorce from secular learning nevertheless proved impossible. One main obstacle derived from the Consistory's own portrayal of the school as an institution of secondary education, which in the French setting involved a classical emphasis. At the same time, the public money the school received prevented completely exempting the school from French educational requirements. To preserve this vital funding, the school's leaders needed to maintain its image of cultural utility by once again promoting its role in integration and regeneration.⁶⁴

Advocating a total elimination of secular studies also raised a logical problem in that it potentially negated one of the main arguments against keeping the school in Metz. The consistorial leaders likely realized the inherent contradiction, for they took care to connect their revisions with the practical benefits of transfer. They assured, for example, that their proposal would not substantially increase the school budget. With a curriculum concentrating on religious studies, a rabbinical school in Paris could operate with only a small increase in its annual government subsidy—perhaps no more than 5,000f even though it would serve additional consistories in Lyon and the African colonies.⁶⁵ Moving the school would cost money in the short term, but the leaders confidently predicted that voluntary contributions would cover all these expenses. The Jews of Paris, they wrote, had already begun preparing for the construction of a new building exclusively for the school, with Jewish donors providing 60,000f to cover the moving and furnishing expenses. Under these circumstances, the government could not raise its likely third objection: that abandoning Metz would entail the total loss of public funds spent on the renovation. The Central Consistory argued that because the government's expenditures would ultimately result in a new rabbinical school, the money spent at Metz would not really have gone to waste.⁶⁶

This time, with clouds of failure shadowing the renovation project and an albatross of debt around its neck, relocation found a sympathetic ear within the Ministry of Religions. In December 1856, the Administration des Cultes non-Catholiques endorsed the transfer proposal. Following a well-worn path, it reminded Rouland of the "defective" condition of rabbinical training at Metz and the inferiority of the town's resources and cultural environment. The official memorandum noted that Judaism, "like the other two Churches [*églises*]" contained an orthodox faction opposed to all religious change and a reform wing comprised primarily of the "Jewish aristocracy, the bankers [and] the scholars." The Metz school was clearly aligned with the "orthodox" Jewish tradition, rejecting "liberal doctrines, religious reforms, [and] essential modifications in the liturgy; it is opposed to the regeneration movement of Judaism." The faculty in turn passed these destructive "prejudices" along to the students.⁶⁷ In Paris, the school would fall under the direct supervision of a reformist Central Consistory seeking to "rejuvenate the Jewish religion, to centralize [its] direction[;] such is the goal of the regulations which it now proposes [and for which it possesses] all the resources imaginable in terms of books and *professeurs*."⁶⁸ While the commission acknowledged the objections of the Metz Consistory, it demonstrated sympathy only for the communal debt of 54,000f incurred during the renovation. Resolving this single issue would clear the path for the school's relocation.[69]

The government's attitude toward moving the school to Paris had thus undergone a complete reversal since the late 1840s. What had changed? Had the logic of the consistorial arguments suddenly persuaded French administrative officials? Perhaps the best answer lay in changes within the government itself. In 1856, Rouland succeeded Fortoul as Minister of Religions and Education, and worked for the next seven years to centralize University authority in Paris.[70] Rouland also set out to curb the influence of French private schools—especially those dominated by the Catholic teaching orders—and to extend the reach of the state school system. Toward these ends, his administration imposed limitations on the membership of religious orders and restricted the methods of funding private religious schools.[71] In this political context, depictions of the Metz Consistory as "orthodox" could just as easily have connoted Christian opposition to Rouland's goals. Moving the rabbinical school to Paris thus fit a ministerial plan that had not existed during the 1840s.

Jewish leaders responded by expressing a more unified opinion that reflected the new political atmosphere. When Rouland polled the departmental consistories on the matter, all but those of Metz and Bordeaux favored the move. The others pointed out Metz's shortcomings while singing the cultural praises of Paris.[72] Marseille's leaders noted that since 1830, the number of Jewish theologians living in Metz had dwindled while Paris had two *grands rabbins,* several communal rabbis, and numerous "other scholars supported by this important community."[73] The Consistory of St. Esprit agreed that Metz could no longer claim to be the French center of Jewish theological scholarship.[74] The Strasbourg leadership predicted that studying in Paris would expose French rabbinical students to "the immense literary and scientific resources of the capital," significantly raising the level of studies. In Paris, the school would soon become "a remarkable theological institution, capable of [producing] pastors . . . distinguished by their enlightened piety."[75] The Paris Consistory boasted that the capital's "great literary and scientific institutions" would provide a "precious" resource to French rabbinical students for the completion of their "indispensable secular studies."[76]

As momentum built, Paris began to assume a broader symbolic significance. The meaning of relocation went beyond improving French rabbinical training and fortifying the school's financial situation. Leaving Metz for Paris also represented the liberation of the rabbinate (and thus, French Judaism) from the constraints and stereotypes of the past. Paris symbolized the new, the "modern," the seat of a French Judaism validated by the presence of the rabbinical school. In the words of the Strasbourg leaders, "Is Paris not . . . the central point towards which all of the great arteries of progress and civilization converge?"[77]

Hosting the school would also stamp Parisian Jewry with the mark of Jewish authenticity; not only *could* they support the rabbinical school financially, they were *morally worthy* of doing so. The St. Esprit Consistory observed that while Paris's Jewish population did not yet numerically surpass that of Metz, it was nonetheless on the rise and—contrary to the views of the Metz leadership—Parisian Jews observed their religion with "solemnity and piety." Consequently, the primary factors justifying the school's location in Metz no longer applied.[78] Finally, while a majority of French Jews still resided in the northeastern departments, by mid-century Paris had clearly become the country's economic, political, and cultural center. Moving the rabbinical school to the capital would therefore affirm the alignment between French Judaism and the French nation. This reconstituted, reinvigorated French Judaism would flow from Paris to the provinces in the person of the enlightened French rabbi.

Jewish leaders also saw Paris as a favorable setting for healing religious divisions between the Sephardic and Ashkenazic communities. The St. Esprit leadership, for example, complained that the École Rabbinique at Metz taught only the Ashkenazic ritual dominant in the northeast. Consequently, young rabbis might find their authority and effectiveness undermined when they arrived at posts in the south with only limited knowledge of Sephardic pronunciation or liturgical practices. The Central Consistory went further, predicting that the Parisian environment would help rabbinical students from Alsace and Lorraine, who "bring with them a very pronounced German accent that [their] stay in . . . Metz cannot attenuate."[79] The Strasbourg Consistory addressed this issue more cryptically, observing that supervision of rabbinical training would prove easier and more effective in Paris. The *grand rabbin* of the Central Consistory could, for example, closely oversee both "the development and precision of studies . . . and the conservation of the ecclesiastic spirit."[80] For the Sephardic population of France, Paris represented "neutral ground where the two rites that divide the Jews are practiced equally."[81]

As important as it might have been to transfer's proponents, ritual tension did not divide the opposing camp. Leaders of both the Sephardic Bordeaux Consistory and the Ashkenazic Metz Consistory focused more on the potential moral dangers of the Parisian setting. The Bordeaux group feared that an extended sojourn in Paris would expose rabbinical students—most of whom would eventually serve small communities in the northeast—to the temptations of urban life. In Paris, rabbinical students would lose their "simplicity of taste, these habits of a modest life without ambition [which is] only proper for those disposed to the life of privations and sacrifices which awaits them in the *petites localités* where they will carry out their ministry."[82] Spoiled by five or six years in Paris, French rabbis would find it difficult to adjust to the simpler lifestyle of the provinces.

An individual, more detailed objection came from the Bordeaux businessman Benjamin Gradis. In a letter to Rouland, Gradis—who earlier had taken the Central Consistory to task over classical studies—elaborated upon Paris's adverse influences, portraying rabbinical students as passive vessels into which the vices of their surroundings flowed at will. Paris, he alleged, was "the least moral and the least religious city in France" where "seductions and bad examples" most abounded. Assuring the proper behavior of young rabbinical students would prove extremely difficult "in a city where traps are set beneath their steps and where even virtue and piety are often ridiculed."[83] Living in Paris promised to be "essentially corrupting and perverting," and graduates of a Parisian rabbinical school would leave imbued with "the love of pleasure [and] of expense, [and with] an aversion to the quiet and modest provincial existence without ambition." This moral corruption would encourage a majority of French rabbis to abandon their calling, depriving provincial communities of religious leadership. One knew, he wrote, that "everybody who has lived in Paris for a certain time is completely disgusted by [the prospect of] living elsewhere."[84]

Gradis extrapolated the moral benefits of simple living to the broader material situation of French Judaism. He opposed the move, "in the interest of not enlarging the religious budget [and for] the invaluable benefits . . . of being a religion at a reasonable price!" Most seriously, he predicted that the cost of operating the rabbinical school in Paris would triple due to the scarcity of certain religious items and the "habits of luxury that [the students would] contract." The government, the students' families, and the consistories all would have to subsidize the school through "special allocations and by voluntary or compulsory contributions." French Judaism's humble economic condition, in his view, lent it a "purity" of morals that the capital would undermine.[85] Finally, since the school already owned the Metz building, Gradis thought it illogical to move to Paris. If the École Rabbinique lacked good professors—which he was not willing to concede—it would certainly prove easier to send better teachers to Metz than to move the entire operation to Paris.[86]

In a last valiant (but ultimately doomed) flurry, the Metz leadership tried to refute all of the academic complaints that had piled up over the years. They argued that the school possessed more than adequate academic resources. The school's faculty included two *agregés* of the University, and "Talmudists and Hebraists are no rarer in Metz than elsewhere." If the Central Consistory wanted to educate "scholars, linguists, or men of letters," it should certainly move to Paris; but the school's mission called for the training of "enlightened and pious rabbis." The École Rabbinique could accomplish this goal in Metz, just as French Protestants did in their *facultés de théologie* in Strasbourg and Montauban.[87] While the school had its problems, most of them had little to do with geographic location. Shortcomings in the secular curriculum resulted more from the school's recruitment patterns. Most rabbinical students came from small communities in Alsace and Lorraine that lacked secondary educational institutions. Consequently, upon enrollment many had to devote significant time to secular studies with little bearing on their rabbinical duties.[88]

The Metz leaders also echoed Gradis's moral concerns. While Paris surely offered rich educational opportunities, it could not provide the student body with "the traditions and the habits which engender lasting religious callings." Indeed, the Paris Consistory had only produced one qualified student from its district in the entire history of the institution: Lazare Wogue, who had arrived in Metz in 1831 when he was only thirteen![89] Since then, the Parisian leadership had found it necessary to ask the Metz Consistory to designate a candidate to fill its vacancy, a practice common for other consistories as well. The lack of students from Paris led the Metz leadership to believe that "the distractions of the capital, the preoccupations of business and the desire to push into the world, or even the exclusive taste for the arts and sciences move young men away from the idea of dedicating themselves to the holy ministry." Finally, recently ordained rabbis often had to wait for a vacancy to become available. In the interim, they supported themselves by conducting classes in religious instruction or by preaching. In Paris, however, after absorbing the influence of University coursework, how many rabbis would resist the temptation of forsaking an uncertain rabbinical career for the immediate security of public or private teaching or other more lucrative and secure activities? Defections from the rabbinate, the Metz Consistory warned, would eventually compromise both the school's existence and the general health of French Judaism.[90]

With consistorial and governmental opinion stacked against it, however, the Metz protest had no chance. The problem's resolution illustrated the divergence in consistorial and governmental priorities. In April, ministerial officials recommended that Rouland authorize the transfer, citing the overwhelming approval of the departmental consistories, the deliberations of the Central Consistory, the unanimous vote of the *grands rabbins,* and the hope of improving the school's academic performance.[91]

For all the arguments over the educational and geographic advantages of Paris, government officials focused most on the issues of financial liability. At the head of their list of preconditions for relocation stood settling the reimbursement for the Metz Consistory's debts. In addition, they advised Rouland to demand that the Central Consistory submit a detailed budget proving that the rabbinical school could survive in Paris on the requested 20,000f annual subvention.[92] The recommendations did not discuss specific curricular issues, nor did they consider the role of French rabbis in Jewish regeneration and integration. Rouland's comments also avoided any mention of these issues. Curricular and ritual details remained the preserve of the Jewish administration; these issues became relevant for the civil administration only to the extent that they affected its financial responsibilities toward an institution whose budget it provided. Government interest focused upon legal and financial questions.

Ultimately, Rouland himself brokered the settlement that freed the École Rabbinique to move to Paris. As predicted, determining compensation for the Metz Consistory became the most complicated problem. In his comments on the memorandum of April 27, 1857, Rouland had opined that the state held no claim to the renovated building in Metz. The Treasury, he wrote, had only subsidized its construction, while the Consistory remained its legal owner.[93] His ministerial cabinet, however, concluded that even though the grounds belonged to the Consistory of Metz, the buildings had been refurbished at state expense. As a result of nearly 15,000f in cost overruns, and the project's general failure, the state could justifiably claim ownership of both the building and the additional land. Consequently, cession of the buildings at Metz required an act of law. Even so, the cabinet doubted the legal capacity of the Metz Consistory to accept the property; such an act seemed rather the function of the Central Consistory.[94]

Jewish leaders, meanwhile, could not agree on an appropriate amount themselves. The Metz Consistory at first asked the Central Consistory for a settlement of 27,000f. It later raised this claim to 80,000f, prompting the Central Consistory to lobby Rouland to help reduce it.[95] The Minister promptly scolded the Metz Consistory for its "exaggerated pretensions," proposing instead a 30,000f indemnity.⁹⁶ He then arranged a meeting between representatives of the Metz and Central Consistories in Paris to iron out a final agreement. On the advice of his cabinet, he asked the Central Consistory to declare its intention to assume all costs of the transfer from Metz and for the procurement of a new building. In return, the Minister agreed to raise the school's annual budget to 20,000f as the Consistory had requested. When the Jewish leadership met his conditions, Rouland promised to authorize the relocation.⁹⁷

The Minister's intervention pushed the two consistories into a lengthy negotiation. A deal was struck only after Albert Cohn, a respected educator and member of the Paris Consistory, served as a mutually approved arbitrator to end the impasse.⁹⁸ Cohn awarded the Metz Consistory the buildings and construction work along with a cash settlement of 42,500f. The Metz leaders grudgingly accepted his decision, even though they complained that the amount stood far below the sum of their financial obligations.⁹⁹ With the main hurdle cleared, the Central Consistory arranged a provisional locale for the rabbinical school in Paris until a new building could be constructed.¹⁰⁰

True to his word, Rouland issued the official decree approving the relocation of the École Rabbinique—which would assume the new name of Séminaire Israélite—on July 1, 1859. The Minister's official report to the Emperor combined the ideological and fiscal arguments for the move, employing practical criteria as support. Rouland had determined that rabbinical education in Metz had become too "narrow [and] formalistic, too out of touch with the culture and the development that it is permitted to require of religious ministers appropriately paid by the state."¹⁰¹ Studying in Paris, he wrote, would enable French rabbis to perform their most important function: "They are called to spread healthy notions of civil and religious life among the populations still indulging in customs and ideas [which represent] the final traces . . . of the inferior condition from which the generosity of the Imperial Government retrieved them at the beginning of this century."¹⁰²

The transfer question thus boiled down to practical matters. The government spent 27,000f each year on the École Rabbinique and its officials thought that neither the state nor the Jews had received a proper return on the investment. A "proper return," in this case, meant rabbis capable of facilitating the regeneration of their less enlightened coreligionists. Ideological goals formed a broad canvas for rabbinical education, while its specific details depended upon state assessments of practical value. These determinations helped to confirm the prototype of the ideal modern French rabbi, around which Jewish debates and decisions would crystallize.

Civil conceptions of utility continued to influence French rabbinical education through the end of the Second Empire. Financial aid not only helped to keep the doors of the rabbinical school open; it established a point of contact between Judaism and state, creating an avenue for civic influence in Jewish affairs. As shown in the previous chapter, consistorial officials needed to align the rabbinical curriculum with French models, portraying compatibility with other religious and educational institutions. Even though consistorial leaders wanted to move the École Rabbinique to Paris much earlier than 1858, the government ultimately determined when relocation became the best option. In reaching the decision to move the school, government officials gave practical utility at least as much weight as ideological issues, and certainly more than any Jewish religious or cultural debates. Under the Third Republic, the subjection of French Judaism to civic interpretations of utility would stimulate profound changes in Jewish education and within the consistorial structure.

III
Toward Separation, 1875–1906

6

Challenges of Equality
Financial Anticlericalism

In 1884 a Parisian Jew named Adolphe Beyfus died, bequeathing gifts to different Jewish institutions in the capital. Among his legacies, Beyfus left a bed in the Jewish hospital, 6,000f for the Jewish charity board (*comité de bienfaisance*), and a lump sum of 1,000f for the Parisian consistorial schools. He also willed his personal library and music collection to the Jewish vocational school and "other similar Jewish establishments most deprived of books."[1] Following standard procedure, the Paris Consistory declared its intention to accept the 1,000f designated for its schools.[2]

On the surface, the Beyfus legacy seemed a routine matter and, had it arisen five years earlier, it would have been. The gift came, however, at a time when an ascendant republican regime had begun to assert its authority over the Catholic church and transform the relationship between religion and state in France. Slowly but surely, the state's tightening grip on the church's public activities began to encompass French Judaism. As in the Catholic case, government officials used money as a tool to redefine the religious activities of the Jewish consistories. This strategy held serious consequences for the Consistory and convinced its leaders to modify their tactical approach to the new regime. They began to employ a portrayal of French Judaism that the consistorial leadership had hitherto rejected: as a unique religion, distinct from and not easily equated with its Christian counterparts.

The struggle for control of France that followed the collapse of the Second Empire in 1871 exacerbated the animosity between French republicans and their monarchist opponents. Catholic leaders joined a resurgent monarchist faction in actively opposing republican ambitions. The church's extensive social and educational operations therefore offered inviting, logical targets in the republicans' struggle for political supremacy. As René Rémond has observed, the alignment and composition of the opposing factions rendered anticlericalism "an elementary reflex" for French Republicans.[3] The establishment of the Third Republic in the 1870s gave a decisive advantage to the Republicans, setting in motion a process that eventually resulted in the law separating church and state in 1905.[4]

Much of the early anticlerical legislation aimed to attack the Catholic church's social and political influence by weakening its presence in the French school system. These measures gradually intensified, producing more extensive action that eventually called the church's public role into question. This escalation, however, also held significant consequences for Protestantism and Judaism in France. French anticlericals were most concerned with weakening the political and social power of the Catholic church; but the political linkage between the three authorized religions raised questions about the consistency of anticlerical legislation. As the radicals confronted the larger issues of consolidating republican political power and legitimacy, pressure mounted to equate the treatment of Catholicism, Protestantism, and Judaism. Rather than relaxing restrictions on the church, the republican regime imposed equivalent restrictions on the minority religions.

The first anticlerical attacks targeted Catholic school personnel. The educational policies of the Third Republic sought to remove Catholic clerical educators—and religious schools in general—from the prominent position they had enjoyed under the Falloux Law. New measures restricted the church's supervisory power and financial involvement in the schools, and clerical access to the public teaching lectern. One might therefore argue that the Falloux Law created a set of conditions that, while strengthening Catholic education in France in the short run, eventually left it vulnerable to government attack. The points at which the Falloux Law had drawn Catholicism closer to the state eventually provided levers for prying the two apart.

Disrupting the flow of money within the French religious structure—which I will refer to as "financial anticlericalism"—enabled the effective assertion of both republican political power and the broader civil supremacy of the state. By blocking the flow of funds from the church to its subsidiary institutions, the government altered the nature of those institutions. An organization cut off from church money either had to shut its doors or search for secular sources of revenue. The secularization of funding thereby enabled the government to affect the laicization of institutions that it wished to distance from the religious purview. Constricting religious financial channels thus reinforced the legislative limitations upon church activities. Jules Ferry, then Minister of Education, described this logic in 1882: "The law of March 28, 1882 is not an accident, an isolated deed in our legislation: by secularizing the school, it has only extended the common law, and to some extent the same principles of our Constitution, to the organization of national instruction, . . . to the only one of the public services which until now, by a strange contradiction, has preserved [its] confessional tie[s]."[5] Public instruction supported by the French Treasury necessitated the further extension of state influence into the French schools.

Because acceptance of civic funding meant submission to civic authority, laicization traveled down a financial path. The French national budget for primary education totaled more than 40,000,000f in 1864. By 1881, it had grown to approximately 116,000,000f. The source of the money also changed. In 1855, approximately 75 percent of elementary school funding came from the communes themselves. By 1880, the state had assumed responsibility for nearly 66 percent of this spending. Increases in school spending, as Grew and Harrigan point out, meant that communal schools began to rely more on the national budget.[6] As money came from increasingly secular sources, institutions receiving that money would have to adopt a more secular posture, conforming to civic guidelines.[7]

Although separating church and state stood near the center of republican ideology, the Catholic church had become too deeply rooted in French life for full separation to occur in one broad stroke. Anticlericals would have to proceed at a gradual pace, chipping away at individual pillars of church influence until the whole figurative house came crashing down.[8] The Conseil d'État played a crucial role in this dismantling process. Although the Ferry Laws of the 1870s imposed legal and organizational changes upon the French school system, the ultimate definition of their scope rested with the Conseil, the chief interpretive body of French administrative law. Its deliberations reveal the financial focus of French anticlericalism in the early 1880s, and the reasoning behind the eventual extension of the policy to French Judaism.

The importance of the Conseil in the anticlerical campaign became apparent shortly after Republicans gained power. During the early to mid-1870s, the Conseil d'État raised significant obstacles to the political subordination of the Catholic church. In 1874, for example, it upheld the right of the parish Catholic lay councils (*fabriques*) to acquire, receive, and own material goods. *Fabriques,* like the consistories, saw to the maintenance of church buildings and assured the availability of vital religious articles.[9] The Conseil's decision authorized the *fabriques* to receive a wide variety of donations and legacies, opening up a potentially broad source of revenue. They could accept gifts on behalf of Catholic institutions, as well as those intended for "recognized establishments of public utility, whatever their origins and nature, [and] whatever the religious or philosophical principle which had presided at their foundation." Coziness between the Conseil and the church also informed a subsequent ruling blocking attempts to replace clerical teachers with lay instructors in the public schools (a central component of Ferry's later school reforms).[10] For the Republicans, the Conseil d'État represented a source of Catholic reaction whose leaders had used their power to block republican initiatives, especially within the religious arena.[11]

This obstructionist reputation led republican politicians to recast the Conseil d'État after gaining control of the National Assembly in 1879. The "purge," as one author has called it, went along with a general political housecleaning of conservative holdovers throughout the French government.[12] When it came time to appoint new members to the Conseil in 1879, the republican government stacked nominations with its allies. It also expanded the body's membership, assuring continued republican dominance. A number of the sitting members resigned in response, further shrinking the ranks of the opposition, and completing the transformation of the Conseil d'État into a body comprised mostly of anticlerical Republicans.[13]

The reconfigured Conseil proved friendlier to republican objectives regarding the church. In April 1881 the Conseil considered a bequest by a Demoiselle Angelique Bonhoure to the Catholic *fabrique* at Poudis for the maintenance of a Catholic school in the commune. While legacies of this type customarily received routine authorization, the Conseil chose to examine it more closely. Specifically, it questioned whether "the *fabriques* can be authorized to receive gifts for the purpose of founding or maintaining schools[?]"[14] This approach laid the foundation for partially excluding the church from civic education and charity, providing a financial wedge against church involvement in French civic life. The Conseil based its decision upon several premises, all of which pointed toward restricting Catholic educational operations. According to the majority opinion, *fabriques*, "like other public establishments," attained their civil status "in view of the special mission which has been entrusted to them . . . [specifically,] the maintenance and conservation of temples [and] the administration of poor relief."[15] Subsequent legislation had neither modified the character of the *fabriques* nor extended to them "the right to found or maintain schools."

Finances had also defined the legal character of the *fabriques*. By ordering the sale of "assets belonging to the *fabriques* and scholastic establishments," the post-Revolution legislature had made public instruction a state responsibility.[16] "Under these circumstances," the opinion concluded, "the restitution to the *fabriques* of services relative to education cannot be reconciled with the exclusive attribution of these same services to the State or to the communes."[17] Nor could the *fabriques* claim protection under the principle of the "freedom of instruction proclaimed by the laws of the Revolution." These laws affirmed only the "individual right of citizens to teach," and no "collective right" for religious groups. While the Falloux Law of 1850 had empowered religious associations—as groups of individuals—to create confessional schools, this right did not extend to "ecclesiastic establishments" that the law considered administrative arms of a larger religious apparatus. The Conseil therefore disallowed the Bonhoure legacy, ruling that the *fabriques* had been created "exclusively in the interest of the celebration of religion and for the administration of charity" and could only "[possess] goods within the limits of these attributes."[18] This ruling thus asserted state prerogatives by altering the flow of money. Restricting the bequests that *fabriques* could receive limited their scope of activity and redefined their legal status within the French religious structure. Just as money had legitimated the educational role of the *fabriques,* the refusal of money removed that attribute.

Subsequent decisions further narrowed Catholic activities. In June 1881, the Conseil prohibited the *fabriques* from receiving "gifts made for the benefit of the poor."[19] This decision—which also included the Protestant consistories—came after another lengthy debate in which more radical members moved to preclude all charitable legacies to *fabriques* and consistories. The attempt proved unsuccessful largely because, as Émile Flourens argued, such a measure would imperil the very existence of these institutions.[20] Others pointed out that while educational and charitable activities lay beyond the capacities of *fabriques* and consistories, forbidding them from accepting donations would leave charity boards as the sole agents capable of receiving these funds. Expanding the scope of the decision would therefore leave the approximately 23,000 communes without any means of administering and accepting charitable funds.[21]

Despite their gradual and somewhat tentative nature, these rulings gave teeth to the Ferry School Laws enacted between 1878 and 1882. Ferry's agenda involved what Pierre Chevallier has called a "scholastic trinity": obligatory, free, and laic education free from religious (specifically Catholic) influence. *Laïcité*, as Ferry understood it, enabled "the exercise of spiritual and intellectual liberty [and emphasized] the necessary and indispensable respect for all beliefs" without allowing one to impose itself upon the others.[22] On a practical level, all three components asserted civil supremacy in scholastic affairs. By rendering primary education obligatory, the state sought to assure the growth of the system and promote the cultural (and ideally, the political) homogenization of French schoolchildren. Removing distinctions between students based upon wealth and religion promoted the same goals. Consequently, the Ferry school reforms—particularly the law of March 28, 1882—contained provisions designed to push the Catholic teaching orders from the realm of public education.[23]

The ruling of 1881 thus provided both the tools and the rationale for squeezing church educational activities financially. Legislative pressure soon followed. A law of June 1881 established free public education, doing away with student fees while mandating state subsidies for communes unable to meet their educational expenses.[24] These measures aimed to reduce the incentive for municipal councils to turn their schools over to clerical teaching orders, while simultaneously cutting off Catholic schools from an additional funding source. Limiting the financial role of the *fabriques* prevented them from channeling money to a school as a charitable act and thereby evading civil oversight of the school's operation.

While the new jurisprudence expanded state sovereignty over the schools, it also contained potential danger for French Judaism. Most seriously, the threat of decentralization hung over Jewish charitable institutions operated under consistorial auspices. If the Jewish Consistory became legally analogous to the *fabriques* and Protestant consistories, it would relinquish the capacity to administer the schools and other charities. Consistorial subsidiary institutions would in turn lose one of their primary funding sources and the basis for their legal existence. Jewish institutions would then need to apply for individual recognition as public utilities, at which point they would have to operate and raise funds independently. A small organization could not take for granted its ability to obtain state authorization, nor trust that it could meet its future budgetary requirements on its own.

Such a possibility did not escape the Jewish leadership. On the heels of the 1881 rulings, the Consistory of Paris established a special committee to examine the implications of the new jurisprudence. The committee's chairman, Narcisse Leven,[25] reported that the ruling posed no immediate threat to consistorial institutions. Jewish consistories occupied a unique legal category that bore little resemblance to the *fabriques* or the Protestant consistories. In the committee's view, the Consistory's rights in this regard were "perfectly established" and protected from a decision that did not address it directly. A proposal to pursue recognition of different Jewish institutions as public utilities was therefore premature and could be abandoned for the time being. The absence of precise details in Leven's report suggests a consistorial strategy of dismissing the question outright in hopes that it would simply disappear.

Confident in its position, the committee had decided to seek an affirmation of consistorial rights through a test case: the donation of a piece of land.[26] On the surface, the case seemed routine. In 1880, Victor St. Paul's will bequeathed a tract of land valued at approximately 18,480f to the Paris Consistory, of which he was a member. St. Paul had specified that the land be used for the construction of a "charitable establishment," namely a Jewish *salle d'asile*.[27] The Paris Consistory readily approved the gift and applied for the necessary authorization from the government in December 1880.[28]

This test, however, nearly cost the Consistory the very rights it sought to reaffirm. Disagreement clearly existed within government circles over the scope of new financial restrictions. Upon examining the St. Paul case file, the Director of Departmental and Communal Administration in Paris expressed deep misgivings about the gift. He granted that a law of May 25, 1844,[29] had empowered the Consistory to operate and oversee Jewish charitable establishments. Nevertheless, he wrote, "[I]n the presence of the jurisprudence which refuses to the *fabriques* as well as to the [Protestant] churches the capacity to accept gifts having a charitable purpose, it appears to me difficult to recognize this capacity for the Jewish Consistories. Consequently, I deem that there is no reason to approve the donation [of Victor St. Paul]."[30] Fortunately for the Consistory, the Director's opinion did not prove decisive, and the St. Paul gift was eventually authorized.[31]

Although the indecision of the Conseil spared the Jewish consistories from the limitations imposed on Catholicism and Protestantism, the relief proved only temporary. The issues raised by the St. Paul case resurfaced in subsequent years with government officials manipulating past consistorial conceptions of French Judaism. In determining the Consistory's legal attributes, the Conseil d'État employed the traditional criteria of equality and fairness to draw a legal analogy between the Jewish Consistory and its Christian counterparts. Ironically, the same logic that the Consistory had used to lobby for equal benefits under the law left French Judaism subject to equal legal restrictions. These restrictions would subsequently exclude the Consistory from a significant portion of Jewish institutional life, and redefine the public role of French Judaism.

French Judaism came under closer scrutiny in the mid-1880s as anticlerical Republicans sought to consolidate their gains. In October 1886, for example, the Goblet School Law synthesized the various reforms passed under Ferry into a more coherent system of legislation. Most important, it firmly rooted Ferry's commitment to laicizing public elementary schooling and teaching personnel.[32] At the same time the Chamber of Deputies moved aggressively to dissolve the entire religious budget, an action that the more moderate Senate could only partially block. Legislative assaults on the religious structure began to address inconsistencies in the system, focusing on unresolved issues that had escaped the first waves of anticlerical measures. These secondary targets included French Judaism, whose status had remained largely untouched.

This change in attitude manifested itself when the Conseil d'État ruled on the Beyfus legacy. In May 1884, the Paris Consistory announced its intention to accept Beyfus's legacy of 1,000f to the consistorial schools.[33] Following Narcisse Leven's reasoning from 1881, the Consistory maintained that its unique mission in administering Jewish education and charity precluded the legal restrictions enacted against the *fabriques* and the Protestant consistories. Léonce Lehmann, a member of the Paris Consistory and a prominent lawyer, outlined the legal basis for this distinction, claiming that the law clearly demonstrated the "double capacity of the Jewish consistories in matters of education and charity."[34] The philanthropic heritage of French Jewish education, he argued, placed it with other Jewish charities. For example, the Consistory aided indigent Jews in Paris—a growing population, many of whom were immigrants and "victims of antisemitic fanaticism." Besides lending material support, the Consistory helped by "moralizing them through work, opening schools and *asiles* for their children who would have difficulty gaining access to the public schools or would have a hard time staying in them." This philanthropic tradition and "the superior principle of liberty of conscience" had rendered "indispensable" the preservation of consistorial educational rights. The consistories also fulfilled charitable functions that no other institution possibly could. For example, only the Jewish Consistory could credibly oversee the distribution of *matzot* and other foods prepared in accordance with Jewish dietary laws. Given the historical link between Jewish education and Jewish charity, the state could not strip the consistories of their charitable capacities without jeopardizing their educational prerogatives.[35]

Lehmann's argument represented a significant (albeit unacknowledged) departure from previous consistorial lobbying tactics. Earlier in the century, Jewish leaders had emphasized the Consistory's similarity to Catholic and Protestant institutions, maintaining that the state had to extend equal treatment to all three recognized religions. Indeed, this reasoning had formed the cornerstone of their argument for creating the Jewish religious budget.

When the state began to impose religious restrictions, however, consistorial leaders began to claim that special circumstances set French Judaism apart from the Christian religions. Advocates of stronger restrictions on Jewish activities meanwhile called for equal treatment of all religions under French law. The criterion of fairness, hitherto employed to support Jewish claims to the benefits of the common law, thus became a rationale for circumscribing consistorial activities.

In March 1886, the Beyfus case came before the Conseil d'État. While an original draft ruling authorized the gift,[36] ensuing debate yielded quite a different result. The reporter of the majority opinion, Bonthoux,[37] framed the issue clearly: did the Jewish Consistory possess the legal capacity to receive "gifts destined for educational or charitable works?"[38] Recent legal precedents, he noted, suggested that such gifts should not be authorized. In April 1881, the Conseil had ruled that *fabriques* and Presbyterian councils "could neither establish nor maintain schools" because existing law granted them only the right to maintain places of worship.[39] This action came despite Article 20 of the organizing laws of the Protestant consistories, which charged them with maintaining discipline, administering "church assets," and providing aid to the poor. In reaching this decision, the Conseil had specified that Article 20 in no way implied any capacity to establish educational institutions.[40]

The majority stopped short of applying this logic to the Jewish Consistory, placing it in a different legal category. The Consistory's organizing law of December 10, 1806, listed among other functions the regulation of "sums intended for the expenses of the Mosaic religion."[41] In the past, the consistories had included educational expenditures among their general religious expenses (*frais du culte*) without government objection. Furthermore, the consistories had repeatedly claimed civil sanction of their educational functions based upon the ruling of June 29, 1819, which permitted the use of religious taxes to subsidize both primary schools and programs of religious instruction. With the establishment of the Jewish religious budget in 1831, the Consistory retained its capacity to accept voluntary contributions as supplements to *frais du culte* not paid by the state. Because these expenses had always included primary education, the government had implicitly authorized the Jewish consistories to accept donations for the creation of schools. The administrative reorganization of the Consistory in 1844 did not establish any new privileges in this regard; the legislature had merely legalized the existing situation. The law therefore contained "incontestable proof" that the Jewish Consistory's traditional functions included education.[42] On these grounds, the majority voted to authorize the Beyfus bequest.

Despite such lengthy precedents, a dissenting opinion opposed authorization on the grounds of equality. This minority held that approving the Beyfus legacy would grant a power to the Jewish consistories that the Conseil had withheld from the Catholics and Protestants. By consequence, the state would create "a privileged situation" for "a religion that represents only a weak minority [in France]." Because Jewish schools occupied the same administrative category—*écoles libres*—as Christian schools, they should follow the same regulations.[43]

The debate soon crystallized around this legal analogy. Bonthoux attempted to rebut the dissenters by rejecting the comparison between the *fabriques* and the Jewish consistories. The different organizational structures of Catholicism and Judaism, he observed, argued against applying the same regulations to both religions. The Catholic church operated numerous organizations capable of seeing to the needs of its faithful, while French Judaism had no structures besides the consistories. In addition, *fabriques* had a "uniquely religious" interest in administering school donations, a function more suitably served by recognized lay organizations. Comparable Jewish associations did not exist, and so restricting the Consistory's financial role would block donations to Jewish schools altogether. Far from providing French Judaism with an unfair advantage, confirming the capacity of the Jewish consistories to accept donations and bequests would "place the *culte israélite* upon a footing of perfect equality with the *culte catholique*."[44] Bonthoux agreed that, in light of the trend toward the "laicization of charity and education," regulations governing French Judaism should be aligned with those for the Christian religions. The government could attain this goal, however, with a few simple modifications and without overhauling the Consistory's legal definition.[45]

Framing the question on the basis of equality caused some members to change their previous positions. Émile Flourens, for example, who had supported a moderate strategy in dealing with the Catholics and Protestants, now rose to refute the majority opinion. The Conseil, he recalled, had ruled in 1880 that religious institutions lacked the civil capacity "to receive gifts destined for a charitable foundation or the creation of schools." By establishing the Jewish religious budget in 1831, the state created a legal equivalency between Judaism, Protestantism, and Catholicism, acknowledging that exclusion from the common law constituted "an insult to the Jews."[46] Flourens did not deny that the Jewish consistories had the right of "supervision and control over the Jewish schools," and the capacity to raise money for them. Nevertheless, he found no legal basis for the majority's apparent desire to expand this narrow right into a broader capacity "to receive [funds] for any [sort of] establishments."[47]

In a roundabout manner, Flourens employed the fairness argument against the Consistory. The key lay in his analogy between the Consistory and Christian institutions based upon their relationship to the state instead of upon the specific functions they performed. Civic money constituted a primary indicator of the nature of that relationship, and the defining mechanism for the acceptable scope of religious activity. French Judaism's receipt of civic funds implied a legal position equal to that of the Christian religions.[48] All three state religions, Flourens concluded, should therefore adhere to the same rules. His interpretation was by no means novel. The author of the *note* of 1841 had expressed similar views while complaining about the rabbinical curriculum at Metz.[49] Both arguments affirmed that the state's financial involvement with Judaism, Protestantism, and Catholicism obliged the government to equalize its demands on all three religions. The assumption of civic equality left the Consistory little basis for demanding special treatment. Flourens's reorientation of the case proved decisive, and a new ruling emerged.[50] The final decision of April 8 disallowed the Beyfus legacy and blocked the Jewish consistories from accepting future educational bequests. At the same time, the Conseil modified the Consistory's legal attributes, prohibiting it from "the foundation or maintenance of scholastic and charitable establishments."[51]

The Beyfus decision represented a new interpretation of the relationship between utility and equality. The creation of the Jewish religious budget in 1831 linked the equality that state money symbolized with French Judaism's moral and political utility. This connection established an acceptable, albeit evolving, space in which French Judaism could operate within the French civic sphere. By attacking the Consistory's relationship to education, the Beyfus jurisprudence redefined the utility of Judaism even as it affirmed the continuing equality of all three authorized religions. Consequently, French Judaism became vulnerable to the same political forces facing French Catholicism and Protestantism by the century's end. Whereas the financial link had traditionally involved the government more deeply in Jewish affairs, the Beyfus ruling transformed that bond into a wedge that drove the religious and civil entities apart. The Consistory's educational and charitable functions had come under attack and would continue to shrink. With its field of activity becoming ever narrower, the Consistory needed a new strategy to fortify the borders of its remaining civic space.

The Beyfus ruling had an immediate impact upon individual consistories, changing administrative attitudes and the ways in which money moved through the bureaucracy. Educational legacies and gifts now faced enormous, if not insurmountable, legal hurdles. The will of Mayer DuPont, for example, designated 40,000f to the Consistory of Nancy for the creation of a charitable establishment and 1,000f to establish an annual scholarship for the education of "young Jews" demonstrating talent in the sciences, letters, or the arts.[52] Prior to the Beyfus decision, the Ministry of the Interior had expressed an inclination to authorize the bequest, citing the differences between the Jewish Consistory and the *fabriques* and Protestant consistories.[53] The Jewish leadership of Nancy fully expected the government to approve the donation. As a result, the president of the Nancy Consistory, Alfred Fould, wrote to the Minister in a perplexed tone in October 1886, inquiring as to why the government had not yet authorized it.[54]

Fould's concern proved well founded, as the Beyfus ruling eventually derailed the DuPont legacy. In March 1887, the Minister of the Interior wrote to the Prefect of the Meurthe and Moselle to inform him of the Beyfus decision and the subsequent change in bequest procedures. In an attempt to circumvent this new legal barrier, the Section de l'Intérieur asked the DuPont heirs if they would designate another establishment to accept the 40,000f. The heirs, though, refused to alter the will's stipulations and instead decided to use the money to establish their own charitable foundation.[55] The Beyfus decision ultimately blocked all but 1,000f of the original gift from reaching the Nancy Consistory.[56]

As the Beyfus jurisprudence eroded the Consistory's intermediary role, Jewish communal charities reorganized and adapted their operations. After 1886, individual Jewish institutions began to seek recognition as establishments of public utility in their own right, independent from the Consistory. These newly incorporated bodies could directly receive donations, reducing the risk of government meddling. The Beyfus decision stimulated this realignment of Jewish charities, encouraging subsidiary institutions not directly connected to religion—hospitals and bureaus for poor relief, for example—to separate themselves from the official Jewish religious structure.

The material incentive to change could be considerable. One month after the Beyfus ruling, the Conseil d'État refused to authorize the bequest of Meyer Joseph Cahen, who had left 10,000f to the Paris Consistory's charity board and 6,000f to the Rothschild Hospital. It also disallowed Cahen's legacy of 6,000f to charitable works lacking a "legal existence." By contrast, the Conseil did authorize the Director of the General Administration of Public Assistance in Paris to accept the 10,000f left to the civic charity board of the seventh *arrondissement*, owing to its secular status.[57] A memorandum attached to the draft copy of the decree, however, suggested amending the ruling so that the Hôpital Rothschild—which had recently received recognition as a public utility—could pursue authorization of its portion of the legacy independent of the Consistory.[58] Both decisions, in the Minister's view, followed the guidelines set up by the Beyfus decision.[59]

One final case moderated the Beyfus restrictions. Instead of disallowing 25,000f bequeathed by Etienne Joseph Albert "in favor of the religious and charitable Jewish institutions of Paris," the Conseil d'État instructed "the Consistory to direct the legacy either to religious establishments in whose name it is able to receive, or to charitable establishments provided with civil existence."[60] The Consistory could still play a role in the financial life of Jewish charities, but only on behalf of institutions lacking an independent legal status.

Through these rulings, the Conseil d'État used money to redraw the boundaries of consistorial activity. While the Consistory could still raise, receive, and distribute funds, the government set new limits on where that money could come from and where it could go. Excluding the Consistory from the donation process in turn redefined communal schools and other charities as strictly civic, non religious institutions. As Jewish charitable organizations came to possess independent civil status, consistorial activity became more confined to facilitating religious practice and observance. By laicizing funds, the state effectively laicized the segment of the Jewish communal structure supported by those funds.

Ironically, this trend helped to cushion French Judaism against the blow of the Separation Law of 1905. By 1904, a ministerial memorandum could reasonably claim that the Central Consistory's intermediary function had become so irrelevant that separation of church and state would not pose a financial threat to French Jewish institutional life.[61] By the time the general political tide turned decisively toward separation in the 1900s, Jewish institutions had already begun to develop alternative methods of sustaining themselves.

Interestingly, the new state of affairs did not generate any ardent protest within French Jewry. The Jewish press, for example, expressed no fervent opposition to or even criticism of the Beyfus decision. Historical literature has remained similarly mute on the case. In one respect, this general silence is not surprising. Because the ruling extended existing jurisprudence to the Jewish consistories, Jewish officials could not claim any special persecution. Moreover, disagreement over the proper role of the consistories in administering Jewish charitable institutions already existed within French Judaism. Viewed in this light, the Beyfus decision pushed consistorial officials to confront problems that predated the case and defied easy resolution in its aftermath.

By limiting the ability of the consistories to receive bequests, however, the Beyfus decision compounded existing practical problems. As the next chapter shows, its restrictions interacted with budget cuts and Jewish communal dynamics to create new financial difficulties for French Judaism. Even though both were subject to the same laws, Jewish schools landed in a different situation than their Catholic counterparts. At this stage, the historically uneven local support for Jewish schooling limited Jewish educational activities. Cut off from significant civic financial support in most cases, consistorial schools assumed a philanthropic character that enabled them to attract private funding. While existing schools might survive, new educational endeavors took the form of supplementary programs of religious instruction. The Beyfus decision thus accelerated the Consistory's exit from institutional education, throwing up financial walls around a more narrowly defined Jewish religious space.

French Jewish leaders also had to contend with financial anticlericalism in the legislative arena. As the Conseil d'État disrupted the flow of money within the religious infrastructure, the National Assembly—especially the Chamber of Deputies—eroded the financial ties between state religions and the French Treasury by reducing or eliminating religious budgets. Struggling for fiscal survival compelled Jewish leaders to reconsider both the best use of their resources and the mission of French Judaism. In the process, they further redefined the scope of their activities and with it French Jewish religious space.

Like the deliberations in the Conseil d'État, legislative budget battles weighed the principle of equal treatment against the demands of Jewish distinctiveness. Consistorial leaders and moderate politicians sought to protect Jewish religious funding by outlining Judaism's particular circumstances. More radical anticlericals, by contrast, wished to lump all three state religions together. In November 1883, Jules Roche, a radical deputy noted for his outspoken anticlericalism, introduced a bill calling for the complete elimination of scholarships for Catholic seminarians.[62] Martin-Feuillée, the Minister of Religions, vigorously opposed the measure, warning that it would not only hinder the recruitment of Catholic clergy, but also lead to the reduction or suppression of similar funding for Jews and Protestants. He also drew a distinction that would frame much of the subsequent debate, casting the issue as "a question of fact"—meaning an isolated instance—rather than as "a question of law [or] of principle": "[T]he question of principle should be set aside for later; at the present time we have only to examine a question of fact; upon this point, I say to you: the Protestant and Jewish seminaries are in a situation such that they require [the] subventions which are accorded to them by the State in order to survive."[63] If the Assembly wished to address a specific problem, he argued, it should not enact a law with far-reaching (and perhaps unintended) consequences without acknowledging the distinction between Catholicism and non-Catholic religions.

Martin-Feuillée's stance represented a public affirmation of Jewish uniqueness that resonated within Jewish circles and earned him accolades in the French Jewish press. Isidore Cahen applauded the speech, agreeing that Roche's plan needed safeguards to minimize collateral damage to Judaism and Protestantism. Since the law viewed all three state religions equally, restricting one on the basis of a legal principle meant restricting all three. Broadly applied budget reductions aimed at Catholicism would therefore cripple the Séminaire Israélite and the Protestant theological schools. Deciding the budgetary question on "fact" instead of "principle," Cahen wrote, would add flexibility to government policy.[64] A significant contingent among the Deputies concurred and crafted a compromise. Although the Chamber suppressed aid to all French seminaries, it subsequently voted individual grants to Jewish and Protestant seminaries and clergy to maintain existing levels of funding.

While grateful for the deputies' good faith, Cahen sensed the danger of a case-by-case solution. Once the principle of budget reduction gained a legal foothold, French anticlericals could use it to reduce or eliminate all funding for French Judaism. At the same time, French antisemites could portray protection of Jewish institutions as evidence of favoritism or Jewish power.[65] Cahen concluded that, even though the matter had been decided favorably for the time being, "the fears demonstrated by [Martin-Feuillée] remain unresolved." The Chamber, he warned, had left the door open for future incursions on Jewish activities.[66]

Cahen's apprehension proved well founded. As the scope of anticlerical legislation expanded, the "question of principle" regarding Judaism and Protestantism became harder to ignore. In 1884, the budget commission of the Chamber of Deputies recommended extensive funding cuts for all three state religions, including a decrease of 10,000f in rabbinical salaries and administrative supplements and the elimination of several vacant religious positions. Most significant, the commission called for the termination of government subsidies to the Séminaire Israélite in Paris.[67]

Spirited opposition rose from both ministerial and consistorial quarters. The *Univers israélite* noted that Martin-Feuillée reacted in the Chamber "even more energetically than [the previous year]."[68] The leaders of the Central Consistory sent a lengthy memorandum to the commission, predicting "disastrous consequences" for both the rabbinical school in particular and for French Judaism in general.[69] As before, they emphasized the uniqueness of the rabbinical school, seeking to distinguish it as much as possible from the Catholic seminaries. "The Central Consistory," they wrote, "fears that the Commission . . . has been misled by the mirage of the word *séminaire*, which has confused . . . this establishment with institutions of a completely different nature."[70]

This assertion led to the remarkable conclusion that the Séminaire Israélite was a "purely lay establishment." Just because the school had assumed the title of *séminaire* after moving to Paris in 1859, it "did not conserve its original character any less; it did not remain any less subject to the supervision of the civil authority." The government, the Jewish leaders reminded, retained the right to appoint the school's director and faculty and to approve its rules and curriculum. The state alone provided for the school's educational and administrative expenses, while Catholic seminaries relied "exclusively upon the ecclesiastical authorities," save for government scholarships for individual students.[71] State money—and the obligations that accompanied it—had thus marked the Séminaire Israélite as a civic entity, even though it served primarily religious purposes.

Despite the eventual defeat of the recommendations, the Consistory had to fend off repeated financial assaults. In 1885, the Chamber of Deputies proposed slashing the Jewish religious budget from 202,900f to 180,900f, including the 10,000f in rabbinical student scholarships. On top of these cuts, the Deputies called for "a significant reduction" of funds for Jewish and Protestant religious buildings.[72] The measure died in the Senate where a consistorial ally, Edmond de Pressensé, warned of the harm it would do to the Protestant theological schools and the Séminaire Israélite.[73] Echoing the Jewish Consistory, Pressensé declared that these institutions received the bulk of their funding from the French Treasury and lacked the alternative resources available to the Catholic seminaries. The question of equal treatment, he held, was immaterial: the Deputies had already applied the law unequally, suppressing Catholic funds while maintaining support for the Jewish and Protestant seminaries on the grounds that "these seminaries have nothing."[74] In recognizing the unequal status of the institutions, the Deputies had themselves dismissed the equality argument. A majority in the Senate agreed, eventually restoring the seminary's full allotment and even adding 12,000f to the general Jewish religious budget.[75]

This triumph unfortunately proved short-lived. Two weeks later the *Archives israélites* lamented the reinstitution of severe funding reductions by the Deputies, who rejected all of the Senate measures. The new budget reduced the seminary's funding from 32,000f to 22,000f; the total amount of salaries paid to religious personnel from 170,900 to 158,900f; and the allotment for maintaining religious buildings from 70,000f to 40,000f.[76] This adverse turn of events sparked negotiations between the Ministry of Religions and the Central Consistory aimed at minimizing the impact of the cuts.[77] Whatever the final arrangement, Jewish leaders feared "great disarray" in all consistorial districts.[78]

Some Jewish observers foresaw even more serious consequences beyond the direct impact on Judaism. Lazare Wogue predicted that eliminating the entire religious budget would remove all the government's leverage with the Catholic church. "The free church in the free state," he warned, would quickly become "the powerful church in the unarmed state."[79] Liberated from the shackles of government oversight, the Catholic church could expand its influence at the expense of non-Catholic religions. In this regard, Wogue echoed the concerns of numerous French politicians. Even Paul Bert, a Ferry lieutenant and committed anticlerical, doubted the advisability of complete separation. Dissolution of the Concordat, he argued, would break the government's hold on religious finances and do away with its ability to subordinate the church.[80]

Similar fears pervaded the Ministry of Religions. The Director General of Religions protested that the budget proposals lacked any sense of proportion to those suggested for Catholicism and would create serious problems for the Jewish consistories. To avoid drastic salary reductions, the central religious administration urged Martin-Feuillée to cut only administrative expenses; it had even drafted an alternative decree along these lines, though too late for inclusion in the 1885 budget. The 1886 budget, the director assured, would confine the 10,000f reduction entirely to administrative costs.[81]

Despite such endeavors, the movement to reduce government subsidies to French Judaism gained momentum. On March 10, 1885, the Chamber of Deputies rejected all of the Senate's moderate recommendations. Instead, the Deputies reduced the Jewish seminary's budget to 22,000f by eliminating 10,000f in scholarships; they also slashed 12,000f from the budget for religious personnel and 30,000f—nearly one half—of the 70,000f allotment for maintaining religious edifices.[82]

Both the subtleties of jurisprudence and the bludgeon of legislative restrictions strained consistorial finances, prompting an internal reassessment of Jewish priorities and attempts to improve communal fundraising. The Paris Consistory, for example, convened a special session in November 1880 to discuss the problems plaguing its communal charity fund, the *caisse de la communauté*. The Consistory had established the *caisse* to defray the operating costs of Judaism in Paris. Its funds also promoted Jewish education in the capital, providing aid for the Parisian Jewish schools, the Talmud

Torah, and the seminary, and higher education scholarships for worthy Jewish students. The Consistory's president, Gustave de Rothschild, proposed reinvigorating the *caisse* with younger members drawn from the developing fields of commerce and industry.[83] The Consistory agreed and determined to pursue a reorganization of the local committees along these lines.[84]

Two years later, however, little had changed and the *caisse* faced increasing financial pressure. Attrition, financial ruin, and neglect had eroded its traditional donor base, while communal religious expenses had grown and government financial support had diminished. In addition to reductions in the national religious budget, the City of Paris had recently ended its 30,000f subvention to the consistorial schools while the size of the Parisian Jewish population had increased significantly.[85] By 1887, consistorial educational institutions alone had accumulated debts of more than 90,000f. To address these shortfalls, the Consistory had to draw upon other resources, including the *caisse* and the income generated by the sale of kosher meat.[86] These stopgap measures, however, could not solve the long-term problem.

Parisian Jewish institutions thus teetered on the edge of potential disaster. Traditionally, the Consistory had acted as a hub uniting various Jewish charitable organizations. Financial anticlericalism, however, had undermined that unity by restricting the Consistory's role as a conduit for charitable funds. Organizations for which the Consistory could no longer serve as a financial source would henceforth need to seek funding on their own, a prospect that threatened smaller institutions with limited donor networks. In the eyes of the consistorial leadership, their worst fears about the Beyfus restrictions had come true.

Addressing this problem meant redefining the ground on which Jewish charity would stand. The Paris Consistory, for example, decided to receive and disperse donations "without a special destination"; it would also maintain its control over the annual fundraising lottery. Changes in consistorial legal attributes, though, favored "the creation of a mixed commission . . . composed of the president and vice-president of each of the great [charitable and instructional organizations] of the community." This new body would oversee all general questions of charitable work—for example, the creation of new organizations—and administer any general gifts received.[87]

The Paris Consistory's call for a new union of charitable associations apparently fell on deaf ears. Several factors likely tempered enthusiasm for the idea. First, control over Jewish charities in Paris and elsewhere had historically constituted a point of contention, with leaders of individual Jewish institutions expressing resentment over the heavy-handed exercise of consistorial authority.⁸⁸ The details of the Consistory's appeal for change suggested its reluctance to cede this power completely. At the same time, the government's loosening of consistorial control likely received at least tacit approval from many of the subordinate institutions. The Beyfus ruling thus stoked a simmering conflict within Jewish communal affairs, giving the state a decisive role in shaping Jewish communal dynamics. Financial anticlericalism provided an opportunity for individual organizations to free themselves from consistorial control. Further state intervention eventually forced the Consistory into a more specialized communal role.

The possibilities of the new system became apparent rather quickly. In the summer of 1887, a question arose concerning the will of an Isaïe Berr, who had bequeathed 2,000f to the Paris Consistory for either the Jewish communal schools or general charitable services.⁸⁹ Obviously, the terms of the gift conflicted with the new guidelines established by the Beyfus jurisprudence. In order for the transaction to take place, the Paris Consistory had to cede its position as receiver to the local charity board.⁹⁰ This arrangement received resounding approval from the government.⁹¹ Restricted by law, the Paris Consistory found itself pushed aside.

The same process occurred in a concurrent case. A woman named Rose Hirsch had left all her assets to the Paris Consistory for the establishment of a fund whose proceeds would be distributed to the Jewish poor four times each year.⁹² Realizing that the Beyfus decision prevented it from accepting the gift, the Paris Consistory ceded the legacy to the Jewish charity board, which the government had recently recognized as a public utility.⁹³ The two-year delay in issuing this decision indicates the reluctance of the Consistory to relinquish its intermediary function in bequest cases. In the end, however, its leaders had to conform to the new legal requirements so that the funds could reach the community. By circumscribing consistorial financial power, the government effectively limited the Consistory's civic function. The incursions of the Conseil d'État and the National Assembly forced a redefinition of Jewish communal functions and, consequently, of Jewish communal space.

7

JEWISH EDUCATION AND JEWISH SPACE

In the autumn of 1903, the Baroness de Rothschild offered to pay for the expansion of the Paris Consistory's Jewish education courses. Classes would move to more convenient locales; new classes would begin where necessary, and supervision of the lessons would become more systematic.[1] The consistorial leaders agreed, and in January 1904 the Baroness covered the cost of moving the classes held in Montmartre from the rue Nicolet to a larger building on the rue Nobel. She also paid the teachers' salaries and the rent and heating.[2] Altogether, the Baroness de Rothschild committed an initial sum of more than 11,000f, plus future support of 5,000f per year.

The Baroness's contributions symbolized the gradual transformation of consistorial education policy over nearly three decades. By prohibiting the Consistory from accessing certain revenue sources, financial anticlericalism had narrowed the field of consistorial activities and circumscribed Jewish space. Consistorial Judaism found new utility by adapting its role as a moral force that could facilitate the French national goal of immigrant absorption. Yet the Consistory's own goals remained decidedly Jewish. Consistorial teachers prepared Jewish children for the *bar mitzvah* and *intitiation religieuse,* but often outside the civic realm. The narrower definition of Jewish civic space thus required a simultaneous redefinition of both the Consistory's educational priorities and French Judaism's civic presence. The growth of the French school system also encouraged these changes, rendering the goal of a national system of Jewish schools unattainable. Ultimately, the combination of anticlerical politics, financial realities, and shifting sensibilities hemmed in the Consistory, compelling its leaders to refocus their educational mission. In orienting their educational efforts toward supplementary programs of religious instruction, consistorial leaders also reconceived French Jewish space.

Decades of marginalization had insulated Jewish schools against the dynamics of financial anticlericalism. While the Beyfus case made it harder to receive legacies, the absence of a central, fixed system of financial support for Jewish education had forced Jewish school leaders to develop independent sources of revenue. Larger institutions either communalized or located private funding within their local communities. Any civic funds that a Jewish primary school received tended to come from the municipality rather than the state. As a result, fluctuations in the national religious budget had little direct effect on Jewish schooling.

The institutional expansion of public education had a more profound impact. Under the Third Republic, the national system began to dominate French primary education. As Grew and Harrigan have convincingly argued, the growth of the national education budget followed rather than drove the spread of schools. School enrollments led to larger budgets rather than more schools attracting more students.[3] Rising spending on schools thus testifies to increases in the numbers of institutions under state control, deeper government involvement, and to growing acceptance of the system among French parents. Between 1875 and 1907 (two years after passage of the law separating church and state in France) the public education budget grew from 78 million francs to more than 283 million francs. Remarkably, this sum represented twenty-five times the amount spent in 1837, while the total budget for the entire French central government had increased only fourfold during the same period.[4] The city of Paris alone reported a primary school budget of more than 14 million francs in 1900.[5]

Such figures dwarfed consistorial school spending (nearly 100,000f in 1894–95), rendering moot any question of competition between public and Jewish schools. The Ferry Laws rendered primary education both free and obligatory, and gradually moved to eradicate Catholic domination of the system. Equally important, the French public schools represented the most practical avenue for gaining *entrée* to French secondary education. Public education had become more accessible, more affordable, and therefore more appealing. The ideological appeal of the public schools received practical reinforcement from the civil authorities.

Grasping the situation, consistorial leaders abandoned hopes of opening new schools and instead worked to strengthen their existing institutions. In larger cities, Jewish schools tended to assume communal status and were absorbed by the civil educational apparatus. For example, the Paris Consistory's schools for boys and girls at the rue des Rosiers had received municipal subsidies ever since their establishment in 1857. In response to the growth of the schools, the city raised its annual subvention over the years and in 1873 accorded them new quarters at the place des Vosges and the rue des Tournelles.[6] These schools were henceforth generally accepted as communalized in spirit if not in name.

Obviously, the Parisian authorities accepted the utility of these schools enough to incorporate them into their own system. Jewish schools that managed to survive also spoke to a particular perception of utility on the part of their benefactors, students, and instructors. As the idea of religious education itself came under heavier attack, however, consistorial leaders had to rethink their school plans to reinforce their claims to utility. Jewish education implied a specifically *Jewish* process of national integration that preserved French Judaism. Pursuing this course in the face of anticlericalism and laicization required a new justification of Jewish distinctiveness.

The arrival of Eastern European Jewish immigrants in France helped to recast Jewish education in contemporary terms. In the task of absorbing relatively large numbers of Jewish newcomers, Jewish leaders found a new sense of urgency and applicability for their educational institutions. The immigrants, many of whom settled in Paris, formed a new student pool in need of instruction that stimulated an expansion of the capital's consistorial schools. Among these new arrivals, the Jewish writer Théodore Reinach boasted, Jewish education could once again apply the principles of regeneration. "It is precisely the influence of generally poor foreign families, whose children are ignorant of French," he wrote,

> that justifies, as much as the delicate question of the Sabbath, the maintenance of primary schools particular to the Jews. . . . Thrown prematurely into a scholastic *milieu* where everything will be new for them—language, ideas, morals—certain Jewish children would risk exhausting themselves in futile efforts, . . . becoming subjects of distrust and laughter for their Christian peers. By managing [their] transition through special schools, we accelerate . . . the moral naturalization of these young generations; we prepare new and devoted recruits for civilization and for France.[7]

Consistorial school records support Reinach's assessment of the new focus upon the immigrant Jewish poor. An 1884 report from the school on the rue de Lafayette listed fifty-one pupils in the school's second division, only twenty-four of whom had been born in France. The other twenty-seven hailed from eastern European locales such as Riga and Brody.⁸ On a visit to the school on the avenue de Ségur, a consistorial inspector noted the presence of "many foreign children whose parents came to Paris without any resources."⁹ Eastern European immigration thus reinvigorated the concept of regeneration by supplying the Consistory with a new target population among whom it could carry out its mission.¹⁰

Emphasizing regeneration at the consistorial schools also answered critics of separate Jewish education. The onset of financial anticlericalism in the 1880s had punctured the concept of Jewish uniqueness and with it the link between utility and equality. At the same time, Ferry's regime had undertaken a nationalization of French education designed to attack the weaknesses blamed for the military disaster of the Franco-Prussian War. The government subsequently sought to unite French citizens by using the school system as a means of cultural and moral cultivation. State policies also encouraged economic progress through vocational and technical education. In this manner, Republican education policy charted its own course of regeneration for the French nation as a whole.¹¹ The old consistorial mission of Jewish regeneration gained renewed vigor as Jewish educators realigned their curricula with the demands of this new environment. Trends in Jewish schooling reflected this general context, with Jewish vocational education, for example, drawing heavily upon French models.¹² By educating the children of the immigrant and the indigent, consistorial schools could reasonably claim a role in promoting French national well-being.

The curricula of the Parisian Jewish schools reflected this consistorial commitment. All three schools followed the same basic curriculum, with secular studies dominating the school week along the lines of the French public system. At the school on the rue de Lafayette, for example, boys and girls of the *première classe* studied both French and arithmetic for five hours each week. Another eleven hours were divided between classes such as history, calligraphy, geography, and physical education. The only significant difference between the genders in secular subjects was that girls studied needlework for four hours each week while boys studied drawing.¹³ By contrast, the school curriculum devoted only one quarter of each week to religious instruction for boys, who studied Hebrew for three hours a week, "morality and religion" for two hours, and singing for two hours. Girls received slightly less religious instruction, studying Hebrew reading for two hours each week, an unspecified course in "religion" for one hour and singing for two hours.¹⁴ The schools on the rue Claude Bernard (also known as the École Rothschild, after its primary benefactor, Baron Gustave de Rothschild) and on the avenue de Ségur followed comparable patterns, devoting roughly three-quarters of their school week to secular subjects for both boys and girls.[15]

In large part, the subordination of religious studies to secular learning resulted from the need for municipal authorization, which in turn demanded conformity to French educational standards. The course of studies also represented a shift in consistorial conceptions of the relationship between being Jewish and being French, and the logical culmination of nearly a century of negotiation and positioning. The predominance of secular studies assigned significant—but nevertheless limited—space to Judaism, even within schools of a decidedly religious character. French Judaism thus existed as a component of Frenchness: Judaism, as consistorial leaders had traditionally argued, served as a moral foundation enabling French Jews to become loyal, productive citizens of France. While this compartmentalization protected Jewish schools, it also contained an inherent weakness. As we have seen, the idea of equality had led the Conseil d'État to view Judaism and Christianity as legally interchangeable. If Judaism functioned as a moral basis for secular education, it need not have been the sole one. The new application of equality potentially threatened the assumption of uniqueness that had been essential to maintaining the relevance of Jewish education in France.

This problem intersected with other concerns as French Jewish leaders began to reconfigure their educational strategy. During the 1880s, the leaders of the Paris Consistory constantly wrung their hands over local reports of growing Jewish religious indifference. Parental attitudes, a lack of qualified teachers, inadequate resources, and an already crowded school day all argued against trying to address the problem by opening more Jewish schools. Instead, the Consistory opted to encourage the formation of supplemental courses of religious instruction. Like the individual charities that became institutions of public utility after the Beyfus decision, Jewish education needed a new field of operation in order to thrive. Just as those organizations established direct relationships to France, Jewish religious instruction would form a direct connection with French Jews. A system based on supplemental religious instruction enabled Jewish educators to define a purely religious, uniquely Jewish space within French society, extending Judaism's instructional reach.

Spurred by the growth of its Jewish population, Paris became the most active center of consistorial Jewish educational activity and innovation during the Third Republic.[16] By the late 1860s, two consistorial primary schools—along with the four communal schools—served the poorer Jewish children of the capital. In 1879 Baron Gustave de Rothschild, president of the Paris Consistory, endowed a third school on the rue Claude Bernard that came to bear his name.[17] Although the three consistorial schools differed somewhat in size, they were all well attended. In 1888, 242 students attended the school at the rue de Lafayette, with 188 at the avenue de Ségur, and 164 at the École Rothschild.[18]

Even access to a large population that could provide private funding did not prevent financial problems. Despite healthy enrollments, all three schools operated under constant financial pressure. Their philanthropic character meant that they could not rely on student fees. During the academic year of 1883–84, the three consistorial schools had only sixty-two students paying school fees: twenty-six at the rue de Lafayette and eighteen each at the avenue de Ségur and the École Rothschild, where the vast majority of its 191 pupils attended for free.[19] The situation placed an ever-growing burden upon the Consistory's educational resources. School budgets between 1885 and 1890 generally counted only 1,200f from student fees against 56,450f in total income.[20] This amount paled in significance when viewed in terms of the Paris Consistory's total school expenditures of nearly 90,000f in 1885. Measured against its level of income, the consistorial school committee projected a shortfall of 33,510f.[21] These deficits would accrue annually at about the same level throughout the 1890s.

Communal contributions could not make up the entire difference. In Paris, the *caisse de la communauté* contributed 39,000f annually to the consistorial schools from the 1880s onward.[22] Baron Gustave de Rothschild financed the building for the school on the rue Claude Bernard and contributed 8,000f annually to its operation.[23] Most donations, though, tended to be more modest and fluctuated in size and frequency. Whereas the budget proposal for 1885–86 predicted 1,500f from donations, the previous year's budget had projected 4,000f and the 1888 budget predicted 8,500f.[24] While smaller gifts constituted an important source of income for the consistorial schools, they lacked any semblance of regularity. The 8,500f in donations projected for 1888–89, for example, actually amounted to only 4,875f of income.[25] Operating in this unstable atmosphere, the Parisian Jewish schools amassed annual deficits of approximately 30,000f. By 1889, the school committee reported a cumulative debt of more than 100,000f.[26] An additional blow landed in 1881, when the Paris municipal council bowed to anticlerical pressure and rescinded its annual subvention of 30,000f to the consistorial schools.[27] The combination of fiscal shortfalls and an inability to compete with the public system precluded any thoughts of expanding Jewish schools whose resources were already stretched to their limit and whose functions no longer served the needs of most French Jews.

French Judaism also faced threats from other quarters. While government anticlericalism undermined religious access to the public school system, it did little to alleviate Jewish concerns about Catholic proselytism in the classroom; nor did a creeping sense of intellectual and social secularism promise long-range prospects for the survival of French Judaism.[28] Sandwiched between an aggressive government and a diversifying, fragmented Jewish population, Jewish leaders recognized a need for broader religious instruction. Strengthening Jewish religious education, they hoped, could provide French Jewish children with an intellectual means for resisting conversionary tactics while simultaneously fortifying their commitment to Judaism. Zadoc Kahn—then *grand rabbin* of Paris—took up the cause in a pastoral letter of 1881, stressing the need for new initiatives. French Jews' religious laxity, he argued, prevented their children from learning about Judaism at home. As a remedy, Kahn advocated formal programmatic instruction that would equip French Jewish children to see their Jewishness as more than an "accident of birth," and to observe their religion out of "the rational love of Judaism."[29]

Similar concern sprouted elsewhere among French Jews. In 1881, for example, the Jewish journalist (and former rabbinical student) Hippolyte Prague applauded Ferry's circular to the French prefects exhorting them to combat religious proselytism in the schools. Ferry, he wrote, had affirmed that "the public school is above all a school of tolerance and of fraternity," where children would learn to get along before being divided by their religious beliefs as adults. The Ferry Laws, Prague hoped, would relieve pressure upon Jewish and Protestant children "to make professions of faith much less Jewish or Protestant."[30]

Five years later, however, Prague assumed a more critical position. He saw the French school debate as polarized between two camps: "those who wish to make religious education preponderant in the school . . . [and] those who wish to ban it." The opponents of religion in schools had triumphed when the Ferry Law of 1882 declared primary education free, obligatory, and laic. Since then, religion had comprised no part of the primary curriculum and parents had to provide religious instruction for their children on their own. The majority of Jewish parents, however, lacked the resources to obtain private religious education.[31] While Prague accepted the necessity of religious neutrality in the public schools, he nevertheless believed that religious instruction "elevates the soul, cultivates good feelings, and lends a goal and holiness to life." While the school laws protected an individual's liberty of conscience, Prague argued the simultaneous need to include religious study in any scholastic program.[32] Prague's position—characteristic of views expressed in the Jewish press at the time—simultaneously supported government religious neutrality while cautioning against complete secularism. From his vantage point, Jewish religious instruction was critical at a time when religious belief itself lay open to political and intellectual attack.

More traditional minded figures, such as Lazare Wogue, shared Prague's concerns. Like Prague, Wogue—a *grand rabbin* who was also editor-in-chief of the *Univers israélite* and a member of the faculty of the Séminaire Israélite—feared that the anticlerical campaigns could eventually drive religion from every sphere of public life. The laicization of French cemeteries in 1881 struck Wogue as a particularly troubling harbinger of a general "era of laicization": "The time will certainly come when this great revolution will be consummated, when civil society will be that which it ought to be, that is to say essentially *laïque* or neutral, eliminating any exclusive or confessional element from its Constitution, from its institutions, from its laws."[33]

If he sensed inevitability in the process, though, Wogue repeatedly questioned the ability of French society to survive complete laicization. Stripped of its religious roots, what moral power could such a society wield? He, too, warned of the dire results of the Law of March 28, 1882, which laicized the public schools and excised subjects such as religious history and biblical geography from the curriculum.[34] Like Prague, Wogue acknowledged the necessity of religiously neutral public schools; still, he worried about the complete removal of religion from French education. On what other basis, he asked, could one establish moral authority? How could schools instill respect for one's parents or duty to one's country without grounding these values in religious ethics? French schools, he argued, needed to "cultivate" religious sentiment in their pupils in order to provide them with a moral compass for adulthood.[35]

In contrast to Prague, though, Wogue concluded that separate Jewish schools remained the best means of strengthening Jewish religious education and thereby Jewish morality. He urged French Jews to "favor the private Jewish schools as much as possible," for "there alone [lies] the health of Judaism, already so seriously compromised, and whose decline the mixed schools can only hasten."[36] Wogue also saw religious education as a justification of the existing French Jewish religious structure. The Consistory, in his view, remained not only relevant but also vital as the educator of French Jews, and thereby the caretaker and perpetuator of French Judaism. It could carry out this function only within a specifically Jewish context.

Practical realities, though, favored Prague's programmatic approach over Wogue's institutional one. Programs of religious instruction could be delivered more widely, meeting in synagogues or schools and avoiding the expenses of construction and maintenance. In 1879, for example, the consistorial school committee had undertaken a fundraising drive for the construction of the school on the avenue de Ségur, raising upward of 240,000f. This sum, however, only assured the acquisition of the site; installation, furnishings, supplies, and maintenance required additional money.[37] Programs also required fewer books and supplies than schools teaching a comprehensive curriculum. Local teachers, rabbis, or cantors could conduct the classes, possibly in more than one location; the consistories could compensate them by charging modest student fees, as opposed to paying salaries to full-time teachers. The relatively low cost of the programs meant that the consistories could offer them in more locations, potentially reaching a larger audience than Jewish schools ever could. Better yet, anticlerical legislation would have no impact on these programs since they would remain clearly within the consistorial purview.

Political and financial anticlericalism thus stimulated a reconfiguration of Jewish educational space. For most of the nineteenth century, French Jewish leaders had interpreted Jewish space in material terms, concentrating on building physical structures such as schools, synagogues, or cemetery grounds. Prior to the Third Republic, much of the tension between the Consistory and the government stemmed from the meaning assigned to these structures. Government officials tended to consider separate Jewish schools signs of continuing Jewish exclusivity, while Jewish leaders maintained that their schools were not separate at all; rather, as a parallel to non-Jewish establishments, they symbolized both Judaism's equality with other religions and its utility as an integrative moral force. Jewish educational space might have been physically separate, but it did not qualitatively differ from French space.

Third Republic anticlericalism, however, made this idea impractical and eventually untenable. Separating religion and state necessitated qualifying the distinction between Jewish and French space. As the state began to laicize physical territory, Jewish leaders developed a new, more abstract conception of Jewish space that extended beyond the walls of a building. In a political climate focused on wholesale national integration, equality no longer presented as pressing a problem. If anything, reinterpretations of equality now threatened the survival of Jewish institutions, and potentially the long-term health of French Judaism. The anticlerical campaigns thus necessitated a rethinking of French Jewish space as singular rather than synthetic.

In this regard, French Judaism diverged from general trends in French political culture. Avner Ben-Amos's study of state funerals illustrates the tactic of using public space to reinforce the broader agenda of the ruling regime. The leaders of the Third Republic, he concludes, "accentuate[d] the integrative rather than the exclusive" elements of these funerals. In other words, Third Republic state funerals—which incorporated civic space as they wound through the streets of Paris—were designed to communicate a common (and decidedly republican) historical and political narrative.[38] As shown in the previous chapter, this political culture compelled Jewish leaders to emphasize the unique elements of French Jewish space in order to preserve Jewish institutional prerogatives. Some of this space remained physical—synagogues, for example—but as Kahn, Prague, and Wogue had all perceived, Judaism needed to reach beyond the material realm into intellectual and cultural space. Within this context, educational issues took on even greater importance. For both Jewish and non-Jewish leaders, the schools constituted a microcosm of the French nation's social organization, the guardians of both its history and future. Staking out Jewish territory in that history and future—and ensuring the survival of Judaism—meant entering that intellectual space through any available channels.

Adapting to non-structural space led French Jewish leaders to seek new access to Jewish students. Initially, they concentrated on bolstering existing operations such as Jewish chaplaincies at French secondary schools, the *lycées* and *collèges*. These institutions offered fertile ground for Christian proselytism, with outnumbered Jewish students vulnerable to conversionary pressures from their peers and instructors. Jewish chaplains had generally seen to the religious needs of Jewish students; they also provided basic instruction in Hebrew and biblical history for individual Jewish students working toward their *initiation religieuse* (generally, the age of thirteen for boys, twelve for girls).[39] In an environment becoming ever more hostile to religion, continued religious instruction could help to maintain a commitment to Judaism beyond the *initiation*.

Strengthening the presence and prestige of Jewish chaplains meant that consistorial officials had to enlist the help of civic authorities. In February 1875, for example, the Consistory of Paris and the Prefect of the Seine worked out a formal structure for Jewish religious instruction in the department's three municipal secondary schools. This program established a centralized course at the École Turgot for Jewish students from all three institutions. One division would meet from two to three o'clock every Thursday afternoon, with a second division meeting from three to four o'clock the same day. Teachers would receive 400f per year, the same salary as Catholic chaplains in the municipal secondary schools.[40] The following January, the Prefect informed the Consistory that the necessary funds had been included in the 1876 budget.⁴¹ This agreement officially equalized the status of Jewish and Christian religious instruction.

Despite such advances, consistorial officials continued to safeguard Jewish equality by emphasizing Jewish uniqueness. Although the Paris Consistory was generally satisfied with its revamped program of religious instruction, its members still complained about the "anomalous situation [that] obliges Jewish students to attend the lessons given by the pastors of the other religions," a situation to which many Jewish parents objected.⁴² In 1876, the *grand rabbin* of Bordeaux protested that the awarding of prizes in religious instruction at the Bordeaux *lycées* unfairly excluded Jewish students, even as it included Protestant ones.⁴³ The rabbi, S. Lévy, argued that he taught lessons at a level similar to those of the Protestant pastor, with the same frequency and in the same schools. He therefore asked that his students receive recognition at the ceremony on an equal basis with their Christian peers. Indeed, Lévy concluded, "it would be a subject of stunning and embarrassing commentary if we Jews were excluded from [a ceremony in which] the other two [state] religions will receive an official consecration."⁴⁴ The law granted Jews a certain degree of difference, while simultaneously guaranteeing equal treatment. This implicit guarantee legitimized Jewish claims to an equally recognized but nevertheless distinctive intellectual space.

In their discussion of Lévy's petition, the civil authorities focused on the question of equality. Like their predecessors in past governments they examined the issue through the lens of numerical utility. The Rector of the Bordeaux Academy, M. Dabas, noted considerable differences between the Jewish and Protestant courses. Rabbi Lévy had not been officially "charged with a course of religious instruction" and taught only a small number of students. By contrast, the Protestant pastor held the formal office of chaplain at the Bordeaux *lycée* and ministered to a larger group.⁴⁵ The Minister, Henri Wallon, reinforced this quantitative notion of utility when he asked Dabas for the number of Jewish students attending Lévy's course.⁴⁶

In response, Rabbi Lévy tried to prove the utility of his course. He informed Dabas that he conducted religious lessons for fourteen Jewish students who resided at the Bordeaux *lycée*; a larger number of the school's Jewish day students also attended these classes. Lévy carefully connected this utility with equal treatment: "I have no doubt that when my course has the same prerogatives as those possessed by the courses of other . . . religions, as many parents as the regulations allow will request that their children [be permitted to enroll in it]."⁴⁷ Equal treatment would thus render his activities that much more *utile* and effective.

While the documents provide no evidence of the resolution of Lévy's case, Dabas linked equality and utility in a way that foreshadowed the later Beyfus decision. In 1876, Dabas observed, Wallon had denied a similar request by the Protestant pastor of Pau based on the small number of students he taught. Yet even that group of Protestant students outnumbered the present group of Jewish students at the Bordeaux *lycée*. "Therefore," Dabas concluded, "we cannot agree to the one [request] without also agreeing to the other."[48] Legitimacy and utility in the eyes of government officials thus remained tied to size and scope. Equality, meanwhile, remained a malleable concept with which an obstinate government official like Dabas could justify positive or negative attitudes toward Jewish proposals.

Although chaplaincy programs were limited to civic secondary schools, they provided a model for expanding the dissemination of Jewish religious learning more broadly. At first, the consistorial leadership tried to address the issue within its existing operations. In the autumn of 1876, for example, the president of the Paris Consistory, Baron Gustave de Rothschild, called for Parisian rabbis to take more active roles in improving religious instruction. Rothschild wanted rabbis to visit the consistorial schools more frequently in order to supervise the religious lessons, "stimulating the teachers and pupils by these testimonies of [their] interest."[49] Narcisse Leven echoed this sentiment in 1879: "We have complained a great deal about the situation of religious instruction in the *lycées* and [in] the other establishments where [it is conducted] by the rabbis." The consistorial leadership, Leven reported, wanted the rabbis to demonstrate more concern about the weak state of Jewish religious instruction, beginning with regular reports on the programs within their districts.[50]

The Ferry Law of March 1882 changed the dynamics of the situation. Its removal of religious instruction from school curricula left supplementary programs as the only means for Jewish religious instruction outside of parochial schools. The Parisian leadership responded quickly. Concurrent to the law's passage, Zadoc Kahn, Narcisse Leven, and Michel Erlanger lobbied the Paris Consistory for a more formal program of religious instruction. The Consistory answered by placing Leven and Erlanger at the head of a new Commission Spéciale d'Instruction Religieuse, which met periodically from May to October 1882.[51] The commission organized eight elementary religious courses for Parisian Jewish schoolchildren above the age of six. These courses were led by rabbis and met all over the city.[52]

Rabbinical involvement lent credibility to these programs among Jews, but establishing external standing involved reinforcing the equal civic status of Jewish religious instruction. Just as earlier generations of French Jewish educators had lobbied for state authorization and civic financial support, the proponents of religious instruction sought state sanction for their programs. The legitimacy of civic recognition would protect these programs from administrative or legislative discrimination. For example, the Law of March 28, 1882, had mandated that public schools would close two days each week so that students could receive religious instruction outside the classroom.[53] In June, the leaders of the Paris Consistory advocated the designation of Saturday as one of the days off (*jours de congés*). Fixing Saturday as one of the mandatory closure days would allow Jewish children to receive religious instruction when many of them were out of school anyway for the Sabbath. The existing *jours de congés*—Wednesday and Sunday—unfairly deprived Jewish children of an extra day of school each week.[54] The resolution neglected to mention, of course, that many Jewish children might forego the Sabbath to attend school anyway. In any case, the existing system blocked their attendance at religious instruction classes.

The Jewish press also weighed in against the present system. Lazare Wogue predicted that individual municipalities would choose the days according to local convenience and "the confessional composition of [each] school." Schools with entirely Christian populations, for example, would close on Thursdays and Sundays; mixed or Jewish schools would close on Saturdays and Sundays. For Jewish children attending mostly Christian schools, the system would mean an entire weekend of inactivity, contradicting both "the most general custom and the principles of healthy pedagogy."[55] The *Archives israélites* expressed similar concern.[56] Both journals called for fair application of the law, and equal educational opportunities for Jewish children. [57]

The controversy over *jours de congés,* however, did little to ignite new commitments to institutional Jewish education. Even though they issued an official resolution to establish Jewish schools wherever possible, consistorial leaders gradually abandoned the institutional strategy and began to focus more on programs.[58] Considerations of utility redirected efforts to encourage Jewish religious instruction, reshaping the very idea of equality in the process. Equality soon came to denote the unfettered ability to perpetuate Jewish religious life in France instead of a prominent public role for Jewish institutions.

Shifting to a programmatic strategy also required a systematic consolidation and standardization of religious instruction. Ensuring the quality of the courses meant exercising tighter control over teaching credentials, which in turn involved navigating a number of legislative obstacles. Most seriously, the 1881 Ferry Law removing religious subjects from the French teaching certification examinations created a potential lacuna in Jewish education. While the legislation bound communal primary schools to "reserve a certain place" for religious studies, the new regulations allowed instructors to teach religious subjects without any proven competency with the material.[59] Despite the advances of Jewish chaplains, consistorial officials worried that poor instruction would drive students away from their courses and sabotage their efforts. If the consistories wanted to promote religious instruction, they needed to find more qualified religious teachers.

Expanding the pool of qualified teachers forced the Consistory to look beyond the rabbinate and give the Parisian teaching corps a more laic character. In 1881, *grand rabbin* Zadoc Kahn proposed a standardized teacher certification program for lay religious instructors in the Paris schools. The Paris Consistory would initiate an annual examination in Hebrew reading, "religious history until the destruction of the Second Temple, biblical geography, and the articles of faith."[60] The Paris leadership endorsed his recommendations and held the first certification tests in 1883.[61] In 1885, the Consistory adopted Kahn's suggestion to promote several assistant rabbis still conducting courses of religious instruction to supervisory roles, assigning their classes to lay teachers.[62]

Laicization did not completely shut the Parisian rabbinate out of the process, though. In addition to supervising courses, rabbis continued to serve as school chaplains, a role that expanded as more Jewish students began to attend mainstream French secondary schools. In 1885, Octave Gréard—Directeur d'Instruction Publique for the city of Paris—installed a Jewish chaplain who taught two classes of religious instruction each week at the Lycée Janson de Sailly.[63] The following year, Gréard authorized another Jewish chaplaincy at the Lycée la Kanal.[64]

Parisian rabbis also nurtured supplementary education programs. In 1887, Rabbi David Haguenau reported that his class at the consistorial synagogue on the rue Notre Dame de Nazareth was "well attended" and yielded "the best results." Haguenau's work proved so successful that the Consistory permitted him to cede his teaching responsibilities at Fontenay to his brother in order to concentrate on his Parisian classes.[65] In 1891, the Paris Consistory authorized Rabbi Simon Debré to conduct lessons in religious instruction in the suburbs. After a favorable review of his work, the Paris Consistory made Debré's position permanent, complete with a salary and travel expenses.[66] By extending the reach of religious instruction, rabbis took an active part in demarcating Jewish educational space.

By 1894, the Paris Consistory's courses had become larger and better organized with classes meeting in four different locations around the city.⁶⁷ Operating budgets for the courses had also grown, signaling their acceptance and success. In 1883, the Consistory had budgeted 10,000f for religious instruction;⁶⁸ by 1894, this figure had increased to 14,550f.⁶⁹ By 1898, the budget had grown to 16,660f, with the bulk of the money applied to the teachers' salaries.⁷⁰ That year, the Paris rabbinate could report that "religious instruction is given to children frequenting the consistorial schools... the communal schools... [and] the *lycées* and *collèges* of the Seine."⁷¹ Zadoc Kahn himself affirmed that, because of the broad range of religious instruction, "our children arrive well prepared... for the *bar mitzvah* and *initiation religieuse*."⁷²

While courses demanded less substantial and more flexible investments of time, money, and personnel, they did not guarantee universal success. Despite Kahn's laudatory assessment and the commitment of time and resources, dissatisfaction with instructional and curricular standards persisted. While rabbinic supervisors triumphantly lauded the consistorial programs, they sharply criticized the quality of instruction in the communal schools. They attributed this disparity mostly to the overcrowding of certain age brackets: almost ninety students between seven and nine years of age, for example, attended the classes conducted in the communal schools. Congested classrooms undermined the lessons, and examinations for the *initiation religieuse* and *bar mitzvah* demonstrated "a certain inferiority among the students of the communal schools," especially in their knowledge of Hebrew.⁷³

By contrast, courses in the district's secondary schools suffered from poor attendance: only forty-nine Jewish students attended classes in the eight secondary schools that offered them. Class sizes ranged from one student at the Lycée St. Louis to eleven at the Lycée Carnot and the Collège Rollin, whose student body included more than eighty Jews.⁷⁴ Rabbi Julien Weill reported similar conditions at the Collège Rollin, whose Jewish enrollment he estimated as approximately sixty Jewish students.⁷⁵ Most of the other courses had five to seven students each. The lone exception existed at the École Commerciale, where thirty-three of the school's sixty-nine Jewish students took part in religious lessons.

Like Jewish schools, religious instruction programs also varied by location. At the same time that the Paris Consistory expanded its programs in the city, for example, it experienced considerable difficulties establishing new ones in the suburbs. A rabbinical inspection of 1898 counted only five suburban communities offering formal courses of Jewish religious instruction, with only 143 children attending out of an estimated Jewish population of approximately 1,200.⁷⁶ The rabbi attributed the situation to greater religious laxity in the suburbs, reporting that "[Jewish] religious activity is lacking at Boulogne, Asmères, and in the majority of localities" except for Neuilly and St. Denis. Religious indifference bred social fragmentation as "the Jews ignore one another, [and] almost never . . . speak about Judaism."[77]

Success also depended upon the abilities of the local instructors.[78] Rabbi Israél Lévi diplomatically observed, for example, that while the cantor of Ferté-sous-Jouarre had a good voice and led services quite capably, his pedagogical talents and religious knowledge did not approach his musical abilities. After personally examining the children of the community, Lévi concluded that they had only learned to read Hebrew, and knew "neither religious history nor the articles of faith."[79] Religious instruction in Tours suffered from similar problems. Rabbi David Haguenau reported that the Jewish population of Tours had split, primarily because of dissatisfaction over its cantor. Communal dissension made any type of venture—even holding services—difficult, much less any sort of religious education program for its seventeen Jewish schoolchildren. Haguenau emphasized that this situation did not result from a paucity of resources, even given the small Jewish population at Tours. Moreover, he lamented that "this truly alarming state of affairs is not isolated. One would easily find similar situations in other small communities."[80]

Communal strife and poor teaching generated little enthusiasm for religious education among suburban Jewish parents, whom the rabbis described as generally apathetic. Rabbi Julien Weill reported that the Jewish community at Le Hâvre—which numbered about forty families—lacked a regular program of religious instruction. Each time the cantor had tried to organize a course, his efforts failed due to a lack of parental cooperation. Only as the time of the *bar mitzvah* approached did Jewish parents send their sons for religious lessons; religious instruction for girls was neglected completely.[81] Weill himself had advertised his own course at the Collège Rollin directly to parents, but to little avail.[82]

The efficacy and flexibility of Jewish religious education programs, however, enabled them to overcome many of these obstacles and spread throughout the Paris district. If they did not strike root in one community, or met isolated resistance, classes could be moved with no long-term financial liability. In October 1903, the Paris Consistory expanded beyond its own scope of activity in designating a 300f subvention for the Université Populaire Juive. Intended to serve Jewish immigrants, this institution provided French courses for adults and Hebrew and religious instruction for children. The Paris leadership also financed classes conducted by a Rabbi Ginsburger in Orléans.[83] The success of the supplementary approach suggests its compatibility with the sensibilities of French Jewish parents. In shifting from institutions to programs, consistorial leaders gradually gave up on a model of education that combined religious and secular learning within a specifically Jewish environment. In its place, they created a more broadly defined Jewish educational space beyond the reach of French public life.

By the time that the separation of church and state became law in December 1905, supplemental religious instruction had become the top Jewish educational priority in Paris. The aftermath of separation demonstrated the prudence of this reorientation. The Law of Separation dissolved the Consistory as an official arm of the state bureaucracy and mandated the transfer of its material holdings to private organizations. The Jewish consistories thereafter became religious associations (*associations cultuelles*) legally confined to charitable and religious activities. Religious education programs were flexible, mobile, relatively inexpensive to operate, and now a legal educational operation in which the consistories could involve themselves.

8

"Just Proportions"
Financial Anticlericalism and Rabbinical Space

In September 1879, the administrative commission of the Séminaire Israélite sent a report to the Paris Consistory describing a general deterioration of the school's academic program. Many of the problems, they wrote, resulted from circumstances beyond their control. The loss of Alsace and Lorraine in 1871, for example, had cut the school off from its main recruiting ground.¹ For this problem, of course, they could propose no immediate remedy. The commission did, however, intend to address the school's other main difficulty: the "gradual encroachment of secondary classical teaching."² Advanced classical studies now absorbed the majority of the students' time, to the detriment of their religious studies: "All of the lessons devoted to literary exercises of a lower level, to French, to Latin, to Greek, to history [and] mathematics . . . constitute an immeasurable burden upon higher education both sacred and profane, [which is] indispensable in an institution such as ours." Rabbinical students found themselves so pressed for time that all their studies had assumed an "artificial" character of "hasty preparation" that produced only mediocre results. The situation could not continue, they concluded, for "despite the prodigious discoveries of modern science, we still have not found a means of lengthening the twenty-four-hour day by even one minute."³

These remarks contrasted sharply with the accommodationist attitude of previous decades. With the relocation to Paris, a new group of teachers had joined the school's faculty to strengthen secular instruction. Isidore Cahen, editor-in-chief of the *Archives israélites,* taught French history and literature; Cahen's longtime friend, Eugène Manuel, took over the courses in Latin and Greek. Manuel—like Cahen, a graduate of the École Normale Supérieure and a co-founder of the Alliance Israélite Universelle—already held a prestigious position at the Lycée Bonaparte in Paris, and would eventually become Inspector General of the French University. Paul Janet, who assumed the philosophy chair, also taught logic at the elite Lycée Louis le Grand.[4] By the mid-1880s, the leaders of the Central Consistory could boast that nearly all the members of the seminary's faculty also belonged to the University.[5] In addition to traditional religious knowledge, the ordination examination now required three written sections in addition to the oral tests. Candidates had to write "a philosophical essay upon a subject assigned by M. [Adolphe] Franck" (who also assigned a Latin passage for translation), in addition to a Hebrew composition test administered by Lazare Wogue. A student had to pass all three sections in order to reach the oral examination.[6]

Budgetary and political pressures, however, nudged Jewish leaders toward a reformulation of the rabbinical curriculum. Despite the optimistic predictions of the transfer camp, the move to Paris had not completely resolved the school's fiscal problems. While the seminary's annual report for its first full year in the capital noted a balanced budget, this number was a deceiving isolated occurrence.[7] The seminary had received more than 5,700f in student fees that year, an unusually high amount. More significant, under the terms of the transfer agreement, the Ministry of Religions had supplemented the regular budget by approximately 25 percent; it had also raised the school's annual budget to 22,000f.[8]

As critics had warned, the Paris relocation generated higher expenses (though not as the result of the luxurious indulgences feared by Benjamin Gradis). Faculty salaries increased considerably to meet the higher cost of living in the capital. The director's salary more than doubled (from 1,400f in Metz to 3,500f in Paris) and the minimum faculty salary rose to 1,000f.[9] The 1862 payroll totaled 12,500f, nearly 57 percent of the total government subsidy of 22,000f.[10] The 1866 budget of 36,800f far exceeded the government subvention, avoiding a deficit only through student fees and a surplus left over from the previous year.[11] As time passed, the deficit became an annual problem. The proposed budget for 1867, for example, projected a shortfall of 4,550f that the school's administrators hoped to cover through proceeds from the annual communal lottery.[12] Similar deficits continued to accrue for the rest of the century.

The early stirrings of financial anticlericalism also made the relationship between the seminary and the state more contentious. One might assume that the Consistory would have adapted to government standards in order to defuse any conflicts and thus maintain the civic funding vital to the school's survival. The commission's remedy for the school's curricular problems, however, paralleled Jewish efforts to demarcate specifically Jewish space through programmatic religious instruction. The realignment of rabbinical studies emphasized the distinctiveness of French Judaism and reinforced the consistorial reconception of Jewish space. Reducing the classical elements of the curriculum meant straying from state curricular mandates; it also meant strengthening those distinctly Jewish elements of rabbinical education. While the school's administrators could not ignore French standards, they could reinterpret the relationship between secular and rabbinical studies. By reining in classical studies, Jewish leaders redefined the composition as well as the scope of rabbinical activity. As noted in the previous chapter, French rabbis would now act to preserve the distinctiveness of their fellow Jews rather than promoting their rapid integration.

Financial anticlericalism helped to accelerate this distancing. In 1885, the seminary received a potentially crushing blow when the National Assembly voted to cancel the ten 1,000f scholarships traditionally accorded to French rabbinical candidates.[13] From then on rabbinical students would receive no government assistance in meeting their tuition and living expenses. This reduction diminished the seminary's budget by nearly one-third, from 32,000f to 22,000f, pinching the resources of the Paris Consistory. In response, the Consistory pressed the school administration to reduce expenses, resolving to seek the aid of the other departmental consistories.[14] These remedies failed resoundingly. In January 1886 the Central Consistory issued a call for financial aid to the departmental consistories, citing the common interest for each department in assuring the financial security of the seminary and the continued training of competent French rabbis.[15] Its appeal raised a total of 3,005.50f, miniscule in comparison to the seminary's budget deficit of nearly 41,000f.[16] Another appeal the following summer produced equally disappointing results.[17]

By the turn of the century, the Consistory could no longer deny the severity of the problem. At a meeting in January 1899, the Paris Consistory confronted the seminary's debt, which had reached crisis proportions. The consistorial president, Baron Gustave de Rothschild, opened the session by outlining what he called the school's "grave financial situation." At that point, the seminary's budget carried an annual deficit of nearly 50,000f and had accrued a cumulative debt of approximately 400,000f. The House of Rothschild had in the past served as guarantor for the institution, granting the school an open line of credit in order to meet its expenses. Yet even this powerful bank hesitated "to keep open an account so seriously debt-ridden."[18]

These problems led some Jewish leaders to propose narrowing the seminary's mission. Narcisse Leven saw the seminary's financial woes as symptomatic of larger problems. On one hand, the fundraising capacity of Jewish communities badly needed repair. Consistorial calls for aid were mostly unsuccessful, he noted, because all Jewish communities lacked adequate sources of revenue. Besides the fees charged for certain synagogue services—weddings and funerals, for example—the communities had no means of supporting themselves financially. Government policies had drastically reduced the religious budget to such an extent that the situation "impedes the development of the religion." Any long-term solution therefore had to address this essential difficulty.[19]

Leven saw no alternative but to downsize the seminary's educational priorities. A chief target was the Talmud Torah of Paris, which the seminary supported as a preparatory school for aspiring rabbinical candidates. Leven admitted that the Talmud Torah had done a fairly good job of educating its students in both religious and secular subjects. But, he asked, was preparing students for the *baccalauréat* examinations consistent with recruiting them for the French rabbinate? Clearly not, for "the majority of [these] students turn away [from the rabbinate] in order to become lawyers [and] physicians." This situation demanded as much consideration as the budget crisis, for all French Jewish communities were experiencing problems in finding qualified rabbis and cantors. The benefits of the Talmud Torah, in Leven's opinion, did not justify its cost. Baron Rothschild shared this view, questioning the long-term viability of the Talmud Torah in light of the financial situation.[20] Leven also suggested an alternative method for augmenting the school's income: opening the seminary and Talmud Torah to foreign students who would pay full tuition. The only problem with this strategy, he noted, involved assuring that both schools retained their French character.[21]

Subtle as it might have been, Leven's position outlined a new consistorial conception of utility. His pared-down vision of the Talmud Torah mission argued for a more inward-looking French Judaism, concerned less with placating government officials and more with ensuring its own survival. As republican officials moved to sever the state's ties to Judaism, they freed consistorial leaders to assert their distinctiveness more openly and to pursue specifically Jewish religious goals. Rabbis, in this conception, represented more than public religious functionaries whose skills and manners should please French bureaucrats: they needed the skills to reinforce Judaism internally. Consequently, strengthening their religious training had once again become a top priority.

None of the consistorial proposals adequately addressed the situation. As Leven had predicted, fundraising campaigns did little to solve the seminary's perpetual deficit problem. In March 1899, the Central Consistory issued an appeal to the departmental consistories that raised only 2,310f toward a projected 50,000f shortfall.[22] Trying again two years later, the Central Consistory warned, "Today the peril is greater because the deficit has grown and grown annually."[23] Once again, the campaign fell well short of its goal. Interestingly, the school's predicted financial collapse never occurred. The House of Rothschild apparently decided to extend the seminary's line of credit, for no further mention of this problem appears in subsequent records. A cloud of financial uncertainty, however, still hung over the institution.

The school continued to suffer, meanwhile, from a deficient level of religious instruction. In response to this problem, the seminary's administrators issued the report cited above, proposing remedies to the school's ongoing curricular difficulties. Most significant, they suggested making the *bachélier-ès-lettres* degree a prerequisite for admission. This change would remove the need for intensive secondary classical studies, as rabbinical students would obtain this knowledge before entering the seminary. They took care to note that they did not advocate the complete suppression of classical studies. Rather, they sought only the limitation of these subjects "to [their] just proportions" within the rabbinic curriculum.[24]

The definition of "just proportions," though, had changed. Classical study would now serve as a tool for honing the practical skills of French rabbinical students rather than as an end in itself. Under the consistorial proposal, literature classes would split into two divisions. Students in their first three years of study would work to improve their French linguistic style by reading Latin and Greek authors. In the upper division, rabbinical students would focus exclusively on religious studies and "preparing for the holy career" to which they aspired.[25] The upper-level classical curriculum would emphasize oratory and homiletics, concentrating upon the development of skills necessary for a rabbi's public functions. Rabbinical students would read French, Latin, and Greek authors from a specifically "Jewish perspective," with instructors choosing texts based upon their applicability to the rabbinic calling and their relevance to issues in contemporary Jewish life.[26] The proposal erected a flexible but sturdy fence between religious and secular learning, implying a qualitative difference between the two realms of knowledge. While Jewish subjects remained compatible with Frenchness, they nevertheless required their own educational and intellectual space. After nearly fifty years of equivocation, those who trained rabbis could now publicly assert the primacy of their religious knowledge, even as they maintained a fealty to the broader secular educational norm.[27]

In January 1880, the Central Consistory formally submitted its proposals to the Minister of Religions. The final petition advocated deemphasizing classical studies in favor of strengthening "more relevant work" in Hebrew language and oratorical skills.[28] The new rules would not completely dismiss French guidelines, however, since the school would require the *bachélier-ès-lettres* diploma of all new entrants. This requirement would eliminate the most basic secondary studies—including classical subjects—from the rabbinic curriculum, "or at least reduce [them] in noticeable proportions." Literary studies would assume a more advanced character, similar to that of French higher education and thus "more appropriate for a Jewish seminary." Reducing the amount of time devoted to classical subjects would create more opportunities for "sacred studies, religious history, the languages of the East, the criticism and research of modern subjects, [and the study of] Philosophy, homiletics, and preaching."[29]

The consistorial proposals more clearly separated secular and religious learning. Requiring the *bachélier-ès-lettres* degree of incoming students meant that all rabbinical students would arrive at the school as educated Frenchmen. With those credentials established, they could turn their full attention to becoming rabbis. Clearly, the Séminaire Israélite would not sever the ties between secular and Jewish learning. The new regulations would affirm the legitimacy of Jewish knowledge (and, by extension, of Judaism itself) by reserving curricular space for Jewish religious study.

Jewish leaders further asserted Jewish distinctiveness through the creation of a formal rabbinical preparatory program at the Talmud Torah. This strategy had been proposed during the Metz period but had floundered due to a lack of resources.[30] The Parisian attempt proved more successful. Founded in 1853 by the Société des Études Talmudiques of Paris, the Talmud Torah provided secondary education for poor Jewish boys within a distinctively Jewish religious context. In its early years, the school had led a rather tenuous existence, changing locations several times.[31] When the seminary moved into its new building on the rue Vauquelin in 1882, the Talmud Torah moved in with it; at that point, the Paris Consistory assumed financial responsibility for its operation.[32] By 1889, an eight-member commission headed by the *grand rabbin* of the Central Consistory oversaw the school, and the Paris Consistory provided an annual subvention of 8,000f.[33]

The two institutions merged in 1892 with the official annexation of the Talmud Torah to the seminary.[34]

On a practical level, the Talmud Torah filled a void in the Jewish educational system, providing a means for replenishing Jewish religious leadership from within a French educational context. By nurturing this institution, the seminary administration cultivated an integrated recruitment system that fed students into the French rabbinate. Many Talmud Torah graduates later pursued careers as Jewish educators and a number went on to rabbinical study. With this agenda in mind, seminary leaders fashioned the Talmud Torah's curriculum to produce young men with both the religious training necessary for rabbinical studies and the secular learning that lent them public credibility as religious leaders. As early as 1874, the seminary administration informed the Paris Consistory of its desire "to organize the Talmud Torah as a secondary school (*école supérieure*)" and to improve the level of education it provided.[35] In 1880, the Consistory created an additional category of scholarship students (*boursiers*) in a new educational division. These students would be approximately sixteen years old, "too old to remain any longer in the preparatory school of the Talmud Torah . . . [but] too young . . . to enter the seminary." They would instead form "a preparatory class," integrated into the seminary itself and composed of students of superior ability who "would [otherwise] get away from us." The Talmud Torah of Paris would constitute the prime recruiting ground for new rabbis, and the new plan would "enable [it] to attract a greater number of students and to prepare carefully the candidates of an elite [group]."[36]

The coordination of studies at the Talmud Torah and the Séminaire Israélite produced marked improvements in French rabbinical training. According to consistorial reports, the preparatory division helped to alleviate the pressures of secular studies on rabbinical candidates. Between 1878 and 1884, the seminary admitted fourteen new *boursiers*. All but one of the candidates coming from the Talmud Torah—the Algerian *boursier*—had obtained the *bachélier-ès-lettres* prior to admission.[37] When the seminary began to attract a number of foreign-born applicants at the turn of the century,[38] the Talmud Torah helped to equip these students with the secular knowledge required for ordination. Indeed, as mentioned in an earlier chapter, director Joseph Lehman used the institution to facilitate the application of the foreign-born Samuel Danilef in 1904.[39] By 1889, the Talmud Torah functioned as a Jewish secondary school as well as a rabbinical preparatory program. Students entered the school at the age of twelve after passing an entrance exam and studied there for two years.[40] One account holds that of the 130 students attending the Talmud Torah between 1868 and 1889, "a great number" entered the seminary or became teachers. Others entered "liberal, industrial, and commercial careers."[41] The faculty of the Talmud Torah also reflected its higher academic standards. Rabbis taught courses in Hebrew and Talmud, while classes in French, Latin, and Greek were conducted by a *licencé* of the University and two *agregés*.[42] A *licencé-ès-sciences* taught the mathematics course, with ancient history and French history conducted by an *agregé*. The curriculum also included courses in German, writing, singing, and *gymnastique*. At the end of their studies, students were supposed to be able to pass the *bachélier* examinations as well as the Hebrew and Talmud requirements necessary for admission to the seminary.[43]

The transformation of the Talmud Torah represented more, however, than a practical remedy for what ailed French rabbinical education. By forging a link with a secondary institution, the seminary leadership expanded the field of rabbinical study and Jewish space. Although the Séminaire Israélite was a decidedly public institution that received government funds, the Talmud Torah gave it a foothold in the private realm. The rabbinical education system—like the French rabbinate itself—thus connected Jewish and French space, affirming French Judaism's legitimacy in both spheres.

In one respect, these changes signified an attempt to equate the Séminaire Israélite with other institutions of higher learning. At the same time, the details of these internal reforms represented an assertion of Jewish distinctiveness, and the legitimacy of that distinctiveness. Despite ongoing financial problems, the school's move to Paris provided the means to satisfy critics of its pedagogy, opening the capital's vast educational resources to rabbinical candidates. Indeed, instructors of the caliber of Eugène Manuel and Isidore Cahen were not available in Metz. By the mid-1880s, the Central Consistory could boast that nearly all the members of the faculty were also members of the French University.[44] The school's administrators also instituted curricular changes designed to raise the level of rabbinical secular learning, planting the Séminaire Israélite more firmly in the French system.

While conforming to French education standards, the seminary's leaders also consciously distinguished their institution from its Catholic namesakes. In 1889, the Central Consistory even requested permission from the government to change the school's name back to the École Centrale Rabbnique, "which, by its designation, expresses exactly the goal that we had in founding this establishment of elevated rabbinical studies."[45] In short, rabbis were to be educated Frenchmen rather than simply religious functionaries.

This assertion represented a significant departure from past consistorial lobbying tactics. During the first decades of its existence, the Consistory had sought the same legal status and benefits for the rabbinical school that the state accorded to Catholic seminaries. As the process of laicization moved into the budgetary realm during the 1880s, the danger increased that anticlericals would eventually succeed in lumping together the Séminaire Israélite with its Catholic and Protestant counterparts. To preserve its ties to the French Treasury, the rabbinical school had to be distinguished from those Catholic institutions now under attack.

The government's attempt to separate religious and civic finances thus engendered an institutional distancing between Judaism and Catholicism. As French political tides moved decisively toward the separation of church and state in 1905, the consistorial administration highlighted differences whenever possible. When the *Univers israélite* pleaded to preserve state rabbinical pensions threatened by a proposed amendment to the Law of Separation, it adopted this very approach. Authors—ranging from the editor, Lazare Wogue, to the Chief Rabbi of France, Zadoc Kahn—repeatedly stressed "the difference . . . between the situation of the Catholic priests who are pledged to celibacy, and that of the Protestant and Jewish clergymen who, [because they are] married and most often family men, have to bear heavy expenses."[46]

If the curriculum at the Séminaire Israélite moved closer to secular French standards, the school remained a distinctly Jewish institution whose differences now justified its existence and the continuation of public financial support. The distancing process in turn encouraged the consistorial leadership to carve out a distinctively Jewish educational space at the highest level of French Jewish learning. Even as the seminary's leaders attempted to raise the level of secular studies, they subtly deemphasized the classical curriculum. With admission requirements reflecting general French norms, the Séminaire Israélite posed no threat to the sanctity of the French University. These adjustments simultaneously freed the school's leadership to particularize the rabbinical curriculum, declaring the primary importance of Jewish knowledge in rabbinical learning.

Conclusion

This book has argued that Jewish integration in nineteenth-century France involved more than questions of assimilation. Throughout the century, consistorial leaders felt considerable pressure to conform to the standards of individual French regimes; these pressures became all the more acute as the consistorial education system increasingly depended upon civil authorities for financial and political support. At the same time, Jewish leaders dealt with internal disagreements between French Jews over the purpose, conception, and execution of Jewish education.

The history of Jewish education in nineteenth-century France suggests a complicated relationship between French Jews and their cultural *milieu*. First, it calls into question the very notion of French Jewish "assimilation." For acculturated nineteenth-century European Jews the term "assimilation" connoted, as David Sorkin writes, integration "into the political structure of a unified state." Among German-speaking Jews, the assimilation ideal focused on moral regeneration, which constituted "their quid for the quo of [equal] rights."[1] Yet no clear yardstick existed to measure if and when Jews had achieved assimilation. Consequently, Sorkin concludes, culturally integrated but not legally emancipated German Jewish intellectuals created a subculture marked by creative approaches to the prospect of their "incomplete emancipation."[2]

In France, by contrast, the *quo* preceded the *quid,* and the attainment of Jewish equality placed quite a different gloss on the process of integration. French Jewish leaders operated upon an assumption of equal rights and equal treatment under the law. Having achieved emancipation, they saw a smaller divide between the universalism of revolutionary ideals of liberty, equality, and fraternity and the particularism of being Jewish; indeed, the former had subsumed and incorporated the latter. For them, Jewish integration and religious distinctiveness could peacefully coexist. As Jay Berkovitz notes, French Jewish religious rituals "dramatized the experience of citizenship, nationalism, and religious pluralism." Subtle religious changes did occur, but these largely connected Jewish worship to expressions of cultural affability. Within this context, the reinterpretation of religious ritual constituted a conservative tactic designed to preserve traditional practices by adapting them to modern sensibilities.³ French Jewish attitudes toward education fit into this general scheme, promoting Jewish integration while interpreting it within a specifically Jewish framework. French Jewish educators chose to preserve certain types of traditional learning by realigning them with French cultural standards.

The connection between Jewish schools and the French state, however, distinguishes the history of French Jewish education from that of religious change. Ritual adaptations lay largely beyond the purview of government bureaucrats, while education policy remained securely within their jurisdiction. Although no French regime fully embraced Jewish schooling, the consistorial education system enabled French authorities to establish cultural mileposts for successful Jewish integration. Without the "carrot" of emancipation to dangle before French Jewry, government officials wielded the "stick" of political and financial power. The evidence makes clear that, no matter which regime ruled France, government officials expected Jewish educational institutions to conform to French guidelines. Studying French language, French history, and arithmetic would facilitate the participation of Jewish schoolchildren in the national economy and their development as moral, loyal citizens. French rabbinical students also had to conform to the standards for higher education by studying Latin and Greek. Different eras produced different methods for enforcing these guidelines, but the twin goals of cultural unity and political loyalty remained constant throughout the nineteenth century.

Yet conformity had a limited reach. The subordination of Catholicism, Protestantism, and Judaism to state authority linked them to the twists and turns of French politics. Each religion, though, retained its own internal structures within the broader political culture. Parochial schools by their very nature guaranteed that a degree of pluralism would subsist despite the assumption of educational uniformity. Jewish schools, like their Catholic and Protestant counterparts, adhered to general guidelines but with the added goal of perpetuating a specific religious tradition. In this regard, French Jewish education maintained a striking continuity under different French regimes.

If the Falloux Law bolstered the presence of Catholic clergy in the schools, it did not wipe out Jewish education; neither did the marginalization of Jewish schools among French Jews themselves. Pupils in Jewish schools still studied Hebrew and the Bible and learned to reconcile this knowledge with the expectations of French citizenship. Jewish chaplains worked to ensure that Jewish students in non-Jewish settings would do the same. Rabbinical education retained its traditional character even as it absorbed and internalized French cultural features like classical studies. At times, Jewish leaders had to adapt the delivery system for Jewish knowledge while portraying their educational institutions in terms amenable to government authorities. Jewish religious learning continued nonetheless, even as Radical Republican anticlericalism squeezed its resources. Consistorial leaders made their compromises from a pluralistic point of view, legitimating the accommodation of state demands and the perpetuation of Jewish traditions.

Throughout this century-long negotiation, utility and equality remained the currency of discourse between Jewish leaders and state officials. Before the Third Republic, state bureaucrats emphasized the financial and political aspects of utility; meanwhile, Jewish leaders focused on equality as a justification for maintaining a separate Jewish educational space. When the campaign to separate church and state gained momentum in the 1880s, both groups swapped positions: civil officials emphasized the need to treat Judaism, Catholicism, and Protestantism in the same way, while Jews argued the uniqueness of their position.

Jewish integration in France thus did not follow a linear path, but one fraught with cultural fragmentation. The relegation of consistorial elementary schools to the philanthropic realm, for example, resulted from their disjunction with both Jewish traditionalism and acculturation. Professional and social incentives convinced most Jewish parents to send their children to communal schools despite the threat of Christian conversionary pressure; those adhering to traditional learning avoided the consistorial schools as too modern. Those pupils who attended the Jewish schools seemed to have no other choice, being neither academically, culturally, nor economically able to attend the mainstream French schools. This scholastic division reflected a developing sense of Jewish communal connections. As Katy Hazan has pointed out, Jewish school projects constituted "an authentic expression of Jewish life, implying solidarity and mutual responsibility."[4] Many French Jews, however, chose to express their solidarity from a distance, separating themselves culturally and intellectually from their poorer coreligionists.

Reconciling these different attitudes meant accepting a variety of cultural choices within French Jewish life. The history of French Jewish education thus demonstrates that "official" French cultural models did not necessarily become Jewish ones, but rather served as a basis for establishing

Franco-Jewish ideals. Jewish intellectual traditions established the general framework for Jewish education in France, while French cultural expectations tempered Jewish affirmations of religious distinctiveness.

This interpretation nuances Owen Chadwick's classic depiction of "religion" and "science" in nineteenth-century Europe as "balloon duelists," diametrically opposed forces locked in mortal combat.[5] Far from dismissing one or the other field of knowledge, consistorial Jewish schooling sought to integrate the two. Influenced by an active group of French Jewish intellectuals, a critical scientific methodology became an accepted form of studying Jewish religious texts. The scientific approach, as Berkovitz has shown, became relatively standard in scholarly circles and deeply influenced Jewish religious and intellectual attitudes.[6] It also created an intellectual option that preserved ties to Jewish tradition even as the aforementioned economic and social advantages of integration attracted many French Jews.

This evolving cultural sensibility pervaded Jewish elementary and rabbinical school regulations during the nineteenth century. On the pages of curricular guidelines Hebrew stood beside French, biblical exegesis beside arithmetic, and liturgical study beside French history. Each subject contributed to an intellectual whole that merged secular and religious learning into Franco-Judaism. Balancing "Jewish" and "French" thus involved a cultural rather than a theological approach and produced a cultural rather than theological solution.

The persistence of Jewish education in France testifies to a consistorial commitment to maintaining this cultural balance. Despite many challenges, Jewish schools did not fade into oblivion. French Jewish leaders doggedly sustained their schools; when necessary, they adapted from an institutional to a programmatic strategy. Supplemental programs of religious instruction configured a more flexible Jewish space while more clearly reflecting the sensibilities of acculturated French Jews. They allowed upwardly mobile French Jews to differentiate themselves from parochial schools aimed at the poor, while still enabling an assertion of their Jewishness. As such, these courses legitimized Jewishness, carving out specifically Jewish territory in French schools and within secular Jewish life. External factors may have marginalized Jewish education, but internal Jewish opinion determined its final form and eventually reinvigorated it.

The case of Jewish education thus illustrates a curious irony of nineteenth century French history: efforts to impose cultural uniformity encouraged the development of more pluralistic outlooks. Joseph Byrnes has argued that revolutionary efforts to institute secular religious festivals failed to unite French Catholics under a new civil religion. On the contrary, these attempts to "fashion a national identity" from above exacerbated existing social, political, and religious divisions between French citizens.[7] This same pluralistic tendency arose within Judaism even as successive school legislation sought to homogenize French education. Like their Catholic fellow-citizens, French Jews held multiple social, cultural, and religious perspectives, which produced a variety of educational choices.

Consistorial representation of Jews and Judaism marching in unison toward integration belied these internally fragmented Jewish attitudes. French rabbinical students may have studied Latin and Greek, but often grudgingly and against the wishes of at least some of their instructors. In other quarters, critics like Olry Terquem believed that they did not engage in enough secular study. Conflicts over the rabbinical school's location also reflected a diversity of opinion among French Jews regarding the types of rabbis they wanted, no matter the government's expectations. Similarly, the most far-reaching consistorial school plans went awry in practice, largely because French Jews viewed them only as charitable enterprises instead of viable educational options.

The Consistory's adaptation of its education policies during the Third Republic reflected its move toward a more overtly pluralistic approach to Jewish existence in France. With anticlerical politicians attacking the very idea of a religious budget during the 1880s and 1890s, consistorial leaders replaced their appeals for equal treatment with arguments for the uniqueness of the Jewish situation. When, in 1885, Edmond de Pressensé rose in the Senate to protest proposed reductions to the Jewish and Protestant budgets, he dismissed the principle of equal treatment requiring equal legal restriction.[8] His remarks—which had the full blessing of the Central Consistory—represented a significant departure from traditional consistorial rhetoric. Above all, they signaled that the ideal of an internally homogeneous, externally integrated French Jewry had been superseded by a more pluralistic conception. French Judaism, it turned out, constituted a unique entity whose institutions were not in fact equivalent to those of the Christian religions.

If Jews could exist as simultaneously distinct from—but nevertheless united with—other French citizens, the bonds between French Jews could be equally complex. The resolution of Jewish educational questions—the consignment of Jewish schools to the charitable realm, and of religious instruction to supplemental status—reconciled Jewishness and Frenchness while allowing for mutual coexistence and distinctiveness.[9] Such a formulation provided for division and unity simultaneously: French Jews were joined both to France and to each other, even though their *expression* of internal unity might distinguish them from their fellow citizens.

This conclusion also refines Pierre Birnbaum's more dualist interpretation of French Jewish life as an ongoing struggle between communitarianism and citizenship: between prioritizing one's membership in French Jewry or one's duties as a French citizen.[10] Certainly, Jews and non-Jews often posed the question of citizenship in these terms. The history of French Jewish education during this period, however, indicates that the question of belonging did not necessarily have an "either/or answer." The tension between communitarianism and citizenship did not automatically mean that French Jews had to sever ties with one view in order to adopt the other. The success of religious instruction programs, for example, indicates that many French Jews were willing to pursue both paths simultaneously if afforded the appropriate means.

Viewed in this light, the educational negotiations between consistorial leaders and government bureaucrats during the nineteenth century represent efforts to define the interaction between French Jews and their cultural environment. Utility, at least as employed by government officials, implied that the state would tolerate Jewish differences so long as they did not conflict with the national interest. Clearly, these criteria changed as readily as the ruling regimes of nineteenth-century France. The concept of equality, however, transcended simple toleration, presuming an acceptance of—and once again, an inherent compatibility between—cultural or religious differences. Consistorial leaders therefore sought to rise above the shifting sands of utility on the wings of equality, a universal principle that affirmed the rights of French Jewish citizens to preserve some element of distinction. In doing so, they continued an intellectual tradition from the eighteenth century, when Moses Mendelssohn had argued for a division of "right" and "opinion," a separation of "civil felicity" and the thoughts of one's own conscience.[11] The Jewish writer Zalkind Hourwitz had taken this thinking one step further in the years before emancipation: "The Jews are foreigners [in France] neither by nature nor by their religion but only as a result of the injustice of regarding them as such."[12]

The financial relationship between Judaism and state, however, left even this universal principle subject to reinterpretation. Assumptions of equality and expectations of utility compelled both Jewish and government officials to define Jewish space in France, and with it the conditions under which French Judaism would continue. Within this complex web of expectations, money played a key role that transcended its material importance, opening a channel for civil influence in Jewish affairs. The funding process thus consecrated Jewish space as undeniably French, while simultaneously legitimating Jewish claims to that space. Civic authorization meant civic acceptance, not only of the institutions involved, but also of the populations they intended to serve. Far from erasing the question of Jewish status in France, equality challenged French Jews to confront new issues regarding their relationship to their country, to their heritage, and to each other. Resolving these questions produced a Franco-Judaism at once united and divided, but nonetheless resilient.

Notes

Preface and Acknowledgments

1. For a good study of the law, how it came to pass, and contemporary responses to it, see John R. Bowen, *Why the French Don't Like Headscarves: Islam, the State, and the Public Sphere* (Princeton, 2007).

Introduction

1. Consistoire Central to the Ministre des Cultes, September 29, 1811, Archives Nationales, F 11028, AN.
2. Ibid.
3. See, for example, Michael Marrus, *The Politics of Assimilation: A Study of the French Jewish Community at the Time of the Dreyfus Affair* (Oxford, 1971), 93–121; Phyllis C. Albert, *The Modernization of French Jewry* (Hanover, N.H., 1977), 46–95; Jay Berkovitz, *The Shaping of Jewish Identity in Nineteenth-Century France* (Detroit, 1989), 128–49; Michael Graetz, *The Jews in Nineteenth-Century France: From the French Revolution to the Alliance Israélite Universelle* (Stanford, 1996), 17–40.
4. See, for example, Paula S. Hyman, *The Emancipation of the Jews of Alsace* (New Haven, 1991).
5. Ibid., 11–29.
6. Derek Penslar, *Shylock's Children: Economics and Jewish Identity in Modern Europe* (Berkeley, 2001), 92–123.
7. A notable exception to this trend is the important work of Aron Rodrigue on the schools run by the Alliance Israélite Universelle in the French colonies and in Turkey. See his *De l'instruction à l'emancipation* (Paris, 1989). His remains the only book-length study of the subject, though notably dealing with the application of French principles abroad. More recent scholarship has focused on the education of French Jewish girls. See Frances Malino, "The Women Teachers of the Alliance Israélite Universelle, 1872–1940," in Judith Baskin, ed., *Jewish Women in Historical Perspective*, 2nd ed. (Detroit, 1998), 248–69; and Jennifer Sartori, "'Wanted: A Jewish Governess': The Education of Middle-Class Jewish Girls in Nineteenth-Century Paris," *Proceedings of the Annual Meeting of the Western Society for French History* 26 (1999): 24–34.
8. Viviana Zelizer, *The Social Meaning of Money* (New York, 1994), 1–36.

9. The scholarly literature abounds with studies of Jewish identity in modern France, not to mention Europe. While space does not allow for a completely comprehensive list here, standard works in the field include: Marrus, *The Politics of Assimilation;* Patrick Girard, *Les Juifs de France de 1789 à 1860* (Paris, 1976); Albert, *The Modernization of French Jewry;* Hyman, *The Emancipation of the Jews of Alsace* and *From Dreyfus to Vichy: The Remaking of French Jewry* (New York, 1979); Frances Malino and Bernard Wasserstein, ed., *The Jews in Modern France* (Hanover, N.H., 1985); Berkovitz, *The Shaping of Jewish Identity in Nineteenth-Century France;* Michael Graetz, *Les juifs en France au XIXe siècle: de la Révolution à l'Alliance Israélite Universelle* (Paris, 1989); Simon Schwarzfuchs, *Du juif à l'israélite: histoire d'une mutation (1770–1870)* (Paris, 1989); Pierre Birnbaum, *Jewish Destinies: Citizenship, State, and Community in Modern France* (New York, 2000).

10. Adrian Furnham and Michael Argyle, *The Psychology of Money* (London, 1998), 40–41; Victoria Thompson, *The Virtuous Marketplace: Women and Men, Money and Politics in Paris, 1830–1870* (Baltimore, 2000), 2–3, 52–85. A broader overview of the relationship between money and power in French history appears in William Reddy, *Money and Liberty in Modern Europe: A Critique of Historical Understanding* (New York, 1987), esp. the introduction and 34–61, 107–96.

11. Thompson, *Virtuous Marketplace,* 53.

Chapter 1

1. See, for example, Ronald Schechter, *Obstinate Hebrews: Representations of the Jews in France, 1715–1815* (Berkeley, 2003); Birnbaum, *Jewish Destinies;* Schwarzfuchs, *Du juif à l'israélite;* and Paula Hyman's synthesis, *The Jews of Modern France* (Berkeley, 1998).

2. Paula S. Hyman, *The Emancipation of the Jews of Alsace: Acculturation and Tradition in the Nineteenth Century* (New Haven, 1991), 30–33.

3. Hyman, *Emancipation of the Jews of Alsace,* 33–35.

4. Paula S. Hyman, *The Jews of Modern France* (Berkeley, 1998), 10–11.

5. For more on the Gradis family, see Richard Menkis, "Patriarchs and Patricians: The Gradis Family of Eighteenth-Century Bordeaux," in *From East and West: Jews in a Changing Europe, 1750–1870,* ed. Frances Malino and David Sorkin (Oxford, 1990), 11–45.

6. Frances Malino, *The Sephardic Jews of Bordeaux: Assimilation and Emancipation in Revolutionary and Napoleonic France* (Tuscaloosa, 1978), 2–25.

7. Hyman, *The Jews of Modern France,* 6–7; Esther Benbassa, *The Jews of France: A History from Antiquity to the Present,* trans. M. B. DeBevoise (Princeton, 1999), 54–57.

8. Ephraim Karnarfogel, *Jewish Education and Society in the High Middle Ages* (Detroit, 1992), 15–32.

9. Jay Berkovitz, *Rites and Passages: The Beginnings of Modern Jewish Culture in France, 1650–1860* (Philadelphia, 2004), 49–50.

10. Daniel Roche, *France in the Enlightenment* (Cambridge, 1998), 330; two essays in *Éducation et pedagogies au siècle des lumières* (Angers, 1985): René Cailleau,

"La toute-puissance de l'éducation: nature et culture selon Helvétius," 11–27, and Roger Texier, "L'idée de la perfectibilité en education au XVIIIe siécle," 257–75.

11. My categorization of these thinkers follows that of Alyssa Goldstein Sepinwall, who classifies these schools of thought into "impossibilist," unconditionalist," and "conditionalist" schools. See her recent study, *The Abbé Grégoire and the French Revolution: The Making of Modern Universalism* (Berkeley, 2005), 62. See also Arthur Hertzberg, *The French Enlightenment and the Jews* (New York, 1968), 268–313.

12. Frances Malino, *A Jew in the French Revolution: The Life of Zalkind Hourwitz* (Oxford, 1996), 29–59, esp. 52–53.

13. Schechter, *Obstinate Hebrews*, 110–49.

14. For a brief summary of the Napoleonic mode of governing, see Isser Woloch, *The New Regime: Transformations of the French Civic Order, 1789–1820s* (New York, 1994), 46–51.

15. Adrien Dansette, *Histoire religieuse de la France contemporaine: l'Église catholique dans la mêlée politique et sociale* (Paris, 1965), 127–29. Also see Ralph Gibson, *A Social History of French Catholicism, 1789–1914* (London, 1989), 46–49.

16. Hyman, *The Emancipation of the Jews of Alsace*, 15–17; Malino, *The Sephardic Jews of Bordeaux*, 65–68.

17. Malino, *The Sephardic Jews of Bordeaux*; Albert, *Modernization of French Jewry*, 56–57.

18. Jay Berkovitz, *Rites and Passages: The Beginnings of Modern Jewish Culture in France, 1650–1860*, 105; see also his broader discussion of French Jews and the idea of regeneration, 92–107. Grégoire had submitted his treatise, *Essai sur la régénération physique, morale et politique des Juifs*, to the Société Royale des Sciences et des Artes de Metz as an entry in its 1787 competition. The Société had posed the question, "Are there means of rendering the Jews more useful and happier in France?" The first round of submissions having proven unsatisfactory, the Société reopened the competition the following year. This time Grégoire shared the prize with Thierry, a lawyer to the *parlement* of Nancy, and with the lone Jewish entrant, Zalkind Hourwitz. For a comprehensive discussion of the contest and the contents of the different essays, see Malino, *A Jew in the French Revolution*, 14–37; and Sepinwall, *The Abbé Grégoire and the French Revolution*, 56–77.

19. For the most comprehensive discussion of the consistories and their function see Albert, *Modernization of French Jewry*, 45–173.

20. Berkovitz, *The Shaping of Jewish Identity in Nineteenth-Century France*, 150.

21. Schwarzfuchs, *Du juif à l'israélite*, 263–65; Hyman, *The Emancipation of the Jews of Alsace*, 113.

22. As Robert Anderson has written, the Imperial and Bourbon governments considered "primary schools and primary teachers . . . to be only marginally part of the University, and the policy-making machinery [of the central government] was . . . geared to middle-class education." See his *Education in France, 1840–1870* (Oxford, 1975), 6–7.

23. Joseph N. Moody, *French Education Since Napoleon* (Syracuse, 1978), 20–22; Grew and Harrigan, *School, State, and Society*, 47.

24. See Schwarzfuchs, *Du juif à l'israélite*, 268–69.

25. Isser Woloch, *The New Regime: Transformations of the French Civic Order, 1789–1820s* (New York, 1994), 133–42.

26. Hyman, *The Jews of Modern France*, 43.

27. Pierre Birnbaum, *Anti-Semitism in France: A Political History from Léon Blum to the Present*, trans. Miriam Kochan (Oxford, 1992), 29–82.

28. For a brief overview of this school of thought, see Moody, *French Education Since Napoleon*, 18–20.

29. Conflict surrounding the religious content of French public schooling predated the First Empire and continued throughout the nineteenth century. For a summary of the early course of the debate under the Directory and Consulate, see Isser Woloch, *The New Regime*, 194–99. For the Second Empire, see Anderson, *Education in France*. For the Third Republic, see Fritz Ringer, *Fields of Knowledge: French Academic Culture in Comparative Perspective* (Cambridge, 1992), 127–40.

30. Hyman, *The Emancipation of the Jews of Alsace*, 109–11.

31. For more on Terquem's life and activities, see Berkovitz, *The Shaping of Jewish Identity in Nineteenth-Century France*, 119–26, 137–38; Richard Menkis, "Les frères Elie, Olry et Lazare Terquem," *Archives juives* 15 (1979): 58–61; and Michael A. Meyer, *Response to Modernity: A History of the Reform Movement in Judaism* (New York, 1988), 165–67.

32. Berkovitz, *The Shaping of Jewish Identity in Nineteenth-Century France*, 152–53.

33. Hyman, *The Emancipation of the Jews of Alsace*, 101–3. In this regard, the Jewish experience mirrored general French developments. Competition between French private and public schools in general had existed since the Revolution, with the private schools often gaining the advantage. See, for example, Woloch, *The New Regime*, 194–216.

34. See Hyman, *The Emancipation of the Jews of Alsace*, especially 80–85 and 102–3; Albert, *The Modernization of French Jewry*, 254–55, 295–96, and 301–2; and Jonathan Helfand, "French Jewry during the Second Republic and Second Empire (1848–70)," Ph.D. dissertation, Yeshiva University, 1979, 142–44.

35. France, Archives Nationales, F 11014, *Plan d'organisation du culte juif en France*.

36. Ministre des Cultes to the President du Consistoire Central, January 30, 1810, Archives Nationales, F11028.

37. Schwarzfuchs, *Du juif à l'israélite*, 266.

38. Consistoire Central to the Ministre des Cultes, February 7, 1810, Archives Nationales, F 11028.

39. Ibid.

40. Ibid.

41. Consistoire Central to the Ministre des Cultes, September 23, 1810, Archives Nationales, F 11028.

42. Ibid.

43. Consistoire Central to the Ministre des Cultes, September 29, 1811, Archives Nationales, F 11028.

44. Ministre des Cultes to the Consistoire Central des Israélites, January 4, 1812, Archives Nationales, F 11028.

45. Ibid.

46. Ibid.

47. Ibid.

48. Albert, *Modernization of French Jewry*, 124–43. Albert claims that regeneration did include education. Her reading, however, is based on documents from the 1830s—i.e., after Judaism began to receive regular state money—which she reads through the same lens as those from the 1810s.

49. Consistoire Central to the Ministre des Cultes, January 16, 1812, Archives Nationales, F 11028.

50. France, Archives Nationales, F 11028, Consistoire Central, Circulaire to the departmental consistories, March 22, 1812. The *circulaire* was sent under cover of a letter of April 22, 1812.

51. Ibid.

52. The communities of Mulhouse, Plastadt, and Dornach shared their school. The other five were located in Hegenheim, Ribeauville, Bergheim, Durmach, and Belfort. France, Archives Nationales, F 11094 Consistoire de Wintzenheim, *État supplémentaire des dépenses qu'exigent l'administration du culte des communes et l'instruction de la jeunesse pendant l'année 1812*, July 9, 1812 (sent to the Préfet du Haut-Rhine by the Consistoire de Wintzenheim, August 30, 1812).

53. Consistoire de Wintzenheim to the Préfet du Haut-Rhin, August 30, 1812, Archives Nationales, F 11094.

54. France, Archives Nationales, F 11028, Assembly of Consistorial Notables of Wintzenheim, July 9, 1812.

55. Ibid. The scale divided students into three categories: the *première* classe would include students coming from wealthier families, who would pay 30f per year; the *seconde* class would pay 20f per year; the third class would be comprised of poor children who would attend for free. The *troisième* class, though, were not to exceed one-sixth of the total number of students attending the school, which in this case would have been three. Consequently, five-sixths—or fifteen of the eighteen students at full enrollment—would pay at least 20f per year, while at least ten would pay 30f per year. At full capacity, these fees would thus guarantee a theological school at least 300f per year, which would cover the salary of at least one of the *professeurs*.

56. The *agrégation* is a competitive national examination for French University graduates and graduates of the *grandes écoles*. Cahen's placing third in the country was an extremely prestigious academic achievement. For more on the Cahens, see Berkovitz, *The Shaping of Jewish Identity in Nineteenth-Century France*, 90–91, 132; and Graetz, *The Jews of Nineteenth-Century France*, 202–7. Mathieu and Alfred Dreyfus, the sons of an upwardly mobile industrial family in Mulhouse, later attended the local collège for this very reason during the 1860s. See Michael Burns, *Dreyfus: A Family Affair*, 1789–1945 (New York, 1991), 43–44.

57. Albert, *The Modernization of French Jewry*, 255–56.

58. Conseiller de Prefecture du Haut-Rhin to the Ministre des Cultes, July 30, 1812, Archives Nationales, F 11028.

59. Ibid.

60. Ibid.

61. See, for example, Salo W. Baron, "Civil vs. Political Emancipation," in Siegfried Stein and Raphael Loewe, eds., *Studies in Jewish Religious and Intellectual History* (Tuscaloosa, 1977), 29–49; S. Posener, "The Immediate Economic and Social Effects of the Emancipation of the Jews of France," *Jewish Social Studies* 1, no. 1 (1939): 271–326; Marrus, *The Politics of Assimilation*; Robert Badinter, *Libres et égaux: l'émancipation des juifs, 1789–91* (Paris: Fayard, 1989); Frances Malino, "The Right to Be Equal: Zalkind Hourwitz and the Revolution of 1789," in *From East and West: Jews in a Changing Europe, 1750–1870*, ed. Frances Malino and David Sorkin (Oxford, 1990), 57–84.

62. François Furet, *Revolutionary France* (Cambridge, 1992), 273.

63. Gerson-Lévy had been educated in the French system and became a progressive advocate of both moderate religious reform and modern Jewish education. In 1814, he became a bookseller in Metz, where he involved himself in both the École Rabbinique and the Jewish primary school. He also took part in the promotion of general education in the town, serving as secretary of the Comité d'administration des Écoles Israélites de Metz, and as a founding member of the local Société des Amis des Lettres, Sciences et Arts. Berkovitz, *The Shaping of Jewish Identity in Nineteenth-Century France*, 131–32.

64. France, Archives Nationales, F 11028, *Distribution des prix faites aux élèves des écoles israélites de Metz*, October 1, 1819.

65. Ibid.

66. France, Archives Nationales, F 12514, Recteur de l'Académie de Metz, *Rapport* [au Ministre de l'Instruction Publique], July 7, 1825.

67. France, Archives Nationales, F 11031, *Observations du Consistoire israélite de Metz en réponse à la pétition adressée à M. le Préfet de la Moselle par les sieurs Louis Rottembourg et consors, bouchers à Metz*, 1830.

68. Ibid. Despite such high-minded rhetoric, Jewish girls' schools received little more than lip-service in other parts of France, notably in Alsace. See Hyman, *The Emancipation of the Jews of Alsace*, 103–4.

69. Ibid., 103; Zosa Szajkowski, *Jewish Education in France, 1789–1939* (New York, 1980), 17.

70. Under the Empire and Restoration regimes, communes became responsible for administrative expenses ranging from salaries for municipal functionaries such as postal officials to the operating costs of the mayoralty. See Woloch, *The New Regime*, 148–55.

71. France, Archives Nationales, F 12514, Conseil Royale de l'Instruction Publique, *Rapport: secours proposés sur l'exercice 1830 pour les école primaires israélites*, November 17, 1830.

72. Ibid.

73. Ibid.

74. France, Archives Nationales, F 12514, *Rapport [re: secours proposés sur l'exercice 1830 pour les école primaires israélites de Paris]*, November 26, 1830.

75. Ibid. The departmental authorities, however, proved less than cooperative. In November 1830, the Paris Consistory filed its annual request for school aid. The Prefect of the Seine replied, however, that schools separated by religion constituted the product of a "system of intolerance" to which the ascension of King Louis-Phillipe earlier in the year had put an end. If the Jews of Paris wished to maintain separate schools, the cost of maintaining them would not be included in the general municipal expenses. Léon Kahn, "Histoire des écoles consistoriales et communales israélites de Paris (1809–1883)," in *Annuaire de la société des études juives* 3 (1884): 210–11.

76. France, Archives Nationales, F 12514, *Rapport [re: secours proposés sur l'exercice 1830 pour les École primaires israélites de Paris]*, November 26, 1830.

77. Président du Comité des écoles israélites de Strasbourg, Rapport to the Recteur de l'Académie de Strasbourg, December 20, 1831, Archives Nationales, F 12514.

78. Instituteur en Chef Israélite de Haguenau to the Comité des écoles israélites à Strasbourg, February 9, 1829, Archives du Consistoire Central, 4.E.1.

Chapter 2

1. Cottard to the Ministre de l'Instruction publique et des Cultes, January 30, 1832, Archives Nationales, F 12514.

2. Ibid.

3. Jay Berkovitz, *Rites and Passages,* 213–14. See also Paula Hyman, *The Jews of Modern France,* 55.

4. Paula Hyman, *The Emancipation of the Jews of Alsace,* 19–23.

5. See, for example, Sorkin, *The Transformation of German Jewry,* 90–93.

6. Shmuel Feiner, *The Jewish Enlightenment,* trans. Chaya Naor (Philadelphia, 2002), 300–301.

7. France, Archives Nationales, F 11025, Commission administrative de l'École Centrale Rabbinique de France, *Rapport sur la situation de l'école centrale rabbinique de France pour l'année 1846,* March 7, 1847.

8. Grew and Harrigan, *School, State and Society,* 31–32.

9. François Furet and Jacques Ozouf, *Reading and Writing: Literacy in France from Calvin to Jules Ferry* (Cambridge, 1982), 137.

10. François Furet, *Revolutionary France: 1770–1880,* trans. Antonia Nevill (Oxford, 1992), 334–35.

11. See, for example, Laura Sturmingher, *What Were Little Boys and Girls Made of? Primary Education in Rural France, 1830–1880* (Albany, 1983), 7–21.

12. Rebecca Rogers, *From the Salon to the Schoolroom: Educating Bourgeois Girls in Nineteenth-Century France* (University Park, Pa., 2005), 3.

13. Woloch, *The New Regime,* 226; Grew and Harrigan, *School State and Society,* 91–100.

14. Furet and Ozouf, *Reading and Writing,* 137.

NOTES TO CHAPTER 2

15. France, Archives Nationales, F 12514, *Tableau des écoles primaires israélites établies dans les sept arrondissements consistoriales,* September 20, 1831.

16. Pierre Chevallier, B. Grosperrin, and Jean Maillet eds., *l'Enseignement français de la Révolution à nos jours* (Paris, 1968), 73–74. They quote the statistics compiled by Félix Ponteil in his *Histoire de l'enseignement en France, 1789–1965* (Paris, 1965). Ponteil counted approximately 28,000 primary schools in France by 1834.

17. Grew and Harrigan estimate the number of schools in France at about 36,000 by 1829. They caution, however, that this number represents an adjusted estimate, allowing for the practice of neglecting to report the existence of girls' schools and smaller, privately run institutions to the government. See *School, State, and Society,* 31n2.

18. France, Archives Nationales, F 12514, *Tableau des écoles primaires israélites établies dans les sept arrondissements consistoriales,* September 20, 1831. These statistics do not, of course, include the numerous clandestine schools that existed in the eastern departments and even in towns such as Bordeaux.

19. For a brief summary of Cottard's advocacy of Jewish education, see Berkovitz, *The Shaping of Jewish Identity in Nineteenth-Century France,* 161–64.

20. Comité cantonnal des écoles israélites du département du Bas-Rhin to the Ministre de l'Instruction publique et des Cultes, July 25, 1832, Archives Nationales, F 12514.

21. Cottard to the Ministre de l'Instruction Publique, March 19, 1831, Archives Nationales, F 12514.

22. Armand, Recteur de l'Académie de Nancy to Guizot, Ministre de l'Instruction publique, June 2, 1835, Archives Nationales, F 12515.

23. France, Archives Nationales, F 12515, *Extrait des registres des délibérations du conseil municipal de la ville de Nancy,* February 10, 1835.

24. Armand, to the Préfet de la Meurthe, February 23, 1835, Archives Nationales, F 12515.

25. Ibid.

26. Ibid.

27. Conseiller de préfecture délégué, pour le Préfet de la Meurthe, to the Minister de l'Instruction publique, February 25, 1835, Archives Nationales, F 12515.

28. Guizot, to Armand, November 21, 1835, Archives Nationales, F 12515; Guizot, to the Préfet de la Meurthe, November 21, 1835, Archives Nationales, F 12515.

29. France, Archives Nationales, F 12515, *Extrait des registres des délibérations du conseil municipal de la ville de Nancy,* February 10, 1835.

30. Léon Kahn, "Histoire des écoles consistoriales et communales israélites de Paris (1809–1883)," *Annuaire de la société des études juives* 3 (1884): 210–11.

31. Comité communal d'instruction primaire to the Ministre de l'Instruction publique et des Cultes, August 20, 1842, Archives Nationales, F 12515.

32. Ibid. In fact, this request came specifically to help assure the salaries of the two teachers. The committee asked that the Minister officially declare the Sarrebourg school an "a communal primary school, and that the teachers enjoy the salary fixed by the laws and regulations."

NOTES TO CHAPTER 2

33. France, Archives Nationales, F 12515, *Extrait du régistre des déliberations du conseil municipal de la ville de Sarrebourg,* November 6, 1842.

34. Ibid.

35. France, Archives Nationales, F 12515, *Extrait du régistre des déliberations du comité communal d'instruction primaire de la ville de Sarrebourg,* November 9, 1842.

36. Ibid.

37. France, Archives Nationales, F 12515, *Extrait du régistre des déliberations du comité d'instruction primaire de l'arrondissement de Strasbourg,* November 10, 1842, and Decision of the Auditeur au Conseil d'État, Sous-Préfet de l'Arrondissement de Sarrebourg, November 17, 1842.

38. Préfet de la Meurthe to the Ministre de l'Instruction publique, November 24, 1842, Archives Nationales, F 12515. Recteur de l'Académie de Nancy to the Ministre de l'Instruction publique, November 18, 1842, Archives Nationales, F 12515.

39. Ministre de l'Instruction publique to the Recteur de l'Académie de Nancy and le Préfet de la Meurthe, January 4, 1843, Archives Nationales, F 12515.

40. Paula Hyman, *Emancipation of the Jews of Alsace,* 74, 101. Hyman has mentioned the continued existence of numerous "clandestine" Jewish schools in Alsace, where a firmly rooted Jewish religious conservatism contributed to a wariness regarding modern education. This trend mirrored the initial difficulty of public schools in penetrating the French countryside in an effective manner. See, for example, Woloch, *The New Regime,* 195.

41. Szajkowski, *Jewish Education in France, 1789–1939,* 12–15. For more specific statistics on the frequency of Jewish poverty in Alsace, see Hyman, *Emancipation of the Jews of Alsace,* 45–49.

42. President of the Comité israélite de Nancy pour l'Instruction primaire to the Ministre de l'Instruction Publique, June 10, 1831, Archives Nationales, F 12514.

43. Léon Kahn, "Histoire des écoles consistoriales et communales israélites de Paris (1809–1883)," *Annuaire de la société des études juives* 3 (1884): 211.

44. President of the Comité israélite de Nancy pour l'Instruction primaire to the Ministre de l'Instruction Publique, June 10, 1831, Archives Nationales, F 12514.

45. Consistoire de Marseille to the Ministre de l'Instruction publique et des Cultes, October 4, 1832, Archives Nationales, F 12514.

46. France, Archives Nationales, F 12514, Comité consistorial pour les écoles primaires de Bordeaux, *Rapport au recteur de l'académie de Bordeaux,* November 23, 1832.

47. Maire de la Ville de Saint-Esprit to the Recteur de l'Académie de Pau, August 22, 1830, Archives Nationales, F 12514.

48. France, Archives Nationales, F 12514, Comité consistorial pour les écoles primaires de Bordeaux, *Rapport au recteur de l'académie de Bordeaux,* November 23, 1832.

49. Isaac Weille, Commissaire surveillant de la Synagogue de Toulouse to the Préfet de la Haute Garonne, August 4, 1833, Archives Nationales, F 12515.

50. France, Archives Nationales, F 12515, *Extrait des registres des déliberations du conseil général du département de la Haute Garonne,* August 7, 1833; Guizot, to the Préfet de la Haute Garonne January 17, 1834.

51. France, Archives Nationales, F 12515, *Extrait du registre des délibérations du conseil municipal de Toulouse,* May 29, 1834.

52. Recteur de l'Académie de Toulouse to Guizot, November 27, 1834, Archives Nationales, F 12515.

53. France, Archives Nationales, F 11092, *Tableau indiquant les communes du département de la haute garonne qui ont alloué une somme du budget de 1839 pour les besoins du culte israélite,* November 23, 1839.

Chapter 3

1. Consistoire de Strasbourg to the Consistoire Central, March 2, 1869, Archives du Consistoire Central (hereafter CC), 4.E.3.

2. Ibid.

3. Ibid.

4. François Furet, *Revolutionary France, 1770–1880* (Oxford, 1992), 438–91.

5. Patrick J. Harrigan, "Church, State, and Education in France from the Falloux to the Ferry Laws: A Reassessment," *Canadian Journal of History/Annales canadiennes d'histoire* 36, no. 1 (2001): 53–54, 70.

6. Chevallier, Maillet, and Grosperrin, *L'Enseignement français de la Révolution à nos jours,* 91. See also Sarah A. Curtis, *Educating the Faithful: Religion, Schooling, and Society in Nineteenth-Century France* (DeKalb, Ill. 2000), 24.

7. Grew and Harrigan, *School, State and Society,* 95–96.

8. Dimitri Demnard and Dominique Fourment, *Dictionnaire d'Histoire de l'Enseignement* (Paris, 1981), 298–302.

9. Chevallier, Grosperrin, and Maillet, *L'Enseignement français de la Révolution à nos jours,* 95.

10. Curtis, *Educating the Faithful,* 30.

11. Ibid., 21–22.

12. Gabrielle Cadier-Rey, "Les protestants, Orthez, et l'enseignement: de la loi Guizot aux lois Ferry," *Bulletin de la société de l'histoire du protestantisme français* 142, no. 4 (October 1996): 740–41.

13. Grew and Harrigan, *School, State, and Society,* 96.

14. Prost writes that coercion was in fact employed as a method of promoting Catholic education. Squires, for example, could threaten their tenant farmers with eviction if their children did not attend the Catholic school. *Histoire de l'enseignement en France,* 181.

15. Curtis, *Educating the Faithful,* 30–39.

16. Consistoire de Paris to the Consistoire Central, April 10, 1851, 4.E.3, CC.

17. Consistoire de la Gironde [Bordeaux] to the Consistoire Central, April 15, 1851, 4.E.3, CC. One of the female teachers, Mlle. Galathée Astruc, had a *brevet de capacité;* the other, Mme. Veuve Cavaillhon, had a *brevet de capacité du degré supérieur.* Elie Paz, the teacher at the private boys' school, also held the *brevet.* The *école gratuite* for boys was led by Abraham Castro, who held a *brevet* but also served as a cantor [*ministre officiant*] in the city. See *Archives israélites,* 1857, 178.

NOTES TO CHAPTER 3

18. Consistoire de la Gironde [Bordeaux] to the Consistoire Central, April 15, 1851, 4.E.3, CC.
19. Consistoire de Nancy to the Consistoire Central, April 30, 1851, 4.E.3, CC.
20. France, Archives Nationales, $F^{17}9110$, December 1851.
21. Ibid.
22. Consistoire de Colmar to the Consistoire Central, January 19, 1869, 4.E.3, CC.
23. Consistoire de Marseille to the Consistoire Central, May 18, 1852, 4.E.3, CC.
24. Consistoire de Colmar to the Consistoire Central, January 19, 1869, 4.E.3, CC.
25. France, Archives Nationales, $F^{17}9113$, *Circulaire,* July 7, 1862.
26. Consistoire de Marseille to the Consistoire Central, May 18, 1852, 4.E.3, CC.
27. Consistoire de St. Esprit to the Consistoire Central, April 21, 1851, 4.E.3, CC.
28. Consistoire de Nancy to the Consistoire Central, April 30, 1851, 4.E.3, CC.
29. France, Archives Nationales, F^{17} 536–711.
30. France, Archives Nationales, F^{17} 743, *Arrêtés* no. 859, March 2, 1850; no 1175, March 23, 1850.
31. See chapter 1, note 32 above.
32. According to Article 64 of the Law of May 25, 1844, that reorganized the Jewish Consistory. France, Archives Nationales, F^{19} 11129, *Délibération du Consistoire de Bayonne,* February 24, 1888. Also see Phyllis Albert, *Modernization of French Jewry,* 62–77.
33. France, Archives Nationales, F^{19} 11001, Napoléon III, *Décret no. 48,* May 16, 1862.
34. Consistoire Central to the Consistoires Départementaux, December 6, 1868, 4.E.3, CC.
35. Consistoire de la Gironde [Bordeaux] to the Consistoire Central, December 24, 1868, 4.E.3, CC.
36. Consistoire de Bayonne to the Consistoire Central, December 27, 1868, 4.E.3, CC.
37. The commune's contribution included 900f earmarked specifically for the salary of the teacher at the Jewish boys' school. Ibid.
38. Consistoire de Colmar to the Consistoire Central, January 19, 1869, 4.E.3, CC.
39. Ibid.
40. Isidore Cahen, "Effets de la nouvelle loi de l'enseignement sur le culte israélite—traitement des rabbins," *Archives israélites* 11 (1850): 617.
41. Ibid.
42. Ibid., 618.
43. Ibid., 618–19.
44. Ibid., 619.
45. Michael Graetz, *The Jews in Nineteenth-Century France: From the French Revolution to the Alliance Israélite Universelle* (Stanford, 1996), 202–4. Also see

André Kaspi, "Note sur Isidore Cahen," *Revue des études juives* 4, no. 121 (1962): 417–25.

46. Isidore Cahen, "Effets de la nouvelle loi de l'enseignement sur le culte israélite—traitement des rabbins," *Archives israélites* 11 (1850): 620.

47. Graetz, *The Jews in Nineteenth-Century France*, 205.

48. *Univers israélite* 4 (1849).

49. For more on the two brothers and their conversions, see Berkovitz, *The Shaping of Jewish Identity in Nineteenth-Century France*, 114–15. On the family's consistorial leadership, see Albert, *Modernization of French Jewry*, 104, 139, and 141.

50. *Univers israélite* 8 (1853): 280.

51. Patrick Girard, *Les juifs de France de 1789 à 1860* (Paris, 1976), 242; Graetz, *The Jews in Nineteenth-Century France*, 2–3; Berkovitz, *The Shaping of Jewish Identity in Nineteenth-Century France*, 244. In France, as Graetz states, the incident served as one of the driving forces leading to the formation of the Alliance Israélite Universelle, of which Isidore Cahen was a founding member.

52. Consistoire Central, Consistoire de Colmar, January 19, 1869, 4.E.3, CC.

53. Ibid.

54. Ibid.

55. Ibid.

56. Ibid.

57. Ibid.

58. Consistoire de Paris, *Renseignements circonstancié sur l'état actuel de l'instruction primaire, religieux et profane, dans les écoles de la circonscription de Paris*, May 4, 1869, 4.E.3, CC. This report consisted of a chart attached to a letter from the Consistoire de Paris to the Consistoire Central of May 3, 1869.

59. Ibid.

60. Consistoire de Lyon to the Consistoire Central, January 27, 1869, 4.E.3, CC.

61. Ibid.

62. Ibid.

63. Ibid.

64. Michael Burns, "Majority Faith: Dreyfus before the Affair," in *From East and West: Jews in a Changing Europe, 1750–1870*, ed. Frances Malino and David Sorkin (Cambridge, 1990), 70–74.

65. Consistoire de Colmar to the Consistoire Central, January 19, 1869, 4.E.3, CC.

Chapter 4

1. *Univers israélite* 19 (1864): 80–82.

2. See, for example, Richard Ayoun, "Une nouvelle conception du métier de rabbin: le rabbin consistorial en France au XIXe siécle," *Archives juives* 35, no. 2 (2002): 123–27. See also the work of Jean-Marc Chouraqui, especially "La loi du royaume est la loi: les rabbins, la politique et l'État en France (1807–1905)," *Pardes* 2 (1985): 57–98; "De l'émancipation des juifs à l'émancipation du judaïsme: le

regard des rabbins français du XIXe siècle," in *Histoire politique des juifs en France,* ed. Pierre Birnbaum (Paris, 1990), 39–57; and "Judaïsme traditionel, science et rationalisme: l'exèmple des rabbins français au XIXe siècle," in *Les études juives en France: situation et perspectives,* ed. Frank Alvarez-Pereye and Jean Baumgarten (Paris, 1990), 33–45.

3. Robert D. Anderson, *Education in France, 1840–1870* (Oxford, 1975), 21–27.

4. Joseph Moody, *French Education Since Napoleon* (Syracuse, 1978), 31–32.

5. The Jewish dispute over these matters also mirrored ongoing disagreement within Jewish communities across nineteenth-century Europe. See, for example, Chouraqui, "Judaïsme traditionel, science et rationalisme"; Perrine Simon-Nahum, "La science du judaïsme en France," in *Les études juives en France: situation et perspectives,* ed. Frank Alvarez-Pereye and Jean Baumgarten (Paris, 1990), 23–32; Meyer, *Response to Modernity,* 62–99; Jacob J. Schacter, "Haskalah, Secular Studies and the Close of the Yeshiva in Volozhin in 1892," *Torah U-Madda Journal* 2 (1990): 76–133.

6. Albert, *Modernization of French Jewry,* 244; Berkovitz, *The Shaping of Jewish Identity in Nineteenth-Century France,* 195.

7. Shlomo Berger, "For Which Types of Speech Would a Jew Have Studied Greek Rhetoric in Seventeenth-Century Amsterdam?" *Studia Rosenthaliana* 34, no. 2 (2000): 153–67.

8. Robert Liberles, *Religious Conflict in Social Context: The Resurgence of Orthodox Judaism in Frankfurt am Main, 1838–1877* (Westport, Conn. 1985), 114.

9. See, for example, Ismar Schorsch, *From Text to Context: The Turn to History in Modern Judaism* (Hanover, 1994), 9–13.

10. Albert, *Modernization of French Jewry,* 169.

11. France, Archives Nationales, F^{19} 11014, *Plan d'organisation du culte juif en France.*

12. Ibid. Also see Albert, *Modernization of French Jewry,* 265–66; and Berkovitz, *The Shaping of Jewish Identity in Nineteenth-Century France,* 192–93.

13. Berkovitz, *The Shaping of Jewish Identity in Nineteenth-Century France,* 194–95.

14. Such permission was mandatory for the establishment of a seminary for any official faith according to the law organizing the Université [March 17, 1808].

15. Consistoire Central to le Grand Maître de l'Université Impériale, Archives Nationales, F^{19} 11028, October 16, 1809. The reasoning described here also reflects that of the *Plan d'organisation* cited above.

16. Ministre des Cultes to the President du Consistoire Central, January 30, 1810, Archives Nationales, F^{19} 11028, Consistoire Central to the Ministre des Cultes, February 7, 1810, Archives Nationales, F^{19} 11028.

17. Consistoire Central to the Ministre des Cultes, September 29, 1811, Archives Nationales, F^{19} 11028.

18. France, Archives Nationales, F^{19} 11028, Consistoire Central, *Circulaire,* March 22, 1812.

19. Ibid.

20. Conseiller de Préfecture du Haut-Rhin to the Ministre des Cultes, July 30, 1812, Archives Nationales, F[19] 11028, F[19] 11028.

21. Françoise Mayeur, *Histoire générale de l'enseignement et de l'éducation en France, tome III, de la Révolution à l'école républicaine* (Paris, 1981), 308–10.

22. François Furet, *Revolutionary France* (Oxford, 1988), 269–306.

23. Ministre de l'Intérieur et des Cultes to M. Royer Collard, Président de la Commission de l'Instruction Publique, September 11, 1816, Archives Nationales, F[19] 11028.

24. Commission de l'Instruction Publique to the Ministre de l'Intérieur, October 10, 1816, Archives Nationales, F[19] 11028.

25. Consistoire de Metz et la Comité Cantonnal des Écoles to the Ministre de l'Intérieur et des Cultes, February 17, 1822, Jewish Theological Seminary of America Archives (hereafter JTS), Box 18 (part 1) #39.

26. Ibid.

27. Jules Bauer, *L'École rabbinique de France* (Paris, 1930), 4–5.

28. Consistoire de Paris to the Consistoire Central, February 11, 1827, Archives Nationales, F[19] 11025.

29. Consistoire de Marseille to the Consistoire Central, September 3, 1827, Archives Nationales, F[19] 11025.

30. Consistoire du bas-Rhin [Strasbourg] to the Consistoire Central, Paris, September 9, 1827, Archives Nationales, F[19] 11025.

31. For more on the basic components of the Reform movement in France, see Michael Meyer, *Response to Modernity* (New York, 1988), 164–71; also Richard Menkis, "Les frères Elie, Olry et Lazare Terquem," *Archives juives* 15, no. 3 (1979): 58–61. On Cahen, see Berkovitz, *The Shaping of Jewish Identity in Nineteenth-Century France,* 130; Berkovitz, *Rites and Passages,* 184–90; and his obituary in the *Archives israélites,* 23 (1862).

32. See, for example, Allan Forrest, "Paris versus the Provinces," in Martin S. Alexander, ed., *French History Since Napoleon* (New York, 1999), 106–26.

33. Steven Kale, *Legitimism and the Reconstruction of French Society, 1852–83* (Baton Rouge, 1992), 233–38.

34. Berkovitz, *Rites and Passages,* 157–61. See also Michael Graetz, *The Jews in Nineteenth-Century France: From the French Revolution to the Alliance Israélite Universelle,* trans. Jane Marie Todd (Stanford, 1996).

35. Bauer, *Le séminaire rabbinique de France,* 6–7.

36. For a brief chronological overview of Metz's rabbinical heritage, see Berkovitz, *Rites and Passages,* 18–34; also Léon Berman, *Histoire des juifs en France* (Paris, 1937), 277–80.

37. Consistoire Central to the Minister de l'Intérieur de France, March 16, 1828, Archives Nationales, F[19] 11025. The consistorial leadership also pointed out that the *ordonnance* of August 20, 1823, said nothing about the qualifications for communal rabbis. Since they had to fulfill the same religious office as the *grand rabbins,* the Consistory suggested that both rabbinical degrees require the same religious knowledge with a less demanding secular program for the communal rabbis.

38. France, Archives Nationales, F¹⁹ 11025, Consistoire Central, *Extrait des registres des délibérations: Projet de réglement organique pour une École centrale israélite de théologie,* March 9, 1828.

39. France, Archives Nationales, Consistoire Central, *Règlement intérieur de l'École centrale israélite de théologie,* May 8, 1828.

40. Ibid.

41. Bauer, *L'École rabbinique de France,* 26.

42. Moody, *French Education Since Napoleon,* 14–15. Also see Prost, *Histoire de l'enseignement en France, 1800–1967,* 159–62.

43. Ministre de l'Intérieur et des Cultes to the Consistoire Central, May 23, 1828, Archives Nationales, F¹⁹ 11025.

44. Albert, *Modernization of French Jewry,* 255–59.

45. Consistoire Central to the Ministre de l'Intérieur, June 1, 1828, Archives Nationales, F¹⁹ 11025. Also referred to in Albert, *Modernization of French Jewry,* 258.

46. Jacques-Olivier Boudon, "L'épiscopat français et le développement des hautes études ecclésistique au XIXe siècle," *Revue d'histoire de l'église de France* 81, no. 206 (January–June 1995): 219–35.

47. France, Archives Nationales, F¹⁹ 11025, Conseil d'État, Comité de l'Intérieur, *Extrait des délibérations du Comité,* July 23, 1828. The full statement reads: "[T]he most efficient and prompt means of obtaining the amelioration in the morals and customs of French *israélites* that we have hoped [to accomplish] by the legislation which has permitted them to enjoy the same civil and political rights as other Frenchmen, is to place them early on into contact with their fellow citizens and . . . to encourage them . . . to have their children taught the first elements of instruction in public establishments."

48. A government memorandum acknowledged this interpretation, observing that by allotting a special subvention to the school in 1829 the Minister had clearly "recognized [its] utility." France, Archives Nationales, F¹⁹11025, Conseiller d'État chargé des affaires des cultes non-catholiques, *Rapport présenté a Son Excellence le Ministre Secrétaire de l'État au Département de l'Intérieur,* March 6, 1829.

49. The provision earmarked 5,000f specifically for the costs of opening the rabbinical school. The remaining 8,500f would then be divided among the different consistorial synagogues, with the understanding that they would then apply these funds toward the school's establishment. France, Archives Nationales, F¹⁹ 11025, Ministre de l'Intérieur, *Règlement pour l'École centrale rabbinique de Metz,* August 21, 1829 [appendix to the Ministerial *Arrêté*]; France, Archives Nationales, F¹⁹ 11025, Consistoire Central, *Compte des recettes et des dépenses de l'École centrale rabbinique de Metz depuis le mois de mai 1830 jusqu'au 31 Décembre suivant,* April 26, 1831.

50. *Ordonnance du Roi,* March 22, 1831, F¹⁹ 11095, AN.

51. Consistoire de Metz to the Préfet de la Moselle, February 1, 1841, Archives Nationales, F¹⁹ 11025.

52. Ministre de la Justice et des Cultes to the Consistoire Central, February 24, 1838, Archives Nationales, F¹⁹ 11025.

53. The 1838 augmentation still failed to cover the bare minimum of the school's operating costs. The shortfall added 525f to the debt, which increased to 2,342f by the beginning of 1839. Consistoire de Metz to the Préfet de la Moselle, February 1, 1841, Archives Nationales, F¹⁹ 11025.

54. France, CC, 3.H.1, Commission Administrative du Séminaire Israélite, *Projet du budget pour l'exercice 1867,* December 18, 1866.

55. Albert, *The Modernization of French Jewry,* 310–11; Hyman, *The Emancipation of the Jews of Alsace,* 138–39.

56. France, Archives Nationales, F¹⁹ 11025, Consistoire israélite de Metz, *Situation générale de l'École rabbinique au 1er septembre 1835,* September 1, 1835.

57. Ibid.

58. *Archives israélites* 2 (February, 1841), 123–24. Albert briefly refers to this article. See *Modernization of French Jewry,* 245.

59. Préfet de la Moselle to the Ministre de la Justice et des Cultes, July 26, 1841, Archives Nationales, F¹⁹ 11025.

60. Ministre de la Justice et des Cultes to the Consistoire Central, March 26, 1841, Archives Nationales, F¹⁹ 11025.

61. France, Archives Nationales, *Note,* Ministère de la Justice et de la Culte, June 30, 1841. Albert mentions this *note,* but says nothing about the financial question. She also cites this memorandum as coming in response to Franck's article. A margin note on the first page of the document, however, mentions only the commission report. *Modernization of French Jewry,* 245–56.

62. France, Archives Nationales, *Note,* Ministère de la Justice et de la Culte, June 30, 1841.

63. Ibid.

64. See for example David Pinkney, *Decisive Years in France, 1840–1847* (Princeton, 1986), especially chapter 3, "Centralization Made Real."

65. Steven D. Kale, *Legitimism and the Reconstruction of French Society, 1852–1883* (Baton Rouge, 1992), 280–81.

66. France, Archives Nationales, *Note,* Ministère de la Justice et de la Culte, June 30, 1841.

67. Ibid.

68. Ibid.

69. Albert, *Modernization of French Jewry,* 245–46.

70. Consistoire Central to Son Excellence Monsieur le Garde des Sceaux, Ministre de la Justice et des Cultes, July 14, 1847, Archives Nationales, F¹⁹ 11025. The Central Consistory forwarded the report as part of this extensive letter.

71. Ibid.

72. Ibid.

73. Ibid.

74. Ibid.

75. Ibid.

76. Morhange possessed the *bachélier-ès-lettres* degree and served as the rabbinical school's secretary. Since 1835, he had conducted the courses in Latin and Greek.

France, Archives Nationales, F[19] 11025, Consistoire israélite de Metz, *Situation générale de l'École rabbinique au 1er septembre 1835,* September 1, 1835.

77. France, Archives Nationales, F[19] 11025, Commission administrative de l'École Centrale Rabbinique de France, *Rapport sur la situation de l'École centrale rabbinique de France pour l'année 1846,* March 7, 1847.

78. Consistoire Central to Son Excellence Monsieur le Garde des Sceaux, Ministre de la Justice et des Cultes, July 14, 1847, Archives Nationales, F[19] 11025.

79. Ibid. Jean-Marc Chouraqui has written extensively regarding the development and importance of sermonizing in the French rabbinate. See, for example, his articles "De l'émancipation des juifs à l'émancipation du judaïsme: le regard des rabbins français du XIXe siècle," in *Histoire politique des juifs en France,* ed. Pierre Birnbaum (Paris, 1990), 39–57; "'Echoes de la Chaire': la prédication israélite en France," *Revue des études juives* 150, nos. 1–2 (January–June 1991): 71–105; and "Le corps rabbinique et sa prédication en France, 1807–1905," *Histoire, Économie, Société* (Autumn 1984): 294–99.

80. Consistoire Central to Son Excellence Monsieur le Garde des Sceaux, Ministre de la Justice et des Cultes, July 14, 1847, Archives Nationales, F[19] 11025.

81. Meyer, *Response to Modernity,* 131–42.

82. Ibid., 165–71.

83. For an overview of the historical importance of the Gradis family, see the article by Richard Menkis, "Patriarchs and Patricians: The Gradis Family of Eighteenth-Century Bordeaux," in *From East and West: Jews in a Changing Europe, 1750–1870,* ed. Frances Malino and David Sorkin (Cambridge, 1991), 11–45.

84. France, CC, 1.H.1, IV, Benjamin Gradis, *Memoire au sujet de l'École rabbinique de Metz,* August 31, 1847.

85. Ibid. Gradis likely was referring implicitly to the presence of a M. Bourgeois on the faculty of the École Rabbinique. Bourgeois, a Catholic, was an instructor at the *lycée* at Metz and taught rhetoric and philosophy at the École Rabbinique.

86. Consistoire de la Gironde [Bordeaux] to the Consistoire Central, September 29, 1847, 1.H.1, IV, CC.

87. Consistoire de Strasbourg to the Consistoire Central, March 28, 1847, 1.H.1, IV, CC.

88. Roger Price, *The French Second Empire: An Anatomy of Political Power* (Cambridge, 2001), 196–97.

89. Moody, *French Education Since Napoleon,* 59–63. See also Furet, *Revolutionary France,* 455–56, 483.

90. Kale, *Legitimism and the Reconstruction of French Society,* 255.

91. See, for example, Furet, *Revolutionary France,* 301–6; 365–66; Owen Chadwick, *The Secularization of the European Mind* (Cambridge, 1975), 1–14. For a later example, see James R. Lehning, *To Be a Citizen: The Political Culture of the Early French Third Republic* (Ithaca, 2001), 35–57.

92. *Univers israélite* 5 (1849): 170–74.

93. Consistoire de Metz to the Consistoire Central, December 26, 1850, 1.H.1, IV, CC.

94. France, Archives Nationales, F^{19} 11025, *Rapport sur la situation de l'École centrale rabbinique de France pendant l'année 1853,* April 7, 1854. Even including an interruption following the school's transfer to Paris, he would occupy this position for most of the next fifty years. See Bauer, *L'École rabbinique de France,* 75.

95. France, Archives Nationales, F^{19} 11025, *Rapport sur la situation de l'École centrale rabbinique de France pendant l'année 1853,* April 7, 1854.

96. Ibid.

97. France, CC, 1.H.1,IV, *Rapport au Consistoire Central des Israélites de France sur l'inspection de l'École centrale rabbinique pour l'année 1856,* December 11, 1856.

98. See the following chapter for details of the move.

99. France, CC, 2.H.3, Commission d'examen, Séminaire israélite, *Procès-verbal pour l'obtention du diplôme de 2e degré rabbinique,* June 18, 1860.

100. France, CC, 2.H.3, Commission d'examen, Séminaire israélite, *Procès-verbal pour l'obtention du diplôme de 2e degré rabbinique,* December 23, 1863.

101. France, CC, 2.H.3, Commission d'examen, Séminaire israélite, *Procès-verbal pour l'obtention du diplôme rabbinique,* August 31, 1864.

102. France, CC, 2.H.3, Commission d'examen du Séminaire Israélite, *Procès-verbal pour l'obtention du diplôme rabbinique,* March 15, 1866.

103. See the articles by Jean-Marc Chouraqui cited in chapter 4, notes 2 and 79.

104. France, CC, 3.H.1, Commission des examens, *Procès-verbal des Commission d'examen du Séminaire Israélite,* September 6, 1867 [attached to minutes of November 19, 1867].

105. Lehman obtained a rabbinic post with the Paris and eventually replaced Isaac Trénel as Director of the Séminaire Israélite. The registry is located in France, CC 2.H.4.

106. Robert Gildea, "Education and the *Classes Moyennes* in the Nineteenth Century," in *The Making of Frenchmen: Current Directions in the History of Education in France, 1679–1979,* ed. Donald Baker and Patrick Harrigan (Waterloo, Ont., 1980), 285; Moody, *French Education Since Napoleon,* 61.

107. Sandra Horvath-Peterson, *Victor Duruy & French Education: Liberal Reform in the Second Empire* (Baton Rouge, 1984), 145–46. At the forefront of the opposition to such reform stood the influential Association pour l'encouragement des études grecques en France, whose founding members included (ironically) Duruy himself, the historian Ernest Renan, and the influential University official Charles Jourdain. The general membership included Guillame Guizot, a high-ranking official of the Education Ministry, and two active members of the Jewish Consistory: Baron Alphonse de Rothschild and Albert Cohn, a respected educator and member of the French University. For a sample list of members, see France, Archives Nationales, F^{17} 9100, Association pour l'encouragement des études grecques en France, *Annuaire de 1867.* In the late 1860s, the Association lobbied the government against Duruy's proposed deemphasis of the Greek sections of the *baccalauréat* examination. See, for example, the Association's *Supplément à l'annuaire de 1868* in the same location.

108. Commission d'examen, Séminaire Israélite, *Procès-verbal pour l'obtention du diplôme de premier degré rabbinique,* September 24, 1883, 2.H.3, CC, *Elèves.*

While the school classified Syriac and Arabic as secular subjects, these languages had practical religious applications. Both languages are used for critical study of the Hebrew Bible; knowledge of Arabic also might have proven useful to rabbis assigned to posts in Algeria.

109. France, CC, 2.H.3, Commission d'examen, Séminaire Israélite, *Procès-verbal pour l'obtention du diplôme de premier degré rabbinique* (undated, but 1888).

110. France, CC, 2.H.3, Commission d'examen, Séminaire Israélite, *Procès-verbal pour l'obtention du diplôme de premier degré rabbinique,* August 5, 1890.

111. France, CC, 2.H.3, Commission d'examen, Séminaire Israélite, *Procès-verbal pour l'obtention du diplôme de premier degré rabbinique,* April 27, 1893. Ironically, Zeitlin scored highest in philosophy (15), Jewish history (15), and Arabic/Syriaque (16.5), while French was his lowest score (11, the same as he got in *dinim oraux*). He passed and received a communal rabbi's diploma.

112. France, CC, 2.H.3, Commission des examens, *Examens de sortie* of students Chostmann, Atébi, and Bach, April 6, 1903.

113. France, CC, 2.H.3, Commission des examens, *Examens de sortie* of Henri Soil. Undated, but Soil was admitted to the school in October 1926; therefore this exam had to have taken place in the early 1930s.

114. Joseph Lehmann, Directeur du Séminaire to Grand-Rabbin Abraham Cahen, directeur du Talmud Torah, May 9, 1904, CC, 3.H.2.

115. Ben Mosché, "Culte: le budget du culte israélite au Sénat," *Archives israélites* 46 (March 5, 1885): 75–76. The government allocation for the school had gradually increased since its inception. In 1847, the budget rose to 15,000f as an encouragement to keep the school in Metz. After the move to Paris, the school's allocation grew to 32,000f.

116. France, CC, 2.H.2, 1, Consistoire Central, *Circulaire,* March, 1899; *Procès-verbaux du Consistoire de Paris,* November 23, 1899, Archives du Consistoire de Paris (hereafter CP), AA.8, 290. The Paris Rothschilds took a deep interest in the Consistory's educational activities, and for years had handled their financial affairs. The absence of any further mention of this deficit problem from the consistorial minutes suggests that the House of Rothschild raised the credit limit as an act of charity. No formal documentation of the act exists in the consistorial archives, however.

117. Joseph Lehmann, directeur du Séminaire, *Rapport sur le Séminaire Israélite et le Talmud-Thora,* February 16, 1902, Lamont Library (hereafter HUL), Film A 300.251.

118. Ibid.

Chapter 5

1. Ronald Schechter, *Obstinate Hebrews: Representations of Jews in France, 1715–1815* (Berkeley, 2003), 13.

2. Sudhir Hazareesingh, *From Subject to Citizen: The Second Empire and the Emergence of Modern French Democracy* (Princeton, 1998), 8–12. His work also cites the classic book by David Thomson, *Democracy in France* (London, 1946),

which coined the term "accumulative" in referring to the formation of citizenship definitions in France.

3. These figures are taken from Albert, *Modernization of French Jewry,* 21.

4. France, Archives Nationales, F^{19} 11026, Directeur de l'Administration des Cultes, *Note sur l'École rabbinique de Metz,* January 25, 1849.

5. Ibid.

6. Ibid.

7. Consistoire Central to the Directeur Général des Cultes, Dumay, April 18, 1850, Archives Nationales, F^{19} 11026.

8. Directeur de l'Administration de Cultes to the Consistoire Central, CC, 1.H.1, IV, April 25, 1851.

9. Consistoire de Metz to the Consistoire Central, CC, 1.H.1, IV, May 25, 1851.

10. Ministre de l'Instruction publique et des Cultes to the Consistoire Central, June 11, 1851, 1.H.1, IV, CC.

11. Ibid.

12. Ministre de l'Instruction publique et des Cultes to the Consistoire Central, July 12, 1851, Archives Nationales, F^{19} 11026. For example, the commission objected to the lack of a direct entry passage to the director's rooms from the main entrance of the building, and the presence of a large number of window casements which it considered not only unnecessary but dangerous to the stability of the supporting walls.

13. Ministre de l'Instruction publique et des Cultes to the Consistoire Central, November 26, 1851, Archives Nationales, F^{19} 11026. See also the letter from the Consistoire de Metz to the Consistoire Central, CC, 1.H.1, IV, December 2, 1851.

14. France, Archives Nationales, F^{19} 11026, Dérobe, Architecte du Département de la Moselle, *Devis estimatif des travaux à éxecuter pour l'établissment de l'École centrale rabbinique, dans une maison appartenant au Consistoire israélite à Metz,* September 29, 1851.

15. Ministre de l'Instruction publique et des Cultes to the Consistoire Central, December 1, 1851, Archives Nationales, F^{19} 11026; Ministre de l'Instruction publique et des Cultes to the Prefét de la Moselle, December 1, 1851, Archives Nationales, F^{19} 11026.

16. Préfet de la Moselle to the Ministre de l'Instruction publique et des Cultes [Fortoul], December 19, 1851, Archives Nationales, F^{19} 11026.

17. Fortoul, Ministre de l'Instruction publique et des Cultes, to the Préfet de la Moselle, December 20, 1851, Archives Nationales, F^{19} 11026.

18. Consistoire de Metz to the Consistoire Central, CC, 1.H.1, IV, August 23, 1852; France, Archives Nationales, F^{19} 11026, Directeur général de l'administration des cultes, *Rapport au Ministre de l'Instruction publique et des cultes* [Fortoul], February 14, 1853.

19. France, Archives Nationales, F^{19} 11026, Directeur général de l'administration des cultes, *Rapport au Ministre de l'Instruction publique et des cultes* [Fortoul], February 14, 1853.

20. Fortoul, Ministre de l'Instruction Publique et des Cultes to the Préfet de la Moselle, February 21, 1853, Archives Nationales, F^{19} 11026.

21. France, Archives Nationales, F^{19} 11026, Préfet de la Moselle, *Adjudication des travaux de construction d'une École centrale rabbinique à Metz,* March 15, 1853; Préfet de la Moselle to Fortoul, Ministre de l'Instruction publique et des Cultes, September 13, 1853, Archives Nationales, F^{19} 11026.

22. Boesvilvald to Fortoul, Ministre de l'Instruction publique et des Cultes, November 25, 1853, Archives Nationales, F^{19} 11026.

23. Directeur général des Cultes to Ministre de l'Instruction publique et des Cultes September 23, 1854, Archives Nationales, F^{19} 11026; Boesvilvald to the Ministre de l'Instruction publique et des Cultes, April 20, 1855, Archives Nationales, F^{19} 11026.

24. Recteur de l'Académie de Nancy to the Ministre des Cultes, November 2, 1853, Archives Nationales, F^{19} 11026.

25. Boesvilvald to the Ministre de l'Instruction publique et des Cultes, April 20, 1855, Archives Nationales, F^{19} 11026.

26. Consistoire de Metz to the Préfet de la Moselle, May 2, 1855, Archives Nationales, F^{19} 11026.

27. Recteur de l'Académie de Nancy to the Ministre des Cultes, November 2, 1853, Archives Nationales, F^{19} 11026.

28. Consistoire de Metz to the Consistoire Central, December 7, 1853, CC, 1.H.1, VII.

29. Consistoire de Strasbourg to the Consistoire Central, January 30, 1854, CC, 1.H.1, VII; Consistoire de Nancy to the Consistoire Central, January 15, 1854, CC, 1.H.1, VII.

30. Consistoire de St. Esprit to the Consistoire Central, January 25, 1854, CC, 1.H.1, VII; Consistoire de Colmar to the Consistoire Central, June 28, 1854, CC, 1.H.1, VII; Consistoire de Colmar to the Consistoire Central, October 18, 1854, CC, 1.H.1, VII; Consistoire de Marseille to the Consistoire Central, October 5, 1854, CC, 1.H.1, VII.

31. Consistoire de Metz to the Consistoire Central, July 31, 1854, CC, 1.H.1, VII.

32. Recteur de l'Académie de Nancy to the Ministre des Cultes, November 2, 1853, Archives Nationales, F^{19} 11026. One might assume that the term "seminary" [*séminaire*] was the rector's term, and not necessarily Lazare's.

33. For Lazare, homiletics served as one of the primary means of communication between a rabbi and the laity. See, for example, Jean-Marc Chouraqui, "Le corps rabbinique et sa prédication en France, 1807–1905," *Histoire Economie Société* 3, no. 2 (1984): 294–99.

34. Recteur de l'Académie de Nancy to the Ministre des Cultes, November 2, 1853, Archives Nationales, F^{19} 11026.

35. Consistoire de Nancy to the Consistoire Central, January 15, 1854, CC, 1.H.1, VII.

36. Olry Terquem to the Consistoire Central, March 4, 1854, CC, 1.H.1, VII.

37. Mardochée Dorsan Astruc to the Consistoire Central, April 30, 1855, CC, 1.H.1, IV. Astruc, who called himself a "banker residing at Bordeaux,"

NOTES TO CHAPTER 5

was the father of Elie Aristide Astruc, a future founder of the Alliance Israélite Universelle.

38. Consistoire de Metz to the Préfet de la Moselle, May 2, 1855, Archives Nationales, F^{19} 11026.

39. Boesvilvald to the Ministre de l'Instruction publique et des Cultes, May 23, 1855, Archives Nationales, F^{19} 11026.

40. Ministre de l'nstruction publique et des Cultes to the Préfet de la Moselle, May 31, 1855, Archives Nationales, F^{19} 11026.

41. Boesvilvald to the Ministre de l'Instruction publique et des Cultes, June 20, 1855, Archives Nationales, F^{19} 11026.

42. France, Archives Nationales, F^{19} 11026, Ministre de l'nstruction publique et des Cultes, *Avis à la Comptabilité* [des Cultes], December 31, 1855.

43. Consistoire de Metz to the Préfet de la Moselle, March 14, 1856, Archives Nationales, F^{19} 11026.

44. Ministre de l'Instruction publique et des Cultes to the Préfet de la Moselle, April 2, 1856, Archives Nationales, F^{19} 11026.

45. Boesvilvald to the Ministre de l'Instruction publique et des Cultes, January 29, 1857, Archives Nationales, F^{19} 11026.

46. Boesvilvald to the Ministre de l'Instruction publique et des Cultes, January 27, 1857, Archives Nationales, F^{19} 11026.

47. Ibid.

48. France, Archives Nationales, F^{19} 11026, *Production d'un devis de travaux supplémentaire* [pour la reconstruction de l'École Rabbinique], submitted to the Commission des Édifices religieux, January 30, 1857.

49. Ibid.

50. Mardochée Dorsan Astruc to the Consistoire Central, April 30, 1855, CC, 1.H.1, IV.

51. Berkovitz, *The Shaping of Jewish Identity in Nineteenth-Century France*, 222–28. For a more expansive examination of the ritual reforms, see Berkovitz, *Rites and Passages*, 191–203. See also Phyllis Cohen Albert, "Non-Orthodox Attitudes in Nineteenth-Century French Judaism," in *Essays in Modern Jewish History: A Tribute to Ben Halpern*, ed. Frances Malino and Phyllis Cohen Albert (East Brunswick, N.J., 1982), 121–41.

52. Consistoire Central to the Ministre de l'Instruction publique et des Cultes [Rouland], January 8, 1857, Archives Nationales, F^{19} 11026. Technically, the vote was unanimous. The *grand rabbin* of Metz, however—who would have cast a dissenting vote—was absent from the meeting due to illness.

53. Consistoire de Metz to the Consistoire Central, January 3, 1856, CC, 1.H.1, VII; Bauer, *L'École rabbinique de France*, 86.

54. Consistoire de Metz to the Consistoire Central, January 29, 1856, CC, 1.H.1, VII.

55. *Procès-verbaux du Consistoire de Paris*, June 11, 1856, CP, AA.5.

56. Ibid.

57. Ibid.

58. Ibid.

59. Consistoire Central to the Ministre de l'Instruction publique et des Cultes, October 31, 1856, Archives Nationales, F^{19} 11026.
60. Ibid.
61. Ibid.
62. Ibid.
63. Ibid.
64. Despite the failure of this approach, the Consistory employed the same arguments in 1879–80. See chapter 7 below.
65. This supplement would raise the school's allotment to 20,000f.
66. Consistoire Central to the Ministre de l'Instruction publique et des Cultes, October 31, 1856, Archives Nationales, F^{19} 11026.
67. France, Archives Nationales, F^{19} 11026, *Note pour le Ministre* [de l'Instruction publique et des Cultes] *sur la demande de translation de l'École rabbinique de Metz,* December 11, 1856.
68. Ibid.
69. Ibid.
70. Prost, *Histoire de l'enseignement en France,* 30.
71. Moody, *French Education since Napoleon,* 67–68.
72. Rouland, Ministre de l'Instruction publique et des Cultes to the Presidents of the Consistoire Central and the Consistoires Départementaux, March 9, 1857, Archives Nationales, F^{19} 11026. For a published summary of the responses, see Bauer, *L'École rabbinique de France,* 104–8.
73. Consistoire de Marseille to the Ministre de l'Instruction publique et des Cultes, April 5, 1857, Archives Nationales, F^{19} 11026.
74. Consistoire de St. Esprit [Bayonne] to the Ministre de l'Instruction publique et des Cultes, April 6, 1857, Archives Nationales, F^{19} 11026.
75. Consistoire de Strasbourg to the Ministre de l'Instruction publique et des Cultes, March 14, 1857, Archives Nationales, F^{19} 11026.
76. Consistoire de Paris to the Ministre de l'Instruction publique et des Cultes, March 13, 1857, Archives Nationales, F^{19} 11026.
77. Consistoire de Strasbourg to the Ministre de l'Instruction publique et des Cultes, March 14, 1857, Archives Nationales, F^{19} 11026.
78. Consistoire de St. Esprit [Bayonne] to the Ministre de l'Instruction publique et des Cultes, April 6, 1857, Archives Nationales, F^{19} 11026.
79. Consistoire Central to Rouland, Ministre de l'Instruction publique et des Cultes, January 8, 1857, Archives Nationales, F^{19} 11026.
80. Consistoire de Strasbourg to the Ministre de l'Instruction publique et des Cultes, March 14, 1857, Archives Nationales, F^{19} 11026.
81. Consistoire Central to Rouland, Ministre de l'Instruction publique et des Cultes, January 8, 1857, Archives Nationales, F^{19} 11026.
82. Consistoire de Bordeaux to the MInistre de l'Instruction publique et des Cultes, March 25, 1857, Archives Nationales, F^{19} 11026.
83. France, Archives Nationales, F^{19} 11026, Benjamin Gradis, *Pétition au sujet de l'École rabbinique,* April 15, 1857.
84. Ibid.

85. Gradis, it should be noted, was a member of a wealthy merchant family of Bordeaux.

86. Ibid.

87. Consistoire de Metz to the Ministre de l'Instruction publique et des Cultes, March, 1857, Archives Nationales, F^{19} 11026.

88. Ibid. Ironically, this same complaint would form the basis of the Central Consistory's efforts to revise the secular section of the curriculum twenty years later.

89. While he entered the École Rabbinique at age thirteen, Wogue remained at the school for eleven years, graduating in 1842 at the age of twenty-five with the degree of *grand rabbin*. He joined the school's faculty in 1852 as professor of Hebrew, theology, and exegesis. Wogue followed the school to Paris, retiring from the faculty in 1895 after forty-three years of service. He also served as an editor and frequent contributor for the more traditionalist Jewish journal *Univers israélite*.

90. Consistoire de Metz to the Ministre de l'Instruction publique et des Cultes, March 1857, Archives Nationales, F^{19} 11026.

91. France, Archives Nationales, F^{19} 11026, Cabinet du Ministre de l'Instruction publique et des Cultes, *Note pour le Ministre* [Rouland], April 27, 1857.

92. Ibid. The administration intended to approve this provision, and eventually did.

93. Ibid.

94. France, Archives Nationales, F^{19} 11026, Cabinet du Ministre de l'Instruction publique et des Cultes, *Note pour le Ministre,* June 12, 1857.

95. France, Archives Nationales, F^{19} 11026, Administration des Cultes non-catholiques, *Note pour le Ministre,* undated. The memorandum is undated, but probably dates from late 1857 or early 1858, when the indemnity issue was under discussion.

96. Rouland, Ministre de l'Instruction publique et des Cultes to the Consistoire Central, February 23, 1858, Archives Nationales, F^{19} 11026.

97. Ibid.

98. Consistoire Central to Rouland, Ministre de l'Instruction publique et des Cultes, March 7, 1859, Archives Nationales, F^{19} 11026.

99. Consistoire de Metz to the Consistoire Central, January 16, 1959, Archives Nationales, F^{19} 11026.

100. Consistoire Central to Rouland, Ministre de l'Instruction publique et des Cultes, March 7, 1859, Archives Nationales, F^{19} 11026.

101. Rouland, Ministre de l'Instruction Publique et des Culte, *Rapport à l'Empereur* [sur la Translation de l'École centrale rabbinique de Metz], June 1859, Archives Nationales, F^{19} 11026.

102. Ibid.

Chapter 6

1. France, Archives Nationales, F^{19} 11124, Conseil d'État, *Avis sur la question de savoir si les Consistoires israélites peuvent être autorisés à accepter les libéralités*

qui leur sont faites en vue de fondation ou d'entretien d'écoles et d'établissements de bienfaisance, April 8, 1886.

2. France, CP, AA.7, *Procès-verbaux du Consistoire de Paris: Délibération,* May 27, 1884.

3. René Rémond, *L'anticléricalisme en France de 1815 à nos jours* (Paris, 1976), 171–72. John McManners offers a similar interpretation. The anticlerical strategy, in his view, enabled the Republicans to take revenge upon the church while simultaneously disarming a potent political opponent. *Church and State in France: 1870–1914* (New York, 1972), 44.

4. The origins and conduct of Third Republic anticlericalism have attracted a considerable amount of historical attention. A significant portion of existing scholarship focuses on either the ideologies of the different parties or the detailed political strategizing that led to the Law of Separation. This body of literature also emphasizes the pre-occupation of Third Republic anticlerical politicians with the assertion of secular political power. See, for example, Adrien Dansette, *Histoire religieuse de la France contemporaine: L'église catholique dans la mêlée politique et sociale* (Paris, 1965); Evelyn Acomb, *The French Laic Laws* (New York, 1967); McManners, *Church and State in France: 1870–1914;* Malcolm O. Partin, *Waldeck-Rousseau, Combes, and the Church: The Politics of Anti-Clericalism, 1899–1905* (Durham, N.C., 1969); Pierre Chevallier, *La séparation de l'église et de l'école* (Paris, 1981); Jacques Gadille, "On French Anticlericalism: Some Reflections," *European Studies Review* 13, no. 2 (1983): 127–44; Maurice Larkin, *Church and State after the Dreyfus Affair* (New York, 1974); Philip Bertocci, *Jules Simon: Republican Anticlericalism and Cultural Politics in France, 1848–1886* (Columbia, 1978); Pierre Barral, *Jules Ferry: un volonté pour la République* (Nancy, 1985). The other main prong of the literature concentrates on the anticlerical campaign's program for secularizing the schools. In addition to Chevallier, see, for example, Sarah Curtis, *Educating the Faithful: Religion, Schooling, and Society in Nineteeth-Century France;* Curtis, "Persécution et résistance: les congregations enseignantes face à la loi sur les associations de 1901," *Revue d'histoire de l'église de France* 88, no. 220 (2002): 175–95; Paul Gerbod, "De l'influence du catholicisme sur les stratégies éducatives des régimes politiques français de 1806 à 1906," in *L'offre d'école: éléments pour une étude comparée des politiques éducatives au XIXe siècle,* ed. Willem Frijhoff (Paris, 1983), 233–43; Yves Poutet, "Les Frères des écoles chrétiennes à l'époque de Jules Ferry: leur politique scolaire à travers le monde, 1869–1903," in *L'offre d'école,* 285–307.

5. France, Archives Nationales, F^{17} 9125, *Circulaire,* November 2, 1882. The law of March 28, 1882, laicized the French primary schools. Henceforth, religious teaching would have no place in the general school program and teaching personnel would have to possess civil certification in order to fill a post. Both provisions aimed at restricting the activities of teaching orders such as the Christian Brothers who, as stated previously, figured prominently in the primary school systems of many localities.

6. Grew and Harrigan, *School, State, and Society,* 210–12. The numbers they cite are the French government figures compiled in the *Statistique de l'enseignement.*

7. This line of reasoning echoed the argument raised by the author of the *note* of 1841, who had railed against the shortcomings of the secular curriculum at the École Rabbinique at Metz based upon the fact that the school's budget came largely from the French Treasury. See chapter 3 above.

8. McManners, *Church and State in France,* 45.

9. Anne Bonzon-Leizerovici, "La fabrique: une institution locale originale dans la France de l'Ancien Régime," *Historiens et Géographes* 341 (1993): 275.

10. J. J. Weiss, "La fin d'une institution," *Révue de France,* September 1879, 29; cited in Vincent Wright, "L'épuration du Conseil d'État," *Révue d'histoire moderne et contemporaine* 19, no. 4 (1972): 627.

11. Wright, "L'épuration du Conseil d'État," 626–27.

12. *Le Conseil d'État: son histoire à travers les documents de l'époque, 1799–1974* (Paris, 1974), 599–607; Wright, "L'épuration du Conseil d'État," 621–53, *passim*. For an overview of the political evolution of the Conseil, see Brigitte Basdevant-Gaudemet, *Le jeu concordataire dans la France du XIXe siècle: le clergé devant le Conseil d'État* (Paris, 1988), 17–20.

13. Wright, "L'épuration du Conseil d'État," 631–33, 645–47.

14. France, Bibliothéque du Conseil d'État (hereafter BCE), Conseil d'État, Section de l'Intérieur, de l'Instruction Publique, des Beaux-Arts et des Cultes, *Procès-verbal, Annèxes,* April 13, 1881.

15. Ibid. Laws dating from the days of the Consulate and First Empire had delineated these limits. The relevant regulations cited in the report were Article 76 of the Law of 18 Germinal an X [1808] and Article 1 of an imperial decree of December 30, 1809.

16. Ibid.

17. Ibid.

18. Ibid.

19. France, BCE, Conseil d'État, Section de l'Intérieur, de l'Instruction Publique, des Beaux-Arts et des Cultes, *Procès-verbal, annèxes,* June 1, 1881.

20. France, BCE, Conseil d'État, Section de l'Intérieur, de l'Instruction Publique, des Beaux-Arts et des Cultes, *Procès-verbal, annèxes,* May 25, 1881. Flourens was the Director General of the Ministry of Religions. He was also the brother of the radical politician Gustave Flourens, and had been named to the *Conseil* in the Republican purge of the body in July 1879. See Wright, "L'épuration du Conseil d'État," 633.

21. France, BCE, Conseil d'État, Section de l'Intérieur, de l'Instruction Publique, des Beaux-Arts et des Cultes, *Procès-verbal, annèxes,* May 25, 1881.

22. Chevallier, *La séparation de l'église et de l'école,* 284.

23. For an examination of the centrality of *laïcité* in Ferry's program and the political battles that the concept engendered, see Chevallier, ibid., 283–341.

24. Demnard and Fourment, ed., *Dictionnaire d'histoire de l'enseignement,* 309–10.

25. Narcisse Leven (1833–1915) was a lawyer who began his career as a republican political activist during the 1848 revolution in France. He later became a trusted assistant to Adolphe Cremieux, the Minister of Justice during the Second Repub-

lic. Leven was also active in Jewish communal affairs, serving as member of the Consistory and as president of the *Alliance Israélite Universelle* from 1898 to 1915. Paul Silberman, "An Investigation of the Schools Operated by the Alliance Israelite Universelle from 1862–1940," Ph.D. diss., New York University, 1973, 39–40.

26. France, CP, AA.9., *Procès-verbaux du Consistoire de Paris,* November 8, 1881.

27. Flourens, Conseiller d'État, Directeur Général des Cultes to the Consistoire Central, May 18, 1881, Archives Nationales, F^{19} 11141; Maire du Neuvième Arrondissement de Paris to the Préfet de la Seine, January 11, 1881, Archives Nationales, F^{19} 11141.

28. France, Archives Nationales, F^{19} 11141, *Delibération prise par le Consistoire de Paris,* October 18, 1880.

29. This law reorganized the Consistory, and redefined some its functions. See Albert, *Modernization of French Jewry,* 66–77, 196–97, 214–19.

30. Directeur du Cabinet et du Personnel, Chargé par intérim de la Direction de l'Administration Départementale et Communale to Flourens, Conseiller d'État, Directeur Général des Cultes, July 30, 1881, Archives Nationales, F^{19} 11141.

31. France, Archives Nationales, F^{19} 11141, Conseil d'État, *Extrait du registre des délibérations de la Section de l'Intérieur, des Cultes, de l'Instruction publique et des Beaux-Arts,* November 16, 1881.

32. For a general overview of the law's provisions, see Françoise Mayeur, *Histoire générale de l'enseignement et de l'éducation en France,* vol. 3, 540–42; and Félix Ponteil, *Histoire de l'enseignement, 1789–1965* (Paris, 1965), 290.

33. France, CP, AA.7, *Procès-verbaux du Consistoire de Paris: Délibération,* May 27, 1884, 89.

34. France, Archives Nationales, F^{17} 11049, Léonce Lehmann, *Memoire pour le Consistoire Israélite de Paris,* 1884.

35. Ibid.

36. France, BCE, Conseil d'État, Section de l'Intérieur, de l'Instruction Publique, des Beaux-Arts et des Cultes, *Procès-verbal, annèxes,* vol. 1, March 25, 1886.

37. Bonthoux had also joined the Conseil in the Republican turnover of the body in July 1879. See Wright, "L'épuration du Conseil d'État," 634.

38. France, BCE, Conseil d'État, Section de l'Intérieur, de l'Instruction Publique, des Beaux-Arts et des Cultes, *Procès-verbal, annèxes,* vol. 1, May 25, 1886.

39. Ibid.
40. Ibid.
41. Ibid.
42. Ibid.
43. Ibid.
44. Ibid.
45. Ibid.
46. Ibid.
47. Ibid.

48. The Consistory, of course, had never framed the issue in quite the same way. In its view, as we have seen, the state's assumption of the Jewish religious budget

NOTES TO CHAPTER 6

had not *established* Jewish religious equality; rather, it had *acknowledged* the equality that already existed under the law.

49. See chapter 4 above.

50. France, BCE, Conseil d'État, Section de l'Intérieur, de l'Instruction Publique, des Beaux-Arts et des Cultes, *Procès-verbal, annèxes,* vol. 1, May 25, 1886.

51. France, Archives Nationales, F^{19} 11124, Conseil d'État, *Avis sur la question de savoir si les Consistoires israélites peuvent être autorisés à accepter les libéralités qui leur sont faites en vue de fondation ou d'entretien d'écoles et d'établissements de bienfaisance,* April 8, 1886.

52. G. Bihourd, Conseiller d'État et Directeur de l'administration départmentale et communale, Ministère de l'Intérieur to the Préfet de Meurthe-et-Moselle, March 17, 1886, Archives Nationales, F^{19} 11127.

53. Ibid.

54. Alfred Fould, Président du Consistoire de Nancy to the Préfet de Meurthe-et-Moselle, October 12, 1886, Archives Nationales, F^{19} 11127.

55. Préfet de Meurthe-et-Moselle to the Ministre de l'Intérieur, March 29, 1887, Archives Nationales, F^{19} 11127.

56. France, Archives Nationales, F^{19} 11159, Jules Grévy, Président de la République, *Décret,* May 26, 1887. Apparently, this last provision posed no difficulty since the money was intended for individuals rather than institutions.

57. France, Archives Nationales, F^{19} 11124, Conseil d'État, *Extrait du registre des Délibérations de la Section de l'Intérieur, de l'Instruction Publique, des Beaux-Arts et des Cultes,* April 13, 1886.

58. France, Archives Nationales, F^{19} 11124, Conseil d'État, Section de l'Intérieur, de l'Instruction Publique, des Beaux-Arts et des Cultes, *Note,* April 13, 1886.

59. Ministre de l'Instruction publique et des Cultes to the Ministre de l'Intérieur, May 11, 1886, Archives Nationales, F^{19} 11124.

60. France, Archives Nationales, F^{19} 11124, Conseil d'État, Section de l'Intérieur, de l'Instruction Publique, des Beaux-Arts et des Cultes, *Note,* April 13, 1886.

61. France, Archives Nationales, F^{19} 11017, Administration des Cultes, *Note sur l'organisation et le rôle du Consistoire Central des Israélites de France,"* January 29, 1904.

62. Isidore Cahen, "Chambre des députés," *Archives israélites* 44, no. 48 (November 29, 1883): 381–82. A lawyer and political journalist, Roche had written for Georges Clémenceau's journal *La Justice.* See Félix Ribeyre, *La nouvelle chambre, 1889–1893: biographie des 576 députés* (Paris, 1890), 508–9.

63. Isidore Cahen, "Chambre des députés," *Archives israélites* 44, no. 48 (November 29, 1883): 381–82.

64. Ibid.

65. Stephen Wilson, *Ideology and Experience* (Toronto, 1982), 537. For the perils of being a Jewish anticlerical politician, see Pierre Birnbaum, *Les fous de la République,* 162–66 and 169–71. For an example of antisemitic lines of argument, see Arthur Meyer, *Ce que mes yeux ont vu* (Paris, 1911), 123–24, 128, 130.

66. Isidore Cahen, "Chambre des députés," *Archives israélites* 44, no. 48 (November 29, 1883): 381–82.

67. France, Archives Nationales, F[19] 11090, *Rapport fait au nom de la Commission du budget chargée d'examiner le projet de loi portant fixation du budget général de l'exercice 1885 [partie relative au service des cultes],* October 20, 1884 (appendix to the *procès-verbal* of the session of October 20, 1884).

68. "Le budget du séminaire israélite," *Univers israélite* 40, no. 6 (December 1, 1884): 180.

69. France, CC, 4.H.3, 1, *Note contre la suppression proposée par la commission du budget.* The *Univers israélite* published the memorandum in its entirety. See "Le budget du séminaire israélite," 180–83.

70. Ibid., 181.

71. Ibid, 182.

72. Ben Mosché, "Culte: le budget du culte israélite au Sénat," *Archives israélites* 46, no. 10 (March 5, 1885): 75–76.

73. Edmond de Pressensé (1821–94) was a religious scholar and historian as well as a politician. He clearly spelled out his moderate views on anticlerical issues in the preface to an intellectual history that he published in 1882: "Throughout my entire public career I have steadily advocated the complete enfranchisement of conscience, and for this I shall ever plead. . . . I shall be truly happy if this book . . . do[es] something to dispel the fatal misconception that science and conscience, liberty and religion, are incompatible. Such an error may be fatal to the life of a country and a people." *A Study of Origins; or the Problems of Knowledge, of Being, and of Duty* (New York, 1884), xii–xiii.

74. Ben Mosché, "Culte: le budget du culte israélite au Sénat," *Archives israélites* 46, no. 10 (March 5, 1885): 75–76.

75. Ibid.

76. Ben Mosché, "Le budget du culte à la Chambre," *Archives israélites* 46, no. 12 (March 19, 1885): 91.

77. Ministre de la Justice et des Cultes to the Consistoire Central, March 21, 1885, Archives Nationales, F[19] 11090; Consistoire Central to the Ministre de la Justice et des Cultes, March 29, 1885, Archives Nationales, F[19] 11090.

78. Consistoire Central to the Ministre de la Justice et des Cultes, March 29, 1885, Archives Nationales, F[19] 11090.

79. Lazare Wogue, "Le budget des cultes," *Univers Israélite* 41, no. 18 (June 1, 1886): 567–68.

80. McManners, *Church and State in France, 1870–1914,* 141.

81. France, Archives Nationales, F[19] 11090, *Note sur la réduction et la répartition nouvelle . . . du crédits affectés par le Chapître 29 du Budget des Cultes (exercice 1885) aux Indemnités pour frais d'administration des Consistoire israélites,* October 26, 1885.

82. Ben Mosché, "Le Budget du Culte à la Chambre," *Archives israélites* 46, no. 12 (March 19, 1885): 91.

83. Harvard University, Lamont Library, *Rapport du comité de la caisse de la communauté* May 15, 1877, Film A 300.102; Ben-Mosché, "Culte: le Rapport du Consistoire Israélite de Paris," *Archives israélites* 41, no. 27 (July 7, 1881): 229–30.

84. France, CP, AA.6, *Procès-verbaux du Consistoire de Paris,* November 16, 1880.

85. France, CP, AA.6, *Procès-verbaux du Consistoire de Paris: réunion du Consistoire avec le comité de la caisse de la communauté,* April 8, 1882.

86. France, CP, AA.7, *Procès-verbaux du Consistoire de Paris,* February 16, 1887.

87. Ibid.

88. See, for example, the incidents cited by Albert, *Modernization of French Jewry,* 177–82, and 238–39.

89. Directeur de l'Assistance Publique [pour le Ministre de l'Intérieur] to the Ministre de l'Instruction publique, des Beaux-Arts, et des Cultes, July 29, 1887, Archives Nationales, F^{19} 11124.

90. Consistoire Central to the Ministre de l'Instruction publique, des Beaux-Arts, et des Cultes, September 12, 1887, Archives Nationales, F^{19} 11124.

91. Ministre des Cultes to the Ministre de l'Intérieur, September 26, 1887, Archives Nationales, F^{19} 11124; Archives Nationales, F^{19} 11124.*Décret,* no. 48, October 1887, Président de la République.

92. Ibid.

93. France, Archives Nationales, *Délibération prise par le Consistoire Israélite de Paris,* May 20, 1889.

Chapter 7

1. France, CP, AA.9, *Procès-verbaux du Consistoire de Paris,* November 26, 1903.

2. Ibid., January 28, 1904.

3. Grew and Harrigan, *School, State, and Society,* 211.

4. Ibid., 210.

5. Gaston Cadoux, *Les finances de la ville de Paris de 1798 à 1900* (Paris, 1900), 640.

6. Léon Kahn, *Histoire des écoles communales et consistoriales israélites de Paris (1809–1884)* (Paris, 1884), 71–72.

7. Théodore Reinach, "Instruction Publique: l'instruction élémentaire chez les juifs," *Archives israélites* 46, no. 5 (January 29, 1885): 37–38.

8. France, CP, F4, *Liste des Élèves de la classe de l[école de] la rue Lafayette, Garçons, 2ème classe, année scolaire 1883–84.*

9. France, CC, F5, *Procès-verbaux de la Comité d'Inspection des Écoles Consistoriales de Paris,* January 17, 1888.

10. For a good summary of the philanthropic relationship between immigrant and "native" Jews in Paris during the nineteenth century, see Nancy L. Green, "Jewish Migrations to France in the Nineteenth and Twentieth Centuries: Community or Communities?" *Studia Rosenthaliana* 23, no. 2 (1989): 140–46.

11. Moody, *French Education Since Napoleon,* 87–99; George Chase, "Ferdinand Buisson and Salvation by National Education," in *L'offre d'école: éléments pour une étude comparée des politiques éducatives au XIXe siècle,* ed. Willem Frijhoff (Paris, 1983), 263–75.

12. As Lee Shai Weissbach has concluded, Jewish apprenticeship programs during the Third Republic constituted "as much a part of a larger French social action movement as they were a manifestation of the Jewish desire for respectability and acceptance." Lee Shai Weissbach, "The Jewish Elite and the Children of the Poor: Jewish Apprenticeship Programs in Nineteenth-Century France," *Association of Jewish Studies Review* 12, no. 1 (1987): 123–42. The results achieved by French technical education and apprenticeship programs have received differing assessments from historians. Joseph Moody has argued that in the years before World War I, French technical education produced adequate numbers of "middle level industrial personnel." Robert Gildea, however, concludes that "[t]echnical education . . . was less to modernise than to pick up the pieces after rapid economic change . . . the aims of educators and the aims of employers were not always identical; and *déclassement* was increased rather than diminished." See Moody, *French Education Since Napoleon,* 99–104; Gildea, "The Agonies of Modernisation: Some Problems of Technical Education, 1870–1914," in *L'offre d'école,* 223–29.

13. France, CP, F4, École de la rue Lafayette, *Emploi de Temps, garçons du 1ère classe, 1882–1883* and *Emploi de Temps, filles du 1ère classe, 1882–1883*. The Ferry Law of March 28, 1882, had mandated needlework classes for girls in all public schools. It also ordered military exercises for boys. These exercises were instituted at both the Jewish communal schools and eventually at the consistorial schools as well. Such vocational training was designed to prepare these poorer children for eventual entry into an industrializing workforce. See Jeanne Brody, "L'école de la rue des Hospitalières-Saint-Gervais: pratique religieuse et école laïque," 57; also CP, F4, *Procès verbaux de la Comité des Écoles [du Consistoire de Paris],* September 22, 1885.

14. CP, F4, *Procès verbaux de la Comité des Écoles [du Consistoire de Paris],* September 22, 1885. According to an 1885 inspection report, however, Hebrew instruction was limited to a "mnemonic [method] for the translation of the principle texts of the ritual and Pentateuch." France, CP, F4, M. Salomon, *Rapport au président du Comité des écoles consistoriales,* November 5, 1885.

15. France, CP, F4, *Emploi de Temps, classe des garçons [1ère classe], 1882–1883 pour l'École de la rue Claude Bernard,* February 4, 1883; and *Emploi de Temps, classe des garçons, 1ère classe, 1882–1883 pour l'École de l'avenue Ségur,* 1883.

16. After the loss of Alsace-Lorraine in 1871, Paris came to have the largest Jewish population in France. Its numbers rose by additional thousands with the arrival of the Eastern European immigrants between 1881 and 1914. Nancy Green has compiled a composite table drawn from different studies which outlines the growth of both French and Parisian Jewry. See her article, "Jewish Migrations to France in the Nineteenth and Twentieth Centuries: Community or Communities?," 136. For a general estimate of the size of the Jewish immigrant population in Paris during this period, see Green's appendix to her *The Pletzl of Paris: Jewish Immigrant Workers in the Belle Époque,* 203–4. Green outlines the difficulties of arriving at any exact population figure due to the lack of accurate record-keeping on the subject, and therefore draws her inferences from a number of different sources. Nevertheless, it seems safe to say that the immigrants added at least 15,000 souls to a Parisian

Jewish population that grew from more than 25,000 in 1872 to more than 45,000 by 1897.

17. France, Archives Nationales, F^{19} 11002, *Décret no. 12,* January 21, 1879. This *décret* authorized the Paris Consistory to accept the donation from Baron Gustave Samuel James de Rothschild of a site on the rue des Feuillantines, where the new school would be constructed. The *comité des écoles* alternately referred to this school as "l'École Gustave de Rothschild" or "l'école à la rue Claude Bernard."

18. France, CC, F5, Comité des Écoles Consistoriales de Paris, *État numérique des élèves des écoles, 1889.*

19. France, CP, F4, *École de l'Avenue de Ségur: Élèves payants de l'année scolaire 1882–83; École de la rue Claude Bernard: Élèves payants de l'année scolaire 1882–83; École de la rue Lafayette: Élèves payants de l'année scolaire 1882–83;* Fleur, Directeur de l'École de 60 rue Claude Bernard, to the Consistoire Central, January 18, 1883, CP, F4.

20. France, CP, F4, *Projet de budget des écoles pour 1885–1886 [octobre 1, 1885 à septembre 30, 1886],* F4, CP.

21. Ibid.

22. See for example the figures in CP, F4, *Consistoire Israélite de Paris: Projet de budget des écoles pour 1884–1885;* and in CC F7, *Projet de budget des Écoles pour 1894–1895,* June 8, 1894.

23. France, CP, F4, *Consistoire Israélite de Paris: Projet de budget des écoles pour 1884–1885.* Subsequent reports contain the same 8,000f contribution from Rothschild.

24. Ibid; France, CP, F4, Consistoire Israélite de Paris, *Projet du budget des écoles du 1er Octobre 1883 au 30 Septembre 1884;* CC, F5, Comité des Écoles Israélites de Paris, *Projet du budget des Écoles pour 1888–1889,* June 3, 1888.

25. France, CC, F5, Comité des Écoles Israélites de Paris, *Compte générale et définitif de l'exercice 1888–1889,* September 30, 1889.

26. Ibid.

27. France, CP, AA.6, *Procès-verbaux du Consistoire de Paris,* January 3, 1881, 368.

28. Protestant missionaries had a similarly galvanizing effect among Jews in the United States. See Jonathan Sarna, "The Impact of Nineteenth-Century Christian Missions on American Jews," in *Jewish Apostasy in the Modern World,* ed. Todd Endelmann (New York, 1987), 232–54.

29. Zadoc Kahn, *Lettre pastorale,* October 25, 1881, reprinted in *Univers israélite* 37, no. 5 (November 16, 1881): 132–33.

30. Hippolyte Prague, "Questions du jour: la circulaire de M. Ferry," *Archives israélites* 42, no. 7 (February 17, 1881): 51–52.

31. Hippolyte Prague, "La loi sur l'organisation de l'enseignement primaire au Sénat," *Archives israélites* 47, no. 6 (February 11, 1886): 42–43.

32. Ibid.

33. Lazare Wogue, "La question des cimitières," *Univers israélite* 36, no. 17 (May 16, 1881): 523–29.

34. Lazare Wogue, "La loi sur l'enseignement primaire," *Univers israélite* 37, no. 15 (April 16, 1882): 451–55.

35. Ibid.

36. Ibid.

37. France, Archives Nationales, F^{19} 11119, *Délibération du Consistoire de Paris,* March 19, 1879.

38. Avner Ben-Amos, *Funerals, Politics, and Memory in Modern France, 1789–1996* (Oxford, 2000), 18–53.

39. Léon Kahn reports that in 1841, the Consistory decided to implement two ceremonies of *initiation religieuse* for Jewish boys and girls each year: one at the festival of *Pesach* and one at the festival of *Sukkot,* beginning with *Pesach* of 1842. Boys would participate at age thirteen; girls at age twelve. The ceremony took place in the synagogue following the afternoon service on the Saturday of these weeklong festivals. On June 30, 1852, the ceremonies were combined into one, held the Thursday after the holiday of *Shavuot.* Léon Kahn, *Histoire des écoles communales et consistoriales israélites de Paris (1809–1884),* 55n3.

40. France, CP, AA.6, *Procès-verbaux du Consistoire de Paris,* March 4, 1875.

41. Ibid., January 13, 1876.

42. Ibid.

43. The Minister of *Instruction publique* had approved this measure on July 7, 1876. See the margin note on the letter from Dabas, Recteur de l'Académie de Bordeaux, to the Ministre de l'Instruction publique et des Beaux-Arts, July 1, 1876, Archives Nationales, F^{17} 9100. The note reads: "Écrit à M. le Recteur pour autoriser la délivrance des prix, [July 7, 1876]."

44. S. Lévy, Grand rabbin du Consistoire de Bordeaux to Dabas, July 26, 1876, Archives Nationales, F^{17} 9100.

45. Ministre de l'Instruction publique et des Beaux-Arts to Dabas, July 26, 1876, Archives Nationales, F^{17} 9100.

46. Ibid., August 10, 1876.

47. S. Lévy, Grand Rabbin du Consistoire de Bordeaux to Dabas, February 9, 1877, Archives Nationales, F^{17} 9100.

48. Dabas to the Ministre de l'Instruction publique et des Beaux-Arts, February 19, 1877, Archives Nationales, F^{17} 9100.

49. France, CP, AA.6, *Procès-verbaux du Consistoire de Paris,* September 26, 1876.

50. Ibid., April 23, 1879.

51. France, CP, AA.7, *Procès-verbaux du Consistoire de Paris,* February 16, 1882.

52. France, CP, AA.7, *Procès-verbaux du Consistoire de Paris: Commission spéciale d'instruction religieuse,* October 12, 1882.

53. Chevallier, Grosperrin, and Maillet, *L'enseignement français de la Révolution à nos jours,* 124.

54. France, CP, AA.7, *Procès-verbaux du Consistoire de Paris,* June 20, 1882.

55. Lazare Wogue, "La loi sur l'enseignement primaire," *Univers israélite* 37, no. 15 (April 16, 1882): 451–55.

56. Ben Schemouel, "Chronique de la Semaine," *Archives israélites* 43, no. 14 (April 7, 1882): 106–7.

57. Details concerning the final resolution of the matter remain somewhat murky. In June 1882, the Paris Consistory asked the Central Consistory to take up the issue with the Conseil Supérieur de l'Instruction Publique. Jeanne Brody notes that while the minutes of the Conseil acknowledge receipt of such a petition from the Consistory on June 28, they contain no further commentary or discussion regarding the question. From this evidence she concludes that "this suggestion or a variation of it was adopted, which would explain the distinctiveness of [the school on the rue des Hospitalières-Saint-Gervais], the memory of which its former students have retained." Jeanne Brody, "L'école de la rue des Hospitalières-Saint-Gervais: pratique religieuse et école laïque," 57–59.

58. France, CP, AA.7, *Procès-verbaux du Consistoire de Paris,* June 20, 1882. In fact, subsequent events indicate that the public declaration was little more than an attempt to appease two divergent camps of Jewish opinion. The more traditional contingent of French Judaism, such as Lazare Wogue, argued that separate Jewish schools offered the best chance of cultivating religious commitment among French Jews. On the other side stood those such as Narcisse Leven, who emphasized the practical advantages of programs of religious education.

59. Zadoc Kahn, *Rapport présenté au Consistoire israélite de Paris,* October 12, 1881, reprinted in *Univers israélite* 37, no. 5 (November 16, 1881): 133–34.

60. Ibid., 136.

61. France, CP, AA.7, *Procès-verbaux du Consistoire de Paris,* February 14, 1883.

62. Ibid., October 29, 1885.

63. Ibid., January 19, 1885.

64. Ibid., November 16, 1886.

65. Ibid., December 29, 1887.

66. France, CP, AA.8, *Procès-verbaux du Consistoire de Paris,* April 4, 1892.

67. The course at the École de Travail on the rue des Rosiers offered five different levels of classes for both boys and girls alike. At the rue des Tournelles, boys met in six divisions and girls in five. David Haguenau still taught his classes for boys at the synagogue on the rue Notre Dame de Nazareth and another for girls met at the rue Nicolet. France, CC, F7, *Projet de budget des écoles pour 1894–1895,* June 8, 1894.

68. France, CP, AA.7, *Procès-verbaux du Consistoire de Paris,* February 14, 1883.

69. France, CC, F7, *Projet de budget des écoles pour 1894–1895,* Comité des Écoles Consistoriales, June 8, 1894.

70. France, CC, F8, *Projet de budget des écoles pour 1898–1899,* June 5, 1898.

71. France, CP, F8, *Résumé des rapports de Messieurs les Rabbins de Paris,* 1898.

72. Kahn to the Consistoire de Paris, October 12, 1898, CC, F8.

73. France, CP, F8, *Résumé des rapports de Messieurs les Rabbins de Paris,* 1898.

74. Ibid., and M. le Rabbin Raphaël Lévy to the Consistoire de Paris, May 22, 1898, CP, F8.

75. Julien Weill to Zadoc Kahn, February 10, 1898, CP, F8.

76. Ibid.

77. Ibid.
78. Kahn to the Consistoire de Paris, October 12, 1898, CC, F8.
79. Rabbi Israél Lévi to the *Grand rabbin* of Paris, June 20, 1898, CC, F8.
80. Rabbi David Haguenau to J. H. Dreyfuss, June, 1898, CP, F8.
81. Weill to Dreyfuss, June 19, 1898, CC, F8.
82. Weill to Kahn, February 10, 1898, CP, F8.
83. CP, AA.9, *Procès-verbaux du Consistoire de Paris,* May 28, 1903.

Chapter 8

1. France, Archives Nationales, F^{19} 11027, Copie du rapport présenté au Consistoire de Paris par la commission administrative du Séminaire Israélite sur un nouveau projet de réglement et sur un nouveau programme d'études du Séminaire, September 15, 1879.
2. Ibid.
3. Ibid.
4. Consistoire Central to the Minister de l'Instruction Publique et des Cultes, January 13, 1860, Archives Nationales, F^{19} 11027.
5. France, Archives Nationales, F^{19} 11027, *Note pour Messieurs les Membres de la Commission du budget,* June 1884.
6. France, CC, 2.H.2, 2, *Procès verbal d'examine pour l'obtention du diplôme rabbinique* (undated, but ca. 1860s).
7. France, Archives Nationales, F^{19} 11027, *Rapport sur la situation morale et financière du Séminaire pendant l'exercice 1860,* February 9, 1861.
8. Ibid.
9. France, Archives Nationales, F^{19} 11027, Consistoire Israélite de Paris, *Séminaire Israélite: Projet de budget, 1860.*
10. France, Archives Nationales, F^{19} 11027, *Budget du Séminaire Israélite pour l'exercice 1862,* November 19, 1861.
11. France, Archives Nationales, F^{19} 11027, *Séminaire Israélite: Projet du budget pour l'exercice 1866,* December 19, 1865.
12. France, CC, 3.H.1, *Projet du budget pour l'exercice 1867,* December 18, 1866.
13. Ministre de la Justice et des Cultes to the Consistoire Central, March 24, 1885, CC, 4.H.3.1. Also see Bauer, *L'École rabbinique de France,* 154.
14. France, CP, AA.7, *Procès-verbaux du Consistoire de Paris,* April 2, 1885.
15. France, CC, 2.H.2, I, *Circulaire,* June, 1887.
16. Consistoire Central to the Consistoire de Paris, April, 1887, CC, 4.H.3, 1. France, CP, AA.7, *Procès verbaux du Consistoire de Paris,* February 16, 1887.
17. France, CC, 2.H.2, I, *Circulaire,* June, 1887.
18. France, CP, AA.8, *Procès-verbaux du Consistoire de Paris,* January 19, 1899.
19. Ibid.
20. Ibid.
21. France, CP, AA.8, *Procès-verbaux du Consistoire de Paris,* February 16, 1899. Actually, the seminary already accepted foreign students. In his 1896 annual report,

Director Joseph Lehmann reported the presence of two Russians, one *palestinien,* one Turk, and one Bulgarian among the seminary's students. Only three of these five—the Russian, the Turk, and the Bulgarian—were seeking French nationality, implying that the other two intended to return to their countries of origin upon completing their training. France, CC, 3.H.1, *Rapport à la commission administrative du Séminaire, 1896.*

22. France, CC, 2.H.2, 1, *Circulaire,* March, 1899; France, CP, AA.8, *Procès-verbaux du Consistoire de Paris,* November 23, 1899.

23. France, CC, 2.H.2, 1, *Circulaire,* October, 1901.

24. France, F^{19} 11027, *Copie du rapport présenté au Consistoire de Paris par la commission administrative du Séminaire israélite sur un nouveau projet de réglement et sur un nouveau programme d'études du Séminaire,* September 15, 1879.

25. Ibid.

26. Ibid.

27. The Séminaire Israélite thus put a particular French gloss on the Modern Orthodox concept of *Torah im Derekh Eretz.* See, for example, David Ellenson, *Rabbi Asriel Hildesheimer and the Creation of a Modern Jewish Orthodoxy* (Tuscaloosa, 1990), 115–65.

28. Consistoire Central to the Ministre de l'Intérieur et des Cultes, January 12, 1880, Archives Nationales, F^{19} 11027.

29. Ibid.

30. Ibid.

31. France, CC, F5, Albert Lévy, *Monographies pédagogiques no. 55, l'enseignement privé: Écoles israélites,* March 1889. This document is an unbound manuscript.

32. Consistoire Central to the Ministre de la Justice et des Cultes, December 6, 1892, Archives Nationales, F^{19} 11027.

33. Albert Lévy, *Monographies pédagogiques no. 55, l'enseignement privé: Écoles israélites.*

34. Ministre de la Justice et des Cultes to the Consistoire Central, December 30, 1892, Archives Nationales, F^{19} 11027.

35. France, CP, AA.6, *Procès-verbaux du Consistoire de Paris,* July 2, 1874.

36. Ibid.

37. France, Archives Nationales, F^{19} 11027, *Rapport sur la situation morale et financière du Séminaire Israélite pendant les Exercices 1878 à 1883,* February 17, 1884.

38. Bauer, *L'École rabbinique de France,* 170.

39. See chapter 4 above.

40. Albert Lévy, *Monographies pédagogiques no. 55, l'enseignement privé: Écoles israélites.*

41. Ibid.

42. *Licencé* refers to a person who has completed a four-year University degree. *Agregé* refers to one who has passed the *agrégation,* the examination required of secondary school faculty. The title of *agregé* is still prestigious in French academic circles.

43. Albert Lévy, *Monographies pédagogiques no. 55, l'enseignement privé: Écoles israélites.*

44. France, Archives Nationales, F¹⁹ 11027, *Note pour Messieurs les Membres de la Commission du budget,* June 1884 , F¹⁹ 11027.

45. Consistoire Central to Rouland, Ministre de l'Instruction publique et des Cultes, February 12, 1889, Archives Nationales, F¹⁹ 11026.

46. *Univers israélite* 60, part 1 (September 30, 1904–March 30, 1905): 208.

Conclusion

1. David Sorkin, *The Transformation of German Jewry, 1780–1840* (New York, 1987), 39.

2. Ibid., 174–76.

3. Berkovitz, *Rites and Passages,* 238.

4. Katy Hazan, "Du *heder* aux écoles actuelles: l'éducation juive, reflet d'un destin collectif," *Archives juives* 35, no. 2 (2002): 7.

5. Owen Chadwick, *The Secularization of the European Mind in the Nineteenth Century* (Cambridge, 1990), 162–63.

6. Berkovitz, *Rites and Passages,* 166–67.

7. Joseph F. Byrnes, *Catholic and French Forever: Religious and National Identity in Modern France* (State College, Pa., 2005), 68.

8. See chapter 6.

9. This idea echoes Lisa Moses Leff's conclusions regarding Jewish solidarity, connoting a sense of "belonging to a French citizen body . . . sharing a set of moral sentiments," while equating "expressions of 'Jewish solidarity' as a fulfillment of their duties as French citizens." Lisa Moses Leff, "Jewish Solidarity in Nineteenth-Century France: The Evolution of a Concept," *Journal of Modern History* 74, no. 1 (2002): 35.

10. Birnbaum, *Jewish Destinies,* 252–59.

11. Moses Mendelssohn, *Jerusalem, or on Religious Power and Judaism,* trans. Alan Arkush (Hanover, N.H., 1983), 138–39.

12. Excerpted in Frances Malino, *A Jew in the French Revolution,* 49.

Bibliography

Primary Sources

Archives Nationales, Paris
Series F^{19}, Instruction Publique
Series F^{17}, Cultes
Bibliothèque du Conseil d'État
Procès-verbaux, bound volumes, organized chronologically
Archives du Consistoire Central, Paris
Archives du Consistoire de Paris
Brandeis University
French Document Section, Special Collections, Goldfarb Library
Jewish Theological Seminary, New York
French Document Record Group
Cadoux, Gaston. *Les finances de la ville de Paris de 1798 à 1900.* Paris: 1900.
Halphen, Achille-Edmond. *Recueil de lois, décrets, ordonnances, avis du Conseil d'État, arrêtés et règlements concernant les Israélites depuis la Révolution de 1789.* Paris: Wittersheim, 1851.
Kahn, Zadoc. *Sermons et allocutions: adressés à la jeunesse israélite.* Paris: Blum, 1878.
Meyer, Arthur. *Ce que mes yeux ont vu.* Paris: Plon, 1911.
Trénel, Isaac. *Rapport sur la situation morale du séminaire israélite.* Paris: Louis-Guérin, 1867.
Uhry, Isaac. *Recuil des lois, décrets, ordonnances, avis du Conseil d'État, arrêtés et règlements concernant les Israélites depuis 1850.* Bordeaux: Crugy, 1887.
Weill, Alexandre. *Le centenaire de l'emancipation.* Paris, 1888.

Periodicals

Les Archives israélites de France
L'Univers israélite

Reference Works

Choppin, Alain, ed. *Les manuels scolaires en France de 1789 à nos jours—Latin.* Paris: Publications de la Sorbonne, 1988.
Zimmerman, Marie. *Church and State in France: Book Index 1801–1979.*

BIBLIOGRAPHY

Secondary Sources

Albert, Phyllis Cohen. "Ethnicity and Jewish Solidarity in Nineteenth-Century France." In *Mystics, Philosophers, and Politicians: Essays in Jewish Intellectual History in Honor of Alexander Altman,* ed. Jehuda Reinharz and Daniel Swetschinski, 249–74. Durham, N.C.: Duke University Press, 1982.

———. "Israelite and Jew: How Did Nineteenth-Century French Jews Understand Assimilation?" In *Assimilation and Community: The Jews in Nineteenth-Century Europe,* ed. Jonathan Frankel and Steven Zipperstein, 88–109. Cambridge: Cambridge University Press, 1992.

———. "L'intégration et la persistence de l'ethnicité chea les juifs dans la France moderne." In *Histoire politique des juifs de France: entre universalisme et particularisme,* ed. Pierre Birnbaum, 221–43. Paris: Presses de la Fondation nationale des sciences politiques, 1990.

———. *The Modernization of French Jewry: Consistory and Community in the Nineteenth Century.* Hanover, N.H.: Brandeis University Press, 1977.

———. "Nonorthodox Attitudes in Nineteenth-Century French Judaism." In *Essays in Modern Jewish History: A Tribute to Ben Halpern,* ed. Frances Malino and Phyllis Cohen Albert, 121–41. East Brunswick, N.J.: Associated University Presses, 1982.

———. "The Right to be Different: Interpretations of the French Revolution's Promises to the Jews." *Modern Judaism* 12 (1992): 243–57.

Albisetti, James. "The Debate on Secondary School Reform in France and Germany." In *The Rise of the Modern Educational System,* ed. Fritz Ringer, Detlef Mueller, and Brian Simon, 181–96. Cambridge: Cambridge University Press, 1987.

Allen, Edward. "The 'Patriot' *Curés* of 1789 and the 'Constitutional' *curés* of 1791: A Comparison." *Church History* 54 (December 1985): 473–81.

Allier, Raoul, et al. *La séparation des églises et de l'État.* Suresnes: Ernest Payen, 1905.

Anchel, Robert. *Notes sur les frais du culte juif en France de 1815 à 1831.* Paris: Hemmerlé, Petit, 1928.

Anderson, Robert D. "The Conflict in Education: Catholic Secondary Schools (1850–70)." In *Conflicts in French Society,* ed. Theodore Zeldin, 51–93. London: George Allen, 1970.

———. *Education in France, 1848–1870.* Oxford: Clarendon Press, 1975.

———. *France, 1870–1914: Politics and Society.* London: Routledge and Kegan Paul, 1977.

———. "New Light on French Secondary Education in the Nineteenth Century." *Social History* 7, no. 2 (1982): 147–65.

Aston, Nigel. *Religion and Revolution in France, 1780–1804.* Washington, D.C.: Catholic University of America Press, 2000.

———. "Turbulent Priests? The Church and the Revolution." *History Today* 39 (May 1989): 20–25.

Auspitz, Katherine. *The Radical Bourgeoisie: The Ligue de l'enseignement and the Origins of the Third Republic, 1866–1885.* Cambridge: Cambridge University Press, 1982.

BIBLIOGRAPHY

Ayoun, Richard. "Critères d'une élection rabbinique à Paris en 1847." *Yod* 3, fasc. 1 (1er and 2e trimester, 1977): 23–30.

———. *Typologie d'une carrière rabbinque: l'exemple de Mahir Charleville.* Nancy: Presses Universitaires de Nancy, 1993.

———. "Une nouvelle conception du métier de rabbin: le rabbin consistorial en France au XIX siècle." *Archives juives* 35, no. 2 (2002): 123–27.

Badinter, Robert. *Libres et égaux: l'émancipation des juifs, 1789–1791.* Paris: Fayard, 1989.

Baratay, Eric. "Affaire de moeurs, conflits de pouvoir et anticléricalisme: la fin de la congregation des frères de Saint-Joseph en 1888." *Revue d'histoire de l'église de France* 84, no. 213 (1998): 299–322.

Barker, Ernest. *Church, State, and Education.* Ann Arbor: University of Michigan Press, 1957.

Baron, Salo W. "Church and State Debates in the Jewish Community of 1848." In *The Mordecai Kaplan Jubilee Volume,* ed. Moshe Davis, 49–72. New York: Jewish Theological Seminary, 1953.

———. "Civil vs. Political Emancipation." In *Studies in Jewish Religious and Intellectual History,* ed. Siegfried Stein and Raphael Loewe, 29–49. Tuscaloosa: University of Alabama Press, 1979.

Barral, Pierre. *Jules Ferry: un volonté pour la République.* Nancy: Presses Universitaires de Nancy, 1985.

Basdevant-Gaudemet, Brigitte. "Le concordat de 1801: référence pour une politique concordataire." *Revue d'histoire de l'eglise de France* 87, no. 219 (July-December 2001): 393–413.

———. *Le jeu concordataire dans la France du XIXe siècle: le clergé devant le Conseil d'État.* Paris: Presses Universitaires de France, 1988.

Bauer, Jules. *L'École rabbinique de France, 1830–1930.* Paris: Presses Universitaires, 1930.

Baugey, Georges. *De la condition légale du culte israélite en France et en Algérie.* Paris: Rousseau, 1898.

Baye, Jules. "La condition des Juifs en France depuis 1789." *Révue Napoleonne* 4, no. 7 (July 1909): 14–21.

Bellah, Robert. "Legitimation Processes in Politics and Religion." *Current Sociology* 35, no. 2 (1987): 89–99.

Ben-Amos, Avner. *Funerals, Politics, and Memory in Modern France, 1789–1996.* New York: Oxford University Press, 2000.

———. "The Sacred Center of Power: Paris and Republican State Funerals." *Journal of Interdisciplinary History* 22 (Summer 1991): 27–48.

Benbassa, Esther. *The Jews of France: A History from Antiquity to the Present.* Trans. M. B. DeBevoise. Princeton: Princeton University Press, 1999.

Berenson, Edward. *Populist Religion and Left-Wing Politics in France, 1830–1852.* Princeton: Princeton University Press, 1984.

Berg, Roger. *Histoire du rabbinat français.* Paris: Cerf, 1992.

Berg, Roger, and Marianne Urbah-Bornstein. *Les Juifs devant le droit français: législation et jurisprudence de la fin de la 19e siècle à nos jours.* Paris: Belles Lettres, 1984.

Berger, Shlomo. "For Which Types of Speech Would a Jew Have Studied Greek Rhetoric in Seventeenth-Century Amsterdam?" *Studia Rosenthaliana* 34, no. 2 (2000): 153–67.
Berkovitz, Jay. *Rites and Passages: The Beginnings of Modern Jewish Culture in France, 1650–1860.* Philadelphia: University of Pennsylvania Press, 2004.
———. *The Shaping of Jewish Identity in Nineteenth-Century France.* Detroit: Wayne State University Press, 1989.
Birnbaum, Pierre. *Jewish Destinies: Citizenship, State, and Community in Modern France.* New York: Hill and Wang, 2000.
———. *La France imaginée.* Paris: Fayard, 1998.
———. *Les fous de la République.* Paris: Fayard, 1992.
Blackbourn, David. *Class, Religion, and Local Politics in Wilhelmine Germany.* New Haven: Yale University Press, 1980.
Bloch, Maurice. "L'Oeuvre scolaire des juifs français depuis 1789." In *Quatre conférences sur les juifs*, 167–218. Paris: Fischbacher, 1901.
Blumenkranz, Bernhard, ed. *Histoire des juifs en France.* Toulouse: Privat, 1972.
Bonzon-Leizerovici, Anne. "La fabrique: une institution locale originale dans la France d'Ancien Régime." *Historiens et géographes* 341 (1993): 273–85.
Boudon, Jacques-Olivier. "L'épiscopat français et le développement des hautes études ecclésistique au XIXe siècle." *Revue d'histoire de l'église de France* 81, no. 206 (January–June 1995): 219–35.
Bourricaud, François. "Legitimacy and Legitimization." *Current Sociology* 35, no. 2 (1987): 57–67.
Bousquet, Pierre. "Structures administratives et politique scolaire dans l'enseignement primaire urbain. L'exemple de Paris au XIXe siècle." In *L'offre d'école: elements pour une étude comparée des politiques éducatives au XIXe siècle: actes du troisième colloque international*, Sèvres, September 27–30, 1981, ed. Willem Frijhoff and Michel Boulet, 309–17. Paris: Sorbonne.
Bowen, John R. *Why the French Don't Like Headscarves: Islam, the State, and Public Space.* Princeton: Princeton University Press, 2007.
Brody, Jeanne. *La rue des Rosiers: une manière d'être juif.* Autrement, Paris, 1995.
———. "L'école de la rue des Hospitalières-Saint-Gervais: pratique religieuse et école laïque." *Archives Juives* 28, no. 2 (1995): 49–60.
Burney, John M. "The Church, the Provinces, Local Notables, and the Development of French Education." *History of Education Quarterly* 26, no. 2 (1986): 257–64.
Burns, Michael. *Dreyfus: A Family Affair, 1789–1945.* New York: HarperCollins, 1991.
———. "Majority Faith: Dreyfus before the Affair." In *From East and West: Jews in a Changing Europe, 1750–1870,* ed. Frances Malino and David Sorkin, 56–82. Cambridge: Basil Blackwell, 1990.
Byrnes, Joseph F. *Catholic and French Forever: Religious and National Identity in Modern France.* State College: Pennsylvania State University Press, 2005.
Cadier-Rey, Gabrielle. "Les Protestants, Orthez et l'enseignement: de la loi Guizot aux lois Ferry." *Bulletin de la Société de l'histoire du protestantisme français* 142, no. 4 (October 1996): 737–53.

Cahen, Abraham. "Enseignement obligatoire edicté par la communauté israélite de Metz." *Révue des études juives* 2 (April–June 1881): 303–5.

Cailleau, René. "La toute-puissance de l'éducation: nature et culture selon Helvétius." In *Éducation et pedagogies au siècle des lumières: actes du colloque 1983 de l'Institute des sciences de l'education*. Angers: Presses de l'Université Catholique de l'Ouest, 1985.

Campbell, Stuart. *The Second Empire Revisited: A Study in French Historiography*. New Brunswick: Rutgers University Press, 1978.

Caron, Vicki. *Between France and Germany: The Jews of Alsace-Lorraine, 1871–1918*. Stanford: Stanford University Press, 1988.

"Catholics and Politics in 19th Century Germany [Symposium]." *Central European History* 19 (March 1986): 45–122.

Chadwick, Owen. *The Secularization of the European Mind in the Nineteenth Century*. Cambridge: Cambridge University Press, 1975.

Charle, Christophe. *La république des universitaires, 1870–1940*. Paris: Seuil, 1994.

Chase, George. "Ferdinand Buisson and Salvation by National Education." In *L'offre d'école: éléments pour une étude comparée des politiques éducatives au XIXe siècle*, ed. Willem Frijhoff, 263–75. Paris: Sorbonne, 1983.

Chaumet, Pierre-Olivier. "L'administration française des cultes 'non-reconnus' par l'État au XIXe siècle (1802–1905)." *Revue d'histoire droit* 84, no. 1 (2006): 19–45.

Chevallier, Pierre. *La séparation de l'église et l'école*. Paris: Fayard, 1981.

Chevallier, Pierre, Jean Maillet, and B. Grosperrin, ed. *L'Enseignement français de la Révolution à nos jours*. Paris: Mouton, 1968.

Chouraqui, André. *L'Alliance Israélite Universelle et la renaissance juive contemporaine*. Paris: Presses Universitaires, 1965.

Chouraqui, Jean-Marc. "De l'émancipation des juifs à l'émancipation du judaïsme: le regard des rabbins français du XIXe siècle." In *Histoire politique des juifs en France*, ed. Pierre Birnbaum, 39–57. Paris: Presses de la Fondation Nationale des Sciences Politiques, 1990.

———. "'Echoes de la Chaire': la prédication israélite en France." *Revue des études juives* 150, nos. 1–2 (January–June 1991): 71–105.

———. "Judaïsme traditionel, science et rationalisme: l'exèmple des rabbins français au XIXe siècle." In *Les études juives en France: situation et perspectives*, ed. Frank Alvarez-Pereye and Jean Baumgarten, 33–45. Paris: CNRS, 1990.

———. "La loi du royaume est la loi: les rabbins, la politique et l'État en France (1807–1905)." *Pardes* 2 (1985): 57–98.

———. "Le corps rabbinique et sa prédication en France: problèmes et desseins (1808–1905)." *Histoire, économie et société* 3, no. 2 (1984): 293–320.

Clark, Linda. *Schooling the Daughters of Marianne: Textbooks and the Socialization of Girls in Modern French Primary Schools*. Albany: State University of New York Press, 1984.

Coffey, Joan L. "Of Catechisms and Sermons: Church-State Relations in France, 1890–1905." *Church History* 66, no. 1 (1997): 54–66.

Cohen, David. "La Promotion des juifs en France à l'époque du Second Empire (1852–1870)." Dissertation, Université de Provence, 1980.
Collingham, H.A.C. *The July Monarchy: A Political History of France, 1830–1848*. New York: Longman, 1988.
Conseil d'État, *Le Conseil d'État: son histoire à travers les documents d'époque, 1799–1974*. Paris: Centre National de la Recherche Scientifique, 1974.
Curtis, Sarah A. *Educating the Faithful: Religion, Schooling and Society in Nineteenth-Century France*. Dekalb: Northern Illinois University Press, 2000.
———. "Persécution et résistance: les congregations enseignantes face à la loi sur les associations de 1901." *Revue d'histoire de l'église de France* 88, no. 220 (2002): 175–95.
Dansette, Adrien. *Histoire religieuse de la France contemporaine: L'église catholique dans la mêlée politique et sociale*. Paris: Flammarion, 1965.
Dawson, Christopher. *Religion and the Modern State*. London: Sheed and Ward, 1936.
Delmaire, Danielle, and J. M. Delmaire. "Le rapport entre autorité civile et autorité religieuse dans les communautés juives du Nord au XIXe siècle." In *Mélanges à la memoire de Marcel-Henri Prévost*, 319–29. Paris: Presses Universitaires de France, 1982.
Deloye, Yves. *La citoyeneté au miroir de l'école républicain et de ses contestations: politique et religion en France de 1870 à 1914*. Doctoral dissertation, Université Paris-I, 1991.
Demnard, Dimitri, and Dominique Fourment. *Dictionnaire d'histoire de l'énseignement*. Paris: J.-P. Delarge, 1981.
Desan, Suzanne. "Redefining Revolutionary Liberty: The Rhetoric of Religious Revival during the French Revolution." *Journal of Modern History* 60 (March 1988): 1–27.
Despland, Michael. "Des sciences aux sciences religieuses: la programme d'André-Marie Ampère (1834–1843)." *Revue d'histoire et de philosophie religieuses* 77, no. 1 (1997): 67–69.
———. "A Case of Christians Shifting Their Moral Allegiance: France, 1790–1914." *Journal of the American Academy of Religion* 52 (December 1984): 671–90.
Dietrich, Donald J. "Priests and Political Thought: Theology and Reform in Central Europe, 1845–1855." *Catholic Historical Review* 71 (October 1985): 519–46.
Dohrn, Verena. "The Rabbinical Schools as Institutions of Socialization in Tsarist Russia, 1847–1873." *POLIN* 14 (2001): 83–104.
Elms, Elwyn. "The Conseil d'État and the Religious Communities, 1879–1906." *French History* 16, no. 2 (2002): 174–202.
Elwitt, Sanford. *The Making of the Third Republic: Class Politics in France, 1868–1884*. Baton Rouge: Louisiana State University Press, 1975.
Engelmann, Samuel. *Application au culte israélite de la loi du 9 décembre 1905 et du règlement d'administration publique du 16 mars 1906*. Paris: Weill, 1906.
Englund, Steven. "Church and State in France since the Revolution." *Journal of Church and State* 34 (Spring 1992): 325–61.

Eymard, Jean. "La politique financière sous la Restauration (1815–1830)." Thèse pour le doctorat en droit. Paris: Presses Universitaires de France, 1924.

Farr, Ian. "From AntiCatholicism to Anticlericalism: Catholic Politics and Peasantry in Bavaria, 1860–1900." *European Studies Review* 13, no. 2 (1983): 249–69.

Feiner, Shmuel. *The Jewish Enlightenment.* Trans. Chaya Naor. Philadelphia: University of Pennsylvania Press, 2002.

Forrest, Alan. "Paris versus the Provinces: Regionalism and Decentralization since 1789." In *French History since Napoleon*, ed. Martin S. Alexander, 106–26. New York: Arnold, 1999.

Furet, François. *Revolutionary France: 1770–1880.* Cambridge: Blackwell, 1992.

Furet, François, and Jacques Ozouf. *Lire et écrire: l'alphabétisation des français de Calvin à Jules Ferry.* 2 vols. Paris: Editions de Minuit, 1977.

———. *Reading and Writing: Literacy in France from Calvin to Jules Ferry.* Cambridge: Cambridge University Press, 1982.

Furnham, Adrian, and Michael Argyle. *The Psychology of Money.* New York: Routledge, 1998.

Gadille, Jacques. "On French Anticlericalism: Some Reflections." *European Studies Review* 13, no. 2 (1983): 127–44.

Gaillard, Jean-Michel. *Jules Ferry.* Paris: Fayard, 1989.

Gerbod, Paul. "De l'influence du catholicisme sur les stratégies éducatives des régimes politiques français de 1806 à 1906." In *L'offre d'école: éléments pour une étude comparée des politiques éducatives au XIXe siècle,* ed. Willem Frijhoff, 233–43. Paris: Sorbonne, 1983.

———. *La vie quotidienne dans les lycées et collèges au XIXe siècle.* Paris: Hachette, 1968.

Gibson, Ralph. *A Social History of French Catholicism, 1789–1914.* London: Routledge, 1989.

Gildea, Robert. "The Agonies of Modernisation: Some Problems of Technical Education, 1870–1914." In *L'offre d'école: éléments pour une étude comparée des politiques éducatives au XIXe siècle,* ed. Willem Frijhoff, 223–29. Paris: Sorbonne, 1983.

———. "Education and the *Classes Moyennes* in the Nineteenth Century." In *The Making of Frenchmen: Current Directions in the History of Education in France, 1679–1979,* ed. Donald Baker and Patrick J. Harrigan, 275–99. Waterloo, Ont.: Waterloo University Press, 1980.

Giolitto, Pierre. *Histoire de l'enseignement primaire au XIXe siècle.* 2 vols. Paris: Fernand-Nathan, 1983.

Girard, Patrick. *Les Juifs de France de 1789 à 1860.* Paris: Calmann-Lévy, 1976.

———. *Pour le meilleur et pour le pire: vingt siècles d'histoire Juive en France.* Paris: Bibliophane, 1986.

Goodman, Dena. "Public Sphere and Private Life: Toward a Synthesis of Current Historiographical Approaches to the Old Regime." *History and Theory* 31, no. 1 (1992): 1–20.

Graetz, Michael. *Les juifs en France au XIXe siècle: de la Révolution à l'Alliance Israélite Universelle.* Paris: Seuil, 1989.

Green, Andy. *Education and State Formation: The Rise of Education Systems in England, France and the USA.* London: Macmillan, 1990.
Green, Nancy. "Jewish Migrations to France in the Nineteenth and Twentieth Centuries: Community or Communities?" *Studia Rosenthaliana* 23, no. 2 (1989): 135–53.
———. "Les juifs étrangers à Paris." In *Les Paris des étrangers,* ed. André Kaspi and Antoine Marès. Paris: Impression Nationale, 1989 [offprint].
———. *The Pletzl of Paris: Jewish Immigrant Workers in the Belle Époque.* New York: Holmes and Meier, 1986.
Grew, Raymond, and Patrick J. Harrigan. *School, State, and Society: The Growth of Elementary Schooling in Nineteenth-Century France.* Ann Arbor: University of Michigan Press, 1991.
Grew, Raymond, Patrick J. Harrigan, and J. Whitney. "The Availability of Schooling in Nineteenth-Century France." *Journal of Interdisciplinary History* 14, no. 1 (1983): 25–63.
Guilbert, A.-V. *La question du budget des cultes.* Paris: Plon, 1877.
Guillaume, Pierre, ed. *Regards sur les classes moyennes-XIXe et XXe siècles.* Talence: Éditions de la Maison des Science de l'Homme d'Aquitaine, 1995.
Harpaz, Ephraïm. *L'école libérale sous la Restauration: le "Mercure" et la "Minèrve."* Geneva: Droz, 1968.
Harrigan, Patrick J. "The Church and Pluralistic Education: The Development of Teaching in French Catholic Secondary Schools, 1850–1870." *Catholic Historical Review* 64, no. 2 (1978): 185–213.
———. "Church, State, and Education in France from the Falloux to the Ferry Laws: A Reassessment." *Canadien Journal of History/Annales Canadiennes d'Histoire* 36, no. 1 (2001): 52–83.
———. *Mobility, Elites, and Education in French Society of the Second Empire.* Waterloo: Wilfred Laurier University Press, 1980.
———. "The Social Origins, Ambitions, and Occupations of Secondary Students in France during the Second Empire." In *Schooling and Society: Studies in the History of Education,* ed. Lawrence Stone, 206–35. Baltimore: Johns Hopkins University Press, 1976.
———. "Social and Political Implications of Catholic Secondary Education during the Second French Empire." *Societas* 6, no. 1 (1976): 41–59.
Harrison, Carol E. *The Bourgeois Citizen in Nineteenth-Century France: Gender, Sociability, and the Uses of Emulation.* Oxford: Oxford University Press, 1999.
Hause, Steven. "Anti-Protestant Rhetoric in the Early Third Republic." *French Historical Studies* 16 (Spring 1989): 183–201.
Hazan, Katy. "Du *heder* aux écoles actuelles: lééducation juive, reflet d'un destin collectif." *Archives juives* 35, no. 2 (2002): 4–25.
Hazareesingh, Sudhir. *From Subject to Citizen: The Second Empire and the Emergence of Modern French Democracy.* Princeton: Princeton University Press, 1998.
———. "Religion and Politics in the Saint-Napoleon Festivity, 1852–70: Anti-Clericalism, Local Patriotism and Modernity." *English Historical Review* 119, no. 482 (2004): 614–49.

Helfand, Jonathan. "French Jewry during the Second Republic and Second Empire (1848–70)." Ph.D. dissertation, Yeshiva University, 1979.

Hertzberg, Arthur. *The French Enlightenment and the Jews.* New York: Columbia University Press, 1968.

Hilaire, Y. M. "Le recrutement ecclésiastique dans la première moitié du XIXe siècle: le diocèse d'Arras représente-t-il un cas original?" *Bulletin de la Société d'histoire moderne* 67, no. 6 (1968): 13–19.

Hill, Keith. "Belgium: Political Change in a Segmented Society." In *Electoral Behavior: A Comparative Handbook,* ed. Richard Rose, 29–107. New York: Free Press, 1974.

Hope, Nicholas. "The View from the Province: A Dilemma for Protestants in Germany, 1648–1918." *Journal of Ecclesiastical History* 41 (October 1990): 606–21.

Horvath-Peterson, Sandra. *Victor Duruy and French Education.* Baton Rouge: Louisiana State University Press, 1984.

Hyman, Paula S. *The Emancipation of the Jews of Alsace.* New Haven: Yale University Press, 1991.

———. *From Dreyfus to Vichy: The Remaking of French Jewry.* New York: Columbia University Press, 1979.

———. *The Jews of Modern France.* Berkeley: University of California Press, 1998.

———. "The Social Contexts of Assimilation: Village Jews and City Jews in Alsace." In *Assimilation and Community: The Jews in Nineteenth-Century Europe,* ed. Jonathan Frankel and Steven Zipperstein, 110–29. Cambridge: Cambridge University Press, 1992.

Isser, Natalie. "Protestants and Proselytization during the Second French Empire." *Journal of Church and State* 30 (Winter 1988): 51–70.

Izzo, Alberto. "Legitimation and Society: A Critical Review." *Current Sociology* 35, no. 2 (1987): 41–56.

Jaher, Frederic Cople. *The Jews and the Nation: Revolution, Emancipation, State Formation, and the Liberal Paradigm in America and France.* Princeton: Princeton University Press, 2002.

Jourdain, Charles. *Le budget des cultes en France depuis le Concordat de 1801 jusqu'à nos jours.* Paris: Hachette, 1859.

Julia, Dominique, and Paul Pressly. "La population scolaire en 1789: les extravagances statistiques du ministre Villemain." *Annales* 30 (1975): 1516–61.

Kahn, Léon. "Histoire des écoles consistoriales et communales israélites de Paris (1809–1883)." *Annuaire de la société des études juives* 3 (1884): 163–273.

Kale, Steven D. *Legitimism and the Reconstruction of French Society, 1852–1883.* Baton Rouge: Louisiana State University Press, 1992.

Kanarfogel, Ephraim. *Jewish Education and Society in the High Middle Ages.* Detroit: Wayne State University Press, 1992.

Kaufmann, Yvette. "L'attitude du consistoire central Israélite de France et d'Algérie face à la séparation des églises et de l'état." Thèse nouveau régime, Universitaire des Sciences Humaines de Strasbourg, Institut d'Études Hébraïques, October 1991.

Kayser, Jacques. *Les grandes batailles du radicalisme: des origines aux portes du pouvoir, 1820–1901.* Paris: Marcel Rivière, 1962.

Kerner, Samuel. "Acte de fondation d'un collège hébraïque à Metz, 1751." *Archives juives* 7, no. 4 (1970–71).

Koepke, Robert L. "Cooperation, Not Conflict: Curés and Primary School Inspectors in July Monarchy France, 1833–1848." *Church History* 64, no. 4 (1995): 594–609.

———. "Educating Child Labourers in France: The Parliamentary Debates of 1840." *Canadian Journal of History/Annales Canadiennes d'histoire* 27, no. 3 (1992): 502–19.

Kossman, E. H. *The Low Countries, 1780–1940.* Oxford: Oxford University Press, 1978.

Kselman, Thomas. *Death and the Afterlife in Modern France.* Princeton: Princeton University Press, 1993.

———. "Funeral Conflicts in 19th Century France." *Comparative Studies in Society and History* 30 (April 1988): 312–32.

Lafon, Jacques. *Les prêtres, les fidèles, et l'état: le ménage à trois du XIXe siècle.* Paris: Beauchesne, 1987.

Lalouette, Jacqueline. "Dimensions anticléricales de la culture républicaine (1870–1914)." *Histoire, économie et société* 10, no. 1 (1991): 127–42.

Lamberti, Marjorie. "State, Church, and the Politics of School Reform during the Kulturkampf." *Central European History* 19, no. 1 (1986): 63–81.

Larkin, Maurice. *Church and State after the Dreyfus Affair.* New York: Barnes and Noble, 1974.

Leff, Lisa Moses. "Jewish Solidarity in Nineteenth-Century France: The Evolution of a Concept." *Journal of Modern History* 74, no. 1 (2002): 33–61.

Lehning, James R. *To Be a Citizen: The Political Culture of the Early French Third Republic.* Ithaca: Cornell University Press, 2001.

Lepointe, Gabriel. *Les rapports de l'église et de l'état en France.* Paris: Presses Universitaires de France, 1964.

Liberles, Robert. *Religious Conflict in Social Context: The Resurgence of Orthodox Judaism in Frankfurt Am Main, 1838–1877.* Westport, Conn.: Greenwood Press, 1985.

Lorwin, Val. "Belgium: Religion, Class, and Language in National Politics." In *Political Oppositions in Western Democracies,* ed. Robert Dahl, 147–87. New Haven: Yale University Press, 1966.

Lucien-Brun, Henry. *Étude historique sur la condition des Israélites en France depuis 1789.* Paris: Retaux, 1901.

Malino, Frances. *A Jew in the French Revolution: The Life of Zalkind Hourwitz.* Oxford: Blackwell, 1996.

———. "The Right to Be Equal: Zalkind Hourwitz and the Revolution of 1789." In *From East and West: Jews in a Changing Europe, 1750–1870,* ed. Frances Malino and David Sorkin, 57–84. Oxford: Blackwell, 1990.

———. *The Sephardic Jews of Bordeaux.* Tuscaloosa: University of Alabama Press, 1978.

Malino, Frances, and Bernard Wasserstein, eds. *The Jews in Modern France.* Hanover, N.H.: Brandeis University Press, 1985.
Mandrou, Robert. "L'historiographie des minorités en France: bilans et positions de problèmes." In *Les juifs dans l'histoire de France,* ed. Myriam Yardeni, 1–10. Leiden: Brill, 1980.
Marrus, Michael. *The Politics of Assimilation.* Oxford: Oxford University Press, 1971.
Martin, Philippe. "Christianisation? Déchristianisation? Rechristianisation? La question de la sacralisation de l'espace dans la France catholique (XIXe-XXe siècles)." *Kirchliche Zeitgeschichte* 11, no. 1 (1998): 51–68.
May, Anita Rasi. "Disputes over Words and Constitutional Conflict in France, 1730–1732." *French Historical Studies* 14 (Fall 1986): 497–520.
———. "Is *les deux France* a Valid Framework for Interpreting the Nineteenth-Century Church? The French Episcopate as a Case Study." *Catholic Historical Review* 73 (October 1987): 541–61.
Mayeur, Françoise. *Histoire générale de l'enseignement et de l'éducation en France, tome III: de la Révolution à l'école républicaine.* Paris: Nouvelle Librairie de France, 1981.
Mayeur, Jean-Marie. "Jules Ferry et la laïcité." In *Jules Ferry: fondateur de la République,* ed. François Furet, 147–60. Paris: EHESS, 1985.
———. "La laïcité et l'idée laïque au début de la Troisième République." In *Les Opportunistes: les débuts de la République aux républicains,* ed. Léo Hamon. Paris: Éditions de la MSH, 1991.
McBride, Theresa. "Public Authority and Private Lives: Divorce After the French Revolution." *French Historical Studies* 17, no. 3 (1992): 747–68.
McManners, John. *Church and State in France, 1870–1914.* New York: Harper and Row, 1972.
Melamed, Efim. "The Zhitomir Rabbinical School: New Materials and Perspectives." POLIN 14 (2001): 105–15.
Menkis, Richard. "Les frères Elie, Olry, et Lazare Terquem." *Archives juives* 15 (1979): 58–61.
Merrick, Jeffrey. *The Desacralization of the French Monarchy.* Baton Rouge: Louisiana State University Press, 1990.
Metraux, Eva. "Trends in French Thought during the Third Republic." *Science and Society* 5 (1941): 207–21.
Meyer, Michael A. *Response to Modernity: A History of the Reform Movement in Judaism.* New York: Oxford University Press, 1988.
Miller, David. "Armand Gaston Camus and the Civil Constitution of the Clergy." *Catholic Historical Review* 76 (July 1990): 481–505.
Moody, Joseph N. *French Education Since Napoleon.* Syracuse: Syracuse University Press, 1978.
Moreau, Georges. *La question cléricale: le budget des cultes.* Paris: Dentu, 1881.
Neher-Bernheim, Renée. "Sephardim et Ashkenazim à Paris au lieu du XIXe siècle: un essai avorté de fusion des rites." In *Les juifs au regard de l'histoire: mélanges en l'honneur de Bernhard Blumenkranz,* ed. Bernhard Blumenkranz and Gilbert Dahan, 369–82. Paris: Picard, 1985.

Nahon, Monique. "La regénération: école et apprentissage des juifs pauvres de Paris au dix-neuvième siècle." Thèse de la maitrise. Paris VIII, 1983.

Nord, Phillip. "Republicanism and Utopian Vision: French Freemasonry in the 1860s and 1870s." *Journal of Modern History* 63 (June 1991): 213–29.

———. "Three Views of Christian Democracy in *fin de siècle* France." *Journal of Contemporary History* 19 (October 1984): 713–27.

Ozouf, Mona. *L'École, l'église et la République, 1871–1914*. Cana: Jean Offredo, 1982.

Partin, Malcolm O. *Waldeck-Rousseau, Combes, and the Church*: The *Politics of Anticlericalism, 1899–1905*. Durham, N.C.: Duke University Press, 1969.

Penslar, Derek. *Shylock's Children: Economics and Jewish Identity in Modern Europe*. Berkeley: University of California Press, 2001.

Piette, Christine. *Les juifs de Paris: la marche vers assimilation*. Québec: Presses de l'Université de Laval, Cahiers de l'Université de Laval, 1983.

Pinkney, David. *Decisive Years in France, 1840–1847*. Princeton: Princeton University Press, 1986.

Ponteil, Félix. *Histoire de l'enseignement en France, les grandes étapes, 1789–1965*. Paris: Sirey, 1965.

———. *Les institutions de la France de 1814 à 1870*. Paris: Presses Universitaires de Paris, 1966.

Poppel, Steven M. "The Politics of Religious Leadership: The Rabbinate in Nineteenth-Century Hamburg." *Leo Baeck Institute Yearbook* 28 (1983): 439–70.

———. "Rabbinical Status and Religious Authority in Imperial Germany: The German Rabbinical Association." *AJS Review* 9, no. 2 (1984): 185–213.

Posener, S. "The Immediate Economic and Social Effects of the Emancipation of the Jews of France." *Jewish Social Studies* 1, no. 1 (1939): 271–326.

Poteau, Eric. "La société Saint-Bertin de Saint-Omer, une société de prêtres voués à l'éducation au XIXe siècle. Grandeur et decline." *Revue du Nord* 78, no. 316 (1996): 519–27.

Poulat, Émile. *Liberté, laïcité. La guerre des deux France et le principe de la modernité*. Paris: Le Cerf, 1987.

Poutet, Yves. "Les Frères des écoles chrétiennes à l'époque de Jules Ferry: leur politique scolaire à travers le monde, 1869–1903." In *L'offre d'école: éléments pour une étude comparée des politiques éducatives au XIXe siècle: actes du troisième colloque international*, Sèvres, September 27–30, 1981, ed. Willem Frijhoff and Michel Boulet, 285–307. Paris: Sorbonne, 1983.

Price, Roger. *The French Second Empire: An Anatomy of Political Power*. Cambridge: Cambridge University Press, 2001.

———. *A Social History of Nineteenth-Century France*. New York: Holmes and Meier, 1987.

Prost, Antoine. *Histoire de l'enseignement en France, 1800–1967*. Paris: Armand Colin, 1968.

Quartararo, Anne T. "The Perils of Assimilation in Modern France: The Deaf Community, Social Status, and Educational Opportunity, 1815–1870." *Journal of Social History* 29, no. 1 (1995): 5–23.

Raphaël, Freddy, and Robert Weyl. *Juifs en Alsace: culture, société, histoire.* Paris: Privat, 1977.

Rémond, René. *L'anticlericalisme en France de 1815 à nos jours.* Paris: Fayard, 1976.

Ringer, Fritz. *Education and Society in Modern Europe.* Bloomington: Indiana University Press, 1979.

———. *Fields of Knowledge: French Academic Culture in Comparative Perspective, 1890–1920.* Cambridge: Cambridge University Press, 1992.

———. "On Segmentation in Modern European Educational Systems: The Case of French Secondary Education, 1865–1920." In *The Rise of the Modern Educational System,* ed. Fritz Ringer, Detlef Mueller, and Brian Simon, 53–87. New York: Cambridge University Press, 1987.

Roche, Daniel. *France in the Enlightenment.* Trans. Arthur Goldhammer. Cambridge, Mass.: Harvard University Press, 1998.

Rodrigue, Aron. *De l'instruction à l'emancipation.* Paris: Calmann-Lévy, 1989.

Rogers, Rebecca. *From the Salon to the Schoolroom: Educating Bourgeois Girls in Nineteenth-Century France.* University Park: Penn State University Press, 2005.

Rozenblit, Marsha. "Jewish Identity and the Modern Rabbi: The Cases of Isak Noa Mannheimer, Adolf Jellinek, and Moritz G. Demann in Nineteenth-Century Vienna." *Leo Baeck Institute Yearbook* 35 (1990): 103–31.

Sarna, Jonathan. "The Impact of Nineteenth-Century Christian Missions on American Jews." In *Jewish Apostasy in the Modern World,* ed. Todd Endelmann. New York: Holmes and Meier, 1987.

Sartori, Jennifer I. "'Wanted: A Jewish Governess'; The Education of Middle-Class Jewish Girls in Nineteenth-Century Paris." *Proceedings of the Annual Meeting of the Western Society for French History* 26 (1999): 24–34.

Schechter, Ronald. *Obstinate Hebrews: Representations of Jews in France, 1715–1815.* Berkeley: University of California Press, 2003.

Schorsch, Ismar. *From Text to Context: The Turn to History in Modern Judaism.* Hanover, N.H.: Brandeis University Press, 1994.

Schwarzfuchs, Simon. *Du juif à l'israélite: histoire d'une mutation (1770–1870).* Paris: Fayard, 1989.

Sepinwall, Alyssa Goldstein. *The Abbé Grégoire and the French Revolution: The Making of Modern Universalism.* Berkeley: University of California Press, 2005.

Shadal, James. "Emperor, Church, and People: Religion and Dynastic Loyalty during the Golden Jubilee of Franz Joseph." *Catholic Historical Review* 76 (January 1990): 71–92.

Silberman, Paul. "An Investigation of the Schools Operated by the Alliance Israelite Universelle from 1862–1940." Ph.D. diss., New York University, 1973.

Simon, W. M. *European Positivism in the Nineteenth Century.* Ithaca: Cornell University Press, 1963.

Simon-Nahum, Perrine. "La science du judaïsme en France." In *Les études juives en France: situations et perspectives,* ed. Frank Alvarez-Pereye and Jean Baumgarten, 23–32. Paris: CNRS, 1990.

Sorkin, David. *The Transformation of German Jewry, 1780–1840*. New York: Oxford University Press, 1987

Sperber, Jonathan. "Competing Counterrevolutions: Prussian State and Catholic Church in Westphalia during the 1850s." *Central European History* 19 (March 1986): 45–62.

Strumingher, Laura. *What Were Little Girls and Boys Made of? Primary Education in Rural France, 1830–1880*. Albany: State University of New York Press, 1983.

Szajkowski, Zosa. *Jewish Education in France, 1789–1939*. New York: Jewish Social Studies, 1980.

Tauran, Jean-Louis. "Les relations Église-État en France: de la separation impose à l'apaisement négocié." *Revue des sciences morales & politiques; travaux de l'Académie des sciences morales et politiques* 4 (2001): 127–50.

Texier, Roger. "L'idée de la perfectibilité en education au XVIIIe siécle." In *Éducation et pedagogies au siècle des lumières*. Angers: Presses de l'Université Catholique de l'Ouest, 1985.

Thompson, D. G. "General Ricci and the Suppression of the Jesuit Order in France, 1760–64." *Journal of Ecclesiastical History* 37 (July 1986): 426–41.

Thompson, J. M. *Louis Napoleon and the Second Empire*. Oxford: Blackwell, 1954.

Thompson, Victoria E. *The Virtuous Marketplace: Women and Men, Money and Politics in Paris, 1830–1870*. Baltimore: Johns Hopkins University Press, 2000.

Tollet, Daniel, ed. *Politique et religion dans le judaïsme moderne: des communautés à l'émancipation*. Paris: Sorbonne, 1987.

Underwood, Grant. "Mormonism, the Maori and Cultural Authenticity." *The Journal of Pacific History* 35, no. 2 (2000): 134.

Walton, Whitney. *France at the Crystal Palace: Bourgeois Taste and Artisan Manufacture in the Nineteenth Century*. Berkeley: University of California Press, 1992.

Weber, Eugen. *Peasants into Frenchmen*. Stanford: Stanford University Press, 1976.

Weill, Georges. *Histoire de l'idée laïque en France au XIXe siècle*. Paris: Félix Alcan, 1925.

Weinberg, David. *A Community on Trial*. Chicago: University of Chicago Press, 1977.

Weiss, John H. "Origins of the French Welfare State: Poor Relief in the Third Republic, 1871–1914." *French Historical Studies* 13 (Spring 1983): 47–78.

Weissbach, Lee Shai. "The Jewish Elite and the Children of the Poor: Jewish Apprenticeship Programs in Nineteenth-Century France." *Association for Jewish Studies Review* 12, no. 1 (1987): 123–42.

———. "The Nature of Philanthropy in Nineteenth-Century France and the *Mentalité* of the Jewish Elite." *Jewish History* 8, nos. 1–2 (1994): 191–204.

Weisz, George. *The Emergence of Modern Universities in France, 1863–1914*. Princeton: Princeton University Press, 1983.

Willaime, Jean-Paul. "1905 et la pratique d'une laïcite de reconnaissance sociale des religions." *Archives de sciences sociales des religions* 50, no. 129 (2005): 67–82.

Williams, Rosalind H. *Dream Worlds: Mass Consumption in Late Nineteenth Century France.* Berkeley: University of California Press, 1982.

Wilson, Stephen. *Ideology and Experience: Antisemitism in France at the Time of the Dreyfus Affair.* Rutherford, N.J.: Fairleigh Dickinson University Press, 1982.

Woloch, Isser. "Napoleonic Conscription: State Power and Civil Society." *Past & Present* 111 (May 1986): 101–29.

———. *The New Regime: Transformations of the French Civic Order, 1789–1820s.* New York: Norton, 1994.

Wright, Vincent. "L'épuration du Conseil d'État." *Révue d'histoire moderne et contemporaine* 19 (October–December 1972): 621–53.

Zelizer, Viviana A. *The Social Meaning of Money.* New York: Basic Books, 1994.

Zind, Pierre. "La religion dans les lycées sous le régime de la loi Falloux, 1850–1873." In *The Making of Frenchmen: Current Directions in the History of Education in France, 1679–1979,* ed. Donald Baker and Patrick Harrigan, 249–73. Waterloo, Ont.: Waterloo University Press, 1980.

INDEX

Academy of Nancy, 33, 97. *See also* University
Academy of Strasbourg, 28. *See also* University
Administration des Cultes non-Catholiques, 104–5
Albert, Etienne Joseph, 67, 127
Alliance Israélite Universelle, 178n51, 188n37
Alsace, 9, 71, 151
Alsatian Jews, 2, 9–10; corporate communal structure, 10; lower-economic class children in Jewish schools, 39; preservation of traditional ways, 103
Amsterdam, rabbis in, 67
Anderson, Robert, 169n22
anticlericalism: under Radical Republicans, 88–89, 115–33. *See also* Conseil d'État, anticlerical Republican; financial anticlericalism
anticlerical legislation. *See* financial anticlericalism
Archives israélites, 56, 76, 130, 146, 151
Armand, Rector of Academy of Nancy, 33–34
Aron, Jerome, 56
Ashkenazic ritual, 9, 106
Assembly of Jewish Notables, 13–14, 16, 18, 23
assimilation, 160
Astruc, Mardochée, 99, 101, 187n37
Auscher, Jacques, 85
Avignon, 10

baccalauréat, 88
bar mitzvah, 134, 148, 149
Beckert, Heymann, 86

Ben-Amos, Avner, 142–43
Bénédict, Sylvain, 87
Berkovitz, Jay, 11, 29, 67, 161, 163
Berr, Isaac Berr, 13
Berr, Isaïe, 133
Bert, Paul, 131
Beyfus, Adolphe, 115
Beyfus decision, 122, 123, 125, 126–28, 133, 135
Birnbaum, Pierre, 165
Bischeim, 33
Bloch, Abraham, 87
Bloch, Néphtali, 86
Bloch, Simon, 56
Boesvilvald, Émile, 96, 97, 99–100, 100, 101
Bolleviller, 57
Bonaparte, Louis-Napoleon, 82, 173n75. *See also* Napoleon III
Bonhoure, Angelique, 118
Bonnieux, M., 80
Bonthoux, 123, 124
Bordeaux Jewish community, 26. *See also* Consistory, Jewish, Bordeaux
boursiers, 73
brevet de capacité, 51
brevet élémentaire, 51
brévets du degré élémentaire, 52
Brumaltz, 26
budget du culte israélite, 33, 39, 40, 75, 89, 123, 124, 125, 130–31
Byrnes, Joseph, 163–64

Cahen, Abraham, 84–85
Cahen, Emile, 85
Cahen, Isidore, 22, 55–56, 129, 151–52, 158, 178n51

INDEX

Cahen, Meyer Joseph, 126
Cahen, Samuel, 56, 72, 81
caisse de la communauté, 139
Carpentras, 10, 51
Catholic Church: as administrative and moral extension of French state, 13; advantages in communal education system, 47; clerical education, 74; educational domination, 56; opposition to republicans, 116. *See also* schools, Catholic
Catholic proselytism, 140, 143
Cavaillon, 10
Central Consistory. *See* Consistory, Jewish
Cernay, 57
Chadwick, Owen, 163
Chamber of Deputies, 130–31
chaplains, Jewish, at French secondary schools, 143, 145, 147, 162
charities, Jewish: historical link to Jewish education, 122; sought recognition as public utilities independent from consistories, 126
charity boards *(bureaux de bienfaisance),* 20
Chevallier, Pierre, 119
Chief Rabbi of France, 101
Christian Brothers, 32, 40, 47, 191n5
City of Paris, ending of subvention to consistorial schools, 132
"clandestine" schools, 17, 38, 174n18, 175n40
classical studies, debate over, 66–67, 68, 74–75, 76, 81, 82–85, 86, 88
Clercs de St. Viateur, 47
Clermont-Ferrand, Jewish schooling in, 50, 54
Cohn, Albert, 110
Collége Rollin, 138, 149
colléges, 15, 143
Comité Communal d'Instruction Primaire Israélite, 36
Commission de l'Instruction Publique, 70
Commission des Édifices Religieux, 95, 96
communal rabbis, qualifications for, 180n37
concordat, 13, 131

Conseil d'État, 74, 78, 97; anticlerical Republican: blocking of consistories from accepting educational bequests, 125–27; criteria of equality and fairness in determining consistory's legal status, 121, 128–29; importance of in anticlerical campaign, 117–18; prohibition of Catholic *fabriques* from receiving charitable gifts, 118, 119; ruling on Beyfus legacy, 122, 123
Conseil Royale de l'Instruction Publique, 25, 73
Consistory, Jewish, 32; assertion of both Jewish equality and distinctiveness, 3; departmental support for move of rabbinical school to Paris, 105; disagreement with government definitions of Judaism, 91; education as traditional function of, 123; goal of separate Jewish educational system, 21; oversight of distribution of *matzot* and other foods, 122; status of after Separation Law, 150. *See also* education, Jewish
Consistory, Jewish, and rabbinical education: balancing of secular demands of state with traditional rabbinical studies, 66, 90, 103; critique of Metz as location for rabbinical school, 102–3; final plan for rabbinical school, 72–73; forced to address deficiencies in rabbinical school in request for more funding, 80; fundraising campaign among consistories for Metz school, 97–98, 101, 102; fundraising campaigns among consistories for Séminaire Israélite, 153; linking of relocation to curricular reforms, 103–4; linking of relocation to practical concerns, 104; mission to remake French rabbinate, 68; petition for permission to open rabbinical school, 68–69; *Plan d'organisation,* 67, 69, 70; proposals for moving rabbinical school to Paris, 93–94, 98, 102, 106; provisional location for rabbinical school in Paris, 110; reformulation of rabbinical course of study with classical lan-

INDEX

guages, 67; request for funds to renovate Metz school building, 94–95

Consistory, Jewish, post-emancipation: alternative means for providing religious instruction for Jewish children, 41–42; arguments for Jewish education balancing notions of fairness and utility, 36; inability to obtain funding for Jewish education, 40–41; linking of Jewish education to regeneration, 14–15, 22–23, 27, 60; petition to establish national system of Jewish schools, 1–2, 19–20; rebuilding of official Jewish institutions after emancipation, 14; struggle over government funding for Jewish education, 1–2, 5, 6; and two-way obligations of emancipation, 30; utilitarian case for separate Jewish schools, 15–17

Consistory, Jewish, Second Empire: alarm about weakness of Jewish education, 57; establishment of supplementary Jewish religious instruction outside communal schools, 47, 58–59, 60; and ideas of Jewish legitimacy in France, 48; pursuit of communalization of schools, 49; 1868 survey of departmental consistories, 53–54

Consistory, Jewish, Third Republic: argument for rabbinical seminary as lay establishment, 130; attempts to improve communal fundraising, 131–32; focus on distinctiveness of Judaism, 115, 123, 144, 164; focus on supplementary religious instruction, 135, 146; government limits on acceptance of charitable gifts, 125–27; proposal for realignment of rabbinical school curriculum, 155–56; search for new access to Jewish students, 143; threat of decentralization by anticlerical legislation, 120; transformation of educational policy, 134

Consistory, Jewish, Bayonne, 54

Consistory, Jewish, Bordeaux, 40, 54; communalization of Jewish schools, 33, 49–50, 53; focus on moral dangers of Paris as setting for rabbinical school, 106–7; installation of Simon Lévy as rabbi, 65–66; protest of awards in religious instruction to Protestant students, 144–45; and rabbinical school curriculum, 81

Consistory, Jewish, Colmar: inadequacy of Jewish schooling, 50, 54, 57; Jewish population, 93

Consistory, Jewish, Marseille, 40, 51, 71, 105

Consistory, Jewish, Metz: benefits of founding rabbinical school in, 72; decline in influence, 93; focus on moral dangers of Paris as setting for rabbinical school, 106, 107; French *lycée*, 72, 83; frustration with protracted rabbinical school renovations, 100; plans for renovation of rabbinical school, 95–96; protest of transfer of rabbinical school to Paris, 102, 107, 108; and reimbursement for rabbinical school, 109–10; and secular training for *grand rabbins*, 70–71

Consistory, Jewish, Nancy, 33–34, 52; call for relocation of rabbinical school to Paris, 99; and DuPont legacy, 126; Jewish attendance at "mixed schools," 50; municipal council rejection of petitions for assistance by, 33–35, 39–40

Consistory, Jewish, Paris, 58, 71, 93; abilities of lay religious instructors, 149; and Beyfus legacy, 122–23; Commission Spéciale d'Instruction Religieuse, 145–46; committee to examine implications of republican legislation, 120; failure of call for union of charitable associations, 132–33; financial problems, 139–40; government refusal of request for school aid, 35; little support for religious education in suburbs, 149; new conception of utility, 154–55; philanthropic heritage, 122; poor attendance at secondary schools, 138; poor instructional and curricular standards at communal schools, 138; problems with communal charity fund, 131–32; religious indifference in, 138, 149; subvention of Université

223

INDEX

Consistory, Jewish, Paris (*continued*)
  Populaire Juive, 149; supplemental programs of religious instruction, 138, 141–42, 143–44, 147–50; support for move of rabbinical school to Paris, 105; teacher certification exam for lay religious instructors, 147; test case of consistorial rights, 121. *See also* schools, Jewish, Paris
Consistory, Jewish, St. Esprit, 105, 106
Consistory, Jewish, Strasborg, 9, 26, 28, 33, 71, 105, 106; and rabbinical school, 73; report on state of Jewish education, 43–44
Consistory, Uffholtz, 57–58
Consistory, Wintzenheim, 21–22, 23
conversion, Jewish fear of, 56–57
conversos, 10
Cottard, Louis, 28, 29, 30, 33, 36
Curtis, Sarah, 47

Dabas, M., 144–45
Danilef, Samuel, 88, 157
Debré, Simon, 147
Dérobe, M., 95, 96
Dienze, 52
dons et legs, 53
DuPont, Mayer, 125–26
Duruy, Victor, 87, 184n107

Eastern European Jewish immigrants, 136–37, 197n16
École Central Rabbinique de France: attempt to renovate, and government regulations, 95–97, 99–101; budgetary problems, 75, 79–80; conflict over classical studies at, 74–75, 76, 82–85; dissatisfaction with in government and Jewish community, 79; government funding and oversight in nineteenth century, 75, 76, 185n115; insufficient communal funding, 75–76; issue of transfer to Paris and discussions of Jewish integration, 81, 93–94; low faculty salaries and student scholarships, 79; move from Metz to Paris, 85–86; new faculty appointments, 83; physical dilapidation, 93; taught only Ashkenazic ritual, 106; temporary quarters during renovation, 97, 99. *See also* Consistory, Jewish, and rabbinical education; education, rabbinical; Séminaire Israélite
École Commerciale, 148
École Normale Supérieure, 22, 56
écoles communales, 43
écoles congréganistes, 46
écoles laïques, 46
écoles libres, 43, 124
écoles spéciales, 43
École Turgot, 143
education, French system: Catholic, 45–49, 56, 74, 116, 135; changes in during 1830s, 35; and classical studies, 46, 66–67, 68, 74–75, 76, 81, 82–85, 86, 87, 88; communal elementary schools, 117, 122; effects of Guizot school law on, 31, 32; expansion after 1833, 32; and financial anticlericalism, 120, 137, 191n4; and limited possibilities for separate Jewish system, 41–42, 54; mandated stages of moral instruction, 32; as primary agent of national integration, 74; primary education, 15, 25, 30; public education, 87, 134, 135, 170n29; under Second Empire, 46; under Third Republic, 135. *See also* education, Jewish; Falloux Law; Ferry Laws
education, Jewish: communal schools, 45–46, 52–53, 55, 127, 148; consistorial education system, 132, 136–37, 161; elementary education, 11, 162; and French Jewish emancipation, 14–27; girls' schools, 172n68; primary education, 19, 30. *See also* Consistory, Jewish; schools, Jewish
education, Jewish, post-emancipation: and *budget du culte israélite*, 39, 40; communalization of schools, 36; contradictory forces impeding, 29; drop in voluntary contributions to, 40; and government academic and cultural standards, 4–5, 6, 15; under jurisdiction of Education Ministry, 39; lack

224

INDEX

of cooperation from local authorities, 33–35; lack of emphasis on primary schooling, 15; limitations on government aid, 25–26; limited number of state-authorized consistorial schools, 32–33; linked to Jewish legitimacy by notion of utility, 16–17; obstacles in northeast, 28; reluctance of middle-class Jews to send children to private schools, 52; schools viewed as charitable institutions, 39; weak local support, 25, 31–32, 38–39

education, Jewish, Second Empire: conformity demanded by communalization, 51; consolidation and redirection as result of Falloux Law, 44–47, 59–61; limitations of minority status and fiscal constraints, 43–44, 47, 54; move toward program-oriented Jewish education, 53; philanthropic operation aimed at Jewish poor, 47, 49, 60; and redefinition of "equal" and "useful," 47–48; required combination of Jewish and civic support to succeed, 51, 53; weak local support, 49

education, Jewish, Third Republic: absorption of schools by civic educational system, 135–36; Paris as most active center of innovation, 138–39; subordination of religious studies to secular learning, 138; supplemental programs of religious instruction, 141–42, 163

education, rabbinical: competition between Metz and Paris for rabbinical school, 71–72, 92–111; connection of Jewish and French space, 92, 158; and debate over secular learning, 66–67, 68, 74, 75, 76, 81, 82–85, 86, 88; evolution of curriculum during nineteenth century, 90; and government concepts of utility, 67–68, 111; and ideological goals, 110; and Jewish integration, 73, 83, 90; lower-economic class students, 22; new emphasis on homiletics, 66; under policies of French University and French politics, 66; and reformers' call for rabbinate trained in Paris, 71–72; and uniting of French Jewry, 73; weak financial support for, 6, 89–90. *See also* Consistory, Jewish, and rabbinical education; École Central Rabbinique de France; Séminaire Israélite

emancipation: French Jewish, 3, 12, 13, 14–27; German Jewish, 30

equality: criteria in determining consistory's legal status under Republicans, 121, 128–29; and Jewish integration, 160–61; as justification for civic financial support for separate Jewish schools, 60; new meaning as ability to perpetuate Jewish religious life in France, 146, 165; redefinition of, 42; used to justify positive or negative treatment of Jewish proposals, 145. *See also* utility and equality

European Jews: assimilation, 160; classical knowledge of rabbis, 67; debate over legal status, 11–12

fabriques, 117–18, 119, 120, 121, 122, 124

Falloux Law, 44–45, 119, 161; and Catholic influence, 82; and consolidation and redirection for Jewish education, 59–61; emphasis on morality and maintenance of social order, 45; enlargement of elementary teaching pool, 52; granting of control over communal schooling to municipal officials, 45–46, 55; granting of new supervisory powers to Catholic clergy, 46, 55; left Catholic education vulnerable to government attack, 116; mandate for primary curriculum, 51; and representation of Jews on academic councils, 55, 86; undermining of University authority, 45; and vulnerability of Jewish schools to local attitudes, 48, 49

Feiner, Shmuel, 30

Ferry, Jules, 87, 117

Ferry Laws, 45, 87, 118, 119–20, 135, 137, 140; laicization of public elementary schooling and teaching personnel, 120, 122, 192n23; Law of March 28, 1882,

INDEX

Ferry Laws (*continued*)
117, 141, 145, 146–47, 191n5, 197n13; mandated closure of public schools for outside religious instruction, 146; removal of religious instruction from French teaching exams, 146–47; removal of religious instruction from school curricula, 145

Ferté-sous-Jouarre, 149

financial anticlericalism, 115–33, 162, 191n4; equation of treatment of Catholicism, Protestantism, and Judaism, 116, 128; erosion of financial ties between state religions and government, 128–29; importance of Conseil d'État in, 117–18; nationalization of French education, 120, 137, 191n4; and rabbinical education, 151–59; and reconfiguration of Jewish education, 134, 142; severing of link between Jewish utility and equality, 137; slashing of Jewish religious budget, 130–31

Flourens, Émile, 119, 124, 125, 192n20

Fortoul, Hippolyte, 82, 96, 97, 100

Fould, Alfred, 126

frais du culte, 123

France: idea of citizenship in modern, 91; paradoxical social views of money in nineteenth-century, 6

Franck, Adolphe, 76–77, 79, 85, 92, 93, 152

Franco-Judaism, 2

Franco-Prussian War, 44

French antisemites, 129

French cemeteries, laicization of, 141

French enlightenment, 11

French government: attitudes toward Judaism, 5, 77–78; and École Central Rabbinique de France, 75, 76, 79, 95–97, 99–101, 105, 109; expectation that Jews abandon corporate collective existence after emancipation, 12; funding for Jewish education, 1–2, 5, 6, 25–26, 33; guidelines for French schools, 31; and Jewish integration, 2, 14, 39, 92; and Jewish religious budget, 89, 123, 124, 125, 130–31; and rabbinical education, 83, 90, 92, 111; and Séminaire Israélite, 129–30. *See also* financial anticlericalism; municipal authorities; Napoleonic regime; Second Empire; Third Republic

French higher education, and issue of classical languages, 66–67

French Jewry: concentration in three geographical areas, 9–10; disagreement over rabbinical functions, 98; diversity of in nineteenth-century, 4; division between Parisian and rural populations, 72; expected by government to abandon corporate collective existence, 12; full legal emancipation, 3, 12; growing religious indifference within, 1, 46, 52; historians of, 2; historiography, 4; internally fragmented attitudes, 164; polarization between Paris and provinces, 98–99; polarization regarding function and content of Jewish education, 17–18, 38, 50; population at time of French Revolution, 9; preference of middle-class and wealthy for French secondary education, 22; recast image according to French cultural standards, 12; reformist faction, 101; support for rabbinical school in Paris, 71–72, 101; weakened communal structure, 13, 18

French Judaism: adaptation of identity to changing forces, 9; ambiguous scope of legitimate activity, 21; changes in state relations under Second Empire, 47; and concept of Jewish citizenship, 91; debate over legal status, 11, 12; defining the utility of, 29; financial relationship with French state, 2, 5, 80, 92; government attitudes toward, 77–78; inclusion in civil religious administration, 13–14; inclusion in national religious budget of 1831, 39; legitimacy linked to Jewish education by notion of utility, 16; scrutiny by anticlerical Republicans in 1880s, 121–22, 125, 134; weakened communal structure, 13

226

INDEX

French primary education: lack of growth until 1820s, 15; local responsibility for funding under Napoleonic regime, 25

French public education: conflict about religious content of, 170n29; deemphasis on classical studies in secondary education, 87; growth in budget, 135; growth of, 134

French rabbinate: changing roles, 86; creation of civic pedagogical function for, 19–20; dependence on government for salaries, 76, 77; importance of sermonizing in, 183n79; liberation from constraints of past through move of rabbinical school to Paris, 106; as tool for Jewish integration, 68, 72–73; transformation of duties, 66

French Revolution, 30
Frères Maristes, 47
Furet, François, 31, 44

German Jewish emancipation, 30
Gerson-Lévy, 24, 172n63
Ginsburger, Rabbi, 149
Goblet School Law, 122
Gradis, Benjamin, 107–8, 152, 183n85
grand rabbins, 65, 66, 69, 81, 85; conference of, 101
Gréard, Octave, 147
Great Sanhedrin. *See* Napoleonic Sanhedrin
Greek language instruction, 67, 68, 83
Green, Nancy, 197n16
Grégoire, Henri, 12, 14, 30, 169n18
Grew, 31, 117, 135, 174n17
Guizot school law, 29, 39, 44; barrier to development of Jewish educational system, 32; and expansion of French education, 31; greater fiscal responsibilities on communal authorities, 31; movement toward centralized political control, 31

hadarim, persistence of in Upper Rhine, 17
Haguenau, 27, 33

Haguenau, David, 147, 149, 200n67
halakhah, 10
Harrigan, Patrick, 31, 44–45, 117, 135, 174n17
haskalah, 3
Hazan, Katy, 162
Hazareesingh, Sudhir, 91
Hirsch, Emile, 86
Hirsch, Rose, 133
homilectics, 66, 187n33
Hourwitz, Zalkind, 165, 169n18
House of Rothschild, 47, 89, 153, 185n116
Hyman, Paula, 2, 9, 16, 175n40

initiation religieuse, 134, 143, 148
Insming, 52

Jewish clergy, teaching certification of, 52
Jewish immigration, 88
Jewish integration, 42, 78; coexistence with religious distinctiveness, 160–61; concern of municipal authorities, 35–37; and debate about Jewish education, 2; French rabbinate as tool for, 68, 72–73; goal of July Monarchy, 35; goal of Napoleonic regime, 16; government view of Jewish particularism as impediment to, 2; influence of economic and social factors on, 2; in nineteenth-century France, 160; rabbinical education as tool of, 70–71, 73, 90; skepticism toward, 29–30; and transfer of rabbinical school to Paris, 81, 93–94; utility and, 18, 35–36, 60, 69

Jewish particularism: and equality under Third Republic, 115, 123, 144, 164; viewed by government as impediment to integration, 2

Jewish press, 146
Jewish reform, proponents of, 17
Jewish regeneration. *See* regeneration
Jewish vocational education, 137, 197n12
jours de congés, 146
July Monarchy: centralized political control, 31; end of, 42; goal of national unification, 77–78; integration as ultimate utilitarian goal, 35; permanent

227

INDEX

July Monarchy (*continued*)
    appropriation for French Judaism in national budget, 28–29
June Days, 82

kahal, 10
Kahn, Léon, 35, 199n39
Kahn, Zadoc, 89, 140, 147, 148, 159
Kale, Steven, 78, 82
Karo, Joseph, 69
Karpe, Salomon, 87
Klein, Salomon, 17, 52
kosher meat, income generated by sale of, 132

La Bourdonnaye, François Régis de, 73–74
Laferté, 58
laïcité, 119–20
Laine, Joseph, 70
Latin, 67, 68, 83
Lazare, director of Metz rabbinical school, 98
Leff, Lisa Moses, 203n9
Legitimists, 72, 78
Le Hâvre, 58, 149
Lehmann, Joseph, 86, 88, 89, 157
Lehmann, Léonce, 122
Lehmann, Samuel, 85
Léon, Alfred, 65–66
Leven, Narcisse, 120–21, 122, 145, 154, 192n25
Lévy, Marc, 86
Lévy, Néphtali, 85
Lévy, Simon, 65–66, 85, 144
Libourne, Jewish schooling in, 50
l'Isle sur-Sogne, 10–11
Lorraine, 9, 151
Lower Rhine Consistory, 33, 71
Lycée Carnot, 138
Lycée Janson de Sailly, 147
Lycée-Napoleon at Vendée, 56
lycées, 15, 143
Lyon, 11
Lyon Jewish school, 51

Maimonides, 69
Manuel, Eugéne, 152, 158
"marking money," 5

Martin, Henri, 56
Martin-Feuillée, 128–29, 131
maskilim, 3, 30
melammed, 11
Mendelssohn, Moses, 165
Mérilou, Joseph, 26
Meyer, Félix, 87
Michaelis, Johann David, 12
Minister of Religions, 77, 93, 100, 104, 105, 128–29, 131
moral mission, linked Jewish primary schooling and theological academies, 19
Morhange, Louis, 80, 182n76
Mortara, Edgard, 57
municipal authorities: concerns regarding separate Jewish schools and Jewish integration, 35–37; control over communal schooling under Falloux Law, 45–46, 55; prejudicial attitudes toward Jewish schooling, 50–51; sought cheapest school options, 49
municipal ("common") schools, 21
Munk, Salomon, 79

Napoleon Bonaparte: assembly of Jewish leaders, 13–14; negotiation of *concordat* with Pius VII, 13; and regeneration of French Jewry, 1
Napoleonic military campaigns, 25, 70
Napoleonic regime: and class of mid-level civil servants trained in secondary institutions, 15; control over French Catholicism, 13; failure to acknowledge utility of separate Jewish schools, 20; push toward conformity and integration, 16; restrictions on local governments raising additional revenues for schools, 25
Napoleonic Sanhedrin, 13–14, 16, 23, 73, 74
Napoleonic University, 67
Napoleon III, 44, 82
National Assembly, 128–29, 153

Orleanist monarchy, 24, 25, 78

papal Jews, 10–11

228

INDEX

Parisian Jewry: and Jewish authenticity, 106; political influence, 72
Parisian papal Jews, 11
Parisian rabbinate, 147
Peixotto, Esther, 53
pensionnat, 51
Penslar, Derek, 3
Pius IX, Pope, 57
Pius VII, Pope, 13
Plan d'organisation, 67, 69, 70
plan d'organisation du culte juif en France, 18
Portalis, Jean, 13, 18
Portalis Commission, 68
Prague, Hippolyte, 140–41
Prefect of the Moselle, 77, 96, 99, 100
Prémeneu, Félix-Julien-Jean Bigot de, 1–2, 19, 20–21, 23, 69
Pressensé, Edmond, 130, 164, 195n73
Prost, Antoine, 48
Protestantism, 13; schools, 48, 108; theological schools, 129

rabbinical candidates, advised to obtain *bachélier-ès lettres* degree, 70, 88
rabbinical education. *See* education, rabbinical
rabbinical ordination, 69
rabbinical ordination examinations, 84–85, 86, 87, 88, 152
Radical Republicans: anticlerical campaign, 88–89, 115–33; and educational reform, 87; purging of Conseil d'État, 118; redefining of Jewish communal schools as civic institutions, 127; scrutiny of French Judaism, 121–22, 125, 134; struggle for political supremacy after 1871, 116. *See also* Conseil d'État, anticlerical Republican; financial anticlericalism
Rashi, 72
Ratisbonne, Alphonse, 57
Ratisbonne, Auguste, 57
Ratisbonne, Théodore, 57
reform rabbinical conferences, 81
regeneration: government promotion of, 14; mission, 19, 21, 22; in 1830s, 35; tied by Jewish leaders to separate religious instruction, 22, 24. *See also* Jewish integration
Reinach, Théodore, 136
Rémond, René, 116
Restoration regime, and education, 23
Roche, Jules, 128
Rodrigue, Aron, 167n7
Rothschild, Baroness de, 134
Rothschild, Gustav de, 132, 137–38, 138–39, 145, 153, 154, 198n17
Rothschild Hospital, 126–27
Rouland, Gustave, 100, 104, 105, 109, 110

St. Etienne, 58
St. Paul, Victor, 121
salle d'asile, 43, 49, 51, 121
Salomon, Maurice, 83
Sarrebourg: attempt to communalize Jewish school, 36–38; Jewish education under Second Empire, 50
Schechter, Ronald, 12, 91
schools, Catholic: doubling of enrollment between 1850 and 1863, 48; and local philanthropy, 49; rivalry with public schools, 45
schools, Jewish: Marseille, 26, 33; Metz, 24–25, 26, 33, Mulhouse, 9, 54, 58; Nîmes, 51; Paris, 26, 33, 47, 49, 137–38, 139; Phalsbourg, 50; St. Esprit, 40, 51
schools, Protestant, 48, 108
scientific methodology, as form of studying Jewish religious texts, 163
Sèches, Edgard, 88
Second Empire, 50, 115. *See also* Consistory, Jewish, Second Empire; education, Jewish, Second Empire
secular learning, and rabbinical education, 66–67, 68, 71, 74–75, 76, 81, 82–85, 86, 88, 103–4
Séminaire Israélite, 85, 86, 110, *bachélier-ès-lettres* as prerequisite for admission, 155, 156, 157; barrier between religious and secular learning, 155–56; coordination of studies with Talmud Torah, 156–58; distinguished from Catholic seminaries, 158–59; faculty in mid-1880s, 151–52; fiscal

INDEX

Séminaire Israélite (*continued*)
  problems, 152–55; foreign-born applicants, 157; as public institution receiving government funds, 158; realignment of academic program, 151–53; threat of termination of government subsides to, 129–30
Separation Law of 1905, 127, 150, 159
Sephardim Jews of Bordeaux: corporate communal structure, 10; economic success, 10; focus on moral dangers of Paris as setting for rabbinical school, 106–7; insular attitudes toward fellow Jews, 10
Société des Études Talmudiques of Paris, 156
Société pour l'Instruction Primaire, 24
Sorkin, David, 160
Soultz, 33
syndics, 10

Talmud Torah of Hamburg, 67
Talmud Torah of Paris, 88, 154, 156–58
teacher certification: alternative paths to under Falloux Law, 45; exam for lay religious instructors in Paris Consistory, 147; of Jewish teachers, 51–52
teachers: Catholic, hired by municipal councils, 46; Jewish, pattern of discrimination against, 56; lay religious instructors in Paris Consistory, 149
Terquem, Olry, 17, 57, 72, 81, 99, 164
Third Republic: deemphasis on classical study, 87; equation of Judaism with other state religions, 125; national system of French primary education, 135; and relationship between church and state, 115; removal of Catholic clerical educators, 116, 135; state funerals, 142–43. *See also* Consistory, Jewish, Third Republic; education, Jewish, Third Republic; financial anticlericalism
Toland, John, 12
Toulouse, 58
Toulouse municipal council, rejection of separate Jewish school, 41

Ullman, Salomon, 101, 103
Univers israélite, 83, 129, 141, 159, 190n89
University, 22; Academy of Nancy, 33, 97; Academy of Strasbourg, 28; and issue of classical languages, 66–67; and rabbinical education, 66; undermining of authority by Falloux Law, 45
utility: and achievement of integration and regeneration, 18, 60; as an effective government "carrot," 23; linked to Jewish legitimacy through Jewish education, 16; and perceived reluctance of French Jews toward integration, 35–36; and rabbinical role in advancing Jewish integration, 69; and survival of French Judaism, 18, 154, 165
utility and equality: and discourse between Jewish leaders and state, 3, 162; new interpretation of relationship under Third Republic, 125

Vatimesnil, Antoine, 67
Von Dohm, Christian Wilhelm, 12

Wahl, Benjamin, 86
Wallon, Henri, 144, 145
Weil, Isaac, 85
Weill, Emmanual, 85
Weill, Julien, 148, 149
Weille, Isaac, 40–41
Wissembourg, 33
Wogue, Lazare, 108, 131, 141, 146, 152, 159, 190n89, 200n58